ALSO BY ELLEN ULLMAN

Fiction

By Blood
The Bug

Nonfiction

Close to the Machine: Technophilia and Its Discontents

LIFE IN CODE

LIFE IN CODE LIFE IN CO

ELLEN ULLMAN ELLEN ULLM

LIFE IN CODE

A Personal History of Technology

ELLEN ULLMAN

MCD FARRAR, STRAUS AND GIROUX | NEW YORK

MCD

Farrar, Straus and Giroux

18 West 18th Street, New York 10011

Library of Congress Cataloging-in-Publication Data

Names: Ullman, Ellen, author.

Title: Life in code : a personal history of technology / Ellen Ullman.

Description: First edition. | New York : MCD / Farrar, Straus and Giroux, 2017.

Identifiers: LCCN 2017012764 | ISBN 9780374534516 (hardcover) |
    ISBN 9780374711412 (ebook)

Subjects: LCSH: Ullman, Ellen. | Computer programmers—United States—
    Biography. | Computer programming—History. | Internet—History.

Classification: LCC QA76.2.U43 A3 2017 | DDC 005.1092 [B] —dc23

LC record available at https://lccn.loc.gov/2017012764

Designed by Abby Kagan

Our books may be purchased in bulk for promotional, educational, or business
use. Please contact your local bookseller or the Macmillan Corporate and
Premium Sales Department at 1-800-221-7945, extension 5442, or by e-mail
at MacmillanSpecialMarkets@macmillan.com.

www.fsgbooks.com • www.mcdbooks.com

www.twitter.com/mcdbooks • www.facebook.com/mcdbooks

10 9 8 7 6 5 4 3 2 1

Certain names have been changed, whether or not so noted in the text.

To Elliot Ross,
the photographer, my husband, and most loyal, truthful,
and gently demanding editor—with love

Contents

A Note About the Dates   ix

PART ONE: THE PROGRAMMING LIFE

Outside of Time: Reflections on the
    Programming Life   3

Come in, CQ   18

The Dumbing Down of Programming: Some
    Thoughts on Programming, Knowing, and the
    Nature of "Easy"   39

What We Were Afraid of As We Feared Y2K   56

**PART TWO: THE RISE AND FIRST FALL
OF THE INTERNET**

The Museum of Me   81

Fiber Optic Nights   94

Off the High   104

To Catch a Falling Knife   115

PART THREE: LIFE, ARTIFICIAL

Programming the Post-Human: Computer Science
    Redefines "Life"   129

Is Sadie the Cat a Trick?   160

Memory and Megabytes   171
Dining with Robots   181

PART FOUR: THREE STORIES ABOUT WHAT WE OWE THE PAST
While I Was Away   197
Close to the Mainframe   208
The Party Line   223

PART FIVE: THE HAND THAT WRITES THE CODE
Programming for the Millions   237
Boom Two: A Farewell   272

A NOTE ABOUT THE DATES

The years shown on each chapter reflect the time it was written.

The Programming Life

Outside of Time

REFLECTIONS ON THE PROGRAMMING LIFE

1994

I.

People imagine that programming is logical, a process like fixing a clock. Nothing could be further from the truth. Programming is more like an illness, a fever, an obsession. It's like riding a train and never being able to get off.

The problem with programming is not that the computer isn't logical—the computer is terribly logical, relentlessly literal-minded. Computers are supposed to be like brains, but in fact they are idiots, because they take everything you say at face value. I can say to a toddler, "Are yew okay tewday?" and the toddler will understand. But it's not possible for a programmer to say anything like that to a computer. The compiler complains; finds a syntax error; won't translate your program into the zeros and ones of the machine. It's not that a program can't be made to act *as if* it understands—it can. But that's just a trick, a trick of the code.

When you are writing code, your mind is full of details, millions of bits of knowledge. This knowledge is in human form, which is to say rather chaotic, coming at you from one perspective, then another, then a random thought, then something else important, then the same thing with a what-if attached. For example, try to think of everything you know about something as simple as an invoice. Now try to tell an alien how to prepare one. That is programming.

A computer program is an algorithm that must be written down in order, in a specific syntax, in a strange language that is only partially readable by regular human beings. To program is to translate between the chaos of human life and the line-by-line world of computer language.

You must not lose your own attention. As the human-world knowledge tumbles about in your mind, you must keep typing, typing. You must not be interrupted. Any break in your listening causes you to lose a line here or there. Some bit comes; then—oh no—it's leaving, please come back. It may not come back. You may lose it. You will create a bug and there's nothing you can do about it.

Every single computer program has at least one bug. If you are a programmer, it is guaranteed that your work has errors. These errors will be discovered over time, most coming to light after you've moved on to a new job. But your name is on the program. The code library software keeps a permanent record card of who did what and when. At the old job, they will say terrible things about you after you've gone. This is normal life for a programmer: problems trailing behind you through time, humiliation in absentia.

People imagine that programmers don't like to talk because they prefer machines to people. This is not completely true. Programmers don't talk because they must not be interrupted.

This inability to be interrupted leads to a life that is strangely asynchronous with the one lived by other human beings. It's better to send email than to call a programmer on the phone. It's better to leave a note on the chair than to expect the programmer to come to a meeting. This is because the programmer must work in mind-time but the phone rings in real time. Similarly, meetings are supposed to take place in real time. It's not just ego that prevents programmers from working in groups—it's the synchrony problem. To synchronize with other people (or their representation in telephones, buzzers, and doorbells) can only mean interrupting the thought train. Interruptions mean certain bugs. You must not get off the train.

I used to have dreams in which I was overhearing conversations I had to program. Once, I had to program two people making love. In my dream they sweated and tumbled while I sat with a cramped hand writing code. The couple went from gentle caresses to ever-widening passions, and I despaired as I tried desperately to find a way to express the act of love in the computer language called C.

II.

I once had a job where I didn't talk to anyone for two years. Here was the arrangement: I was the first engineer hired by a startup software company. In exchange for large quantities of stock that might be worth something someday, I was supposed to give up my life.

I sat in a large room with two recently hired engineers and three Sun workstations. The fans of the machines whirred; the keys of the keyboards clicked. Occasionally, one or another of us would grunt or mutter. Otherwise, we did not speak. Now and then, I would have a temper outburst in which I pounded the keyboard with my fists, setting off a barrage of beeps. My colleagues might look up but never said anything about this.

Once a week, I had a five-minute meeting with my boss. I liked him; he was genial; he did not pass on his own anxieties about working in a startup. At this meeting I would routinely tell him I was on schedule. Since being on schedule is a very rare thing in software engineering, he would say, "Good, good, see you next week."

I remember watching my boss disappear down the row of cubbyhole partitions. He always wore clothes that looked exactly the same: khaki pants and a checked shirt of the same pattern. So, week to week, the image of his disappearing down the row of partitions remained unchanged. The same khaki pants, the same pattern in the checked shirt. "Good, good, see you next week."

Real time was no longer compelling. Days, weeks, months, and years came and went without much physical change in my surroundings. Surely I was aging. My hair must have grown, I must have cut it; it must have grown again. Gravity must have been working on my sedentary body, but I didn't notice. I only paid attention to my back and shoulders because they seized up on me from long sitting. Later, after I left the company, there was a masseuse on staff. That way, even the back and shoulders could be soothed—all the better to keep you in your seat.

What was compelling was the software. I was making something out of nothing, I thought, and I admit the software had more life for me than my brief love affair, my friends, my cat, my house, my neighbor who was stabbed and nearly killed by her husband. I was creating ("creating"—that is the word we used) a device-independent interface library. One day, I sat in a room by myself surrounded by computer monitors from various manufacturers. I remember looking at the screens of my companions and saying, "Speak to me."

I completed the interface library in two years and left the company. On my last day on the job, the financial officer gave me a check: it was a payment to buy back most of my stock. I knew this was coming. When I was hired I'd signed an agreement: the price of leaving before five years was the return of the stock. Still, I didn't feel free or virtuous. I put the check in my pocket, then got drunk at my farewell party.

Five years later, the company went public. For the engineers who'd stayed, the original arrangement was made good: in exchange for giving up seven years of their lives, they became very, very wealthy. As for me, I bought a car. A red one.

III.

Frank was thinking he had to get closer to the machine. Somehow, he'd floated up. Up from memory heaps and kernels. Up from file systems. Up through utilities. Up to where he was now: an end-user query tool. Next thing, he could find himself working on general ledgers, invoices—God—*financial reports*. Somehow, he had to get closer to the machine.

Frank hated me. Not only was I closer to the machine, I had won the coin toss to get the desk near the window. Frank sat in full view of the hallway, and he was farther from the machine.

Frank was nearly forty. His wife was pregnant. Outside, in the parking lot (which he couldn't see through my window), his new station wagon was heating up in the sun. Soon he'd have a kid, a wife who had just quit her job, a wagon with a child carrier, and an end-user query tool. Somehow, he had to get closer to the machine.

Here are the reasons Frank wanted to be closer to the machine: The machine means midnight dinners of Diet Coke. It means unwashed clothes and bare feet on the desk. It means anxious rides through mind-time that have nothing to do with the clock. To work on things used only by machines or other programmers—that's the key. Programs and machines don't care how you live. They don't care when you live. You can stay, come, go, sleep, or not. At the end of the project looms a deadline, the terrible place where you must get off the train. But in between, for years at a stretch, you are free: free from the obligations of time.

To express the idea of being "closer to the machine," an engineer refers to "low-level code." In regular life, "low" usually signifies something bad. In programming, "low" is good. Low is better.

If the code creates programs that do useful work for regular human beings, it is called "higher." Higher-level programs are called "applications." Applications are things that people use. Although it would seem that usefulness by people would be a good thing, from a programmer's point of view, direct people-use is bad. If regular people, called "users," can understand the task accomplished by your program, you will be paid less and held in lower esteem. In the regular world, the term "higher" may be better, but in programming higher is worse. High is bad.

If you want money and prestige, you need to write code that only machines or other programmers understand. Such code is "low." It's best if you write microcode, a string of zeros and ones that only a processor reads. The next best thing is assembler code, a list of instructions to the processor, but readable if you know what you're doing. If you can't write microcode or assembler, you might get away with writing in the C language or C++. C and C++ are really sort of high, but they're considered "low." So you still get to be called a "software engineer." In the grand programmer scheme of things, it's vastly better to be a "software engineer" than a "programmer." The difference is thousands of dollars a year and a potential fortune in stock.

My office mate Frank was a man vastly unhappy in his work. He looked over my shoulder, everyone's shoulder, trying to get away from the indignity of writing a program used by normal human beings. This affected his work. His program was not all it should have been, and for this he was punished. His punishment was to have to talk to regular people.

Frank became a sales-support engineer. Ironically, working in sales and having a share in bonuses, he made more money. But he got no more stock options. And in the eyes of other engineers, Frank was as "high" as one could get. When asked, we said, "Frank is now in sales." This was equivalent to saying he was dead.

IV.

Real techies don't worry about forced eugenics. I learned this from a real techie in the cafeteria of a software company.

The project team is having lunch and discussing how long it would take to wipe out a disease inherited recessively on the X chromosome. First come calculations of inheritance probabilities. Given a population of a given size, one of the engineers arrives at a wipe-out date. Immediately another suggests that the date could be moved forward by various manipulations of the inheritance patterns. For example, he says, there could be an education campaign.

The six team members then fall over one another with further suggestions. They start with rewards to discourage carriers from breeding. Immediately they move to fines for those who reproduce the disease. Then they go for what they call "more effective" measures: Jail for breeding. Induced abortion. Forced sterilization.

Now they're hot. The calculations are flying. Years and years fall from the final doom-date of the disease.

Finally, they get to the ultimate solution. "It's straightforward," someone says. "Just kill every carrier." Everyone responds to this last suggestion with great enthusiasm. One generation and—bang—the disease is gone.

Quietly, I say, "You know, that's what the Nazis did."

They all look at me in disgust. It's the look boys give a girl who has interrupted a burping contest. One says, "This is something my wife would say."

When he says "wife," there is no love, warmth, or goodness in it.

In this engineer's mouth, "wife" means wet diapers and dirty dishes. It means someone angry with you for losing track of time and missing dinner. Someone *sentimental*. In his mind (for the moment), "wife" signifies all programming-party-pooping, illogical things in the universe.

Still, I persist. "It started as just an idea for the Nazis, too, you know."

The engineer makes a reply that sounds like a retch. "This is how I know you're not a real techie," he says.

V.

A descendant of Italian princes directs research projects at a well-known manufacturer of UNIX workstations. I'm thrilled. In my then five years of being a consultant, the director is the first person to compliment me on what I am wearing to the interview.

It takes me a while, but I soon see I must forget all the usual associations with either Italians or princes. There will be no lovely long lunches that end with deftly peeled fruit. There will be no well-cut suits of beautiful fabrics. The next time I am wearing anything interesting, the director (I'll call him Paolo) tells me I look ridiculous.

Paolo's Italian-ness has been replaced, outer-space-pod-like, with some California New Age, Silicon Valley engineering creature. He eats no fat. He spoons tofu-mélange stuff out of a Tupperware container. Everything he does comes in response to beeps emitted from his UNIX workstation: he eats, goes to meetings, goes rollerblading in the parking lot, buys and sells stock, calls his wife solely in response to signals he has programmed into his calendar system. (The clock on his wall has only the number twelve on it.) Further, Paolo swears he has not had a cold since the day he decided that he would always wear two sweaters. Any day now, I expect to see him get out of his stock-option Porsche draped in garlic.

I know that Paolo has been replaced because I have met his wife.

We are at a team beer-fest in the local programmer hangout on a Friday evening. It's full of men in tee shirts and jeans. Paolo's wife and I are the only people wearing makeup. She looks just the way I expect a no-longer-young Italian woman to look—she has taken time with her appearance, she is trying to talk to people. Across the swill of pitchers and chips glopped with cheesy drippings, she eyes me hopefully: another grown-up woman. At one point, she clucks at Paolo, who is loudly describing the effects of a certain burrito. "The only thing on earth that instantly turns a solid into a gas," he says.

The odder Paolo gets, the more he fits in with the research team. One engineer always eats his dessert first (he does this conscientiously; he wants you—dares you—to say something; you simply don't). Another comes to work in something that looks suspiciously like his pajamas. To join this project, he left his wife and kids back east. He obviously views the absence of his family as a kind of license: he has stopped shaving and (one can't help noticing) he has stopped washing on a regular basis. Another research engineer comes to work in shorts in all weather; no one has ever seen his knees covered. Another routinely makes vast changes to his work the day before deadlines; he is completely unmoved by any complaints about this practice. And one team member screens all email through a careful filter, meaning most mail is deposited in a dead-letter file. This last engineer, the only woman permanently on the project, has outdone everyone on oddness: she has an unlisted work phone. To reach her, you must leave a message with her manager. The officially sanctioned asynchrony of the unlisted phone amazes me. I have never seen anything like it.

These research engineers can be as odd as they like because they are very, very close to the machine. At their level, it is an honor to be odd. Strange behavior is expected, it's respected, a sign that you are intelligent and as close to the machine as you can get. Any decent software engineer can have a private office, come and go at all hours, exist out of normal time. But to be permanently and sincerely eccentric—this is something only a senior research engineer can achieve.

In meetings, they behave like children. They tell each other to shut up. They call each other idiots. They throw balled-up paper. One day, a team member screams at his Korean colleague, "Speak English!" (A moment of silence follows this outburst, at least.) It's like dropping in at the day-care center by mistake.

They even behave like children when their Japanese sponsors come to visit. The research is being funded through a chain of agencies and bodies that culminates in the Board of Trade of Japan. The head of the sponsoring department comes with his underlings. They all wear blue suits. They sit at the conference table with their hands folded neatly in front of them. When they speak, it is with the utmost discretion; their voices are so soft, we have to lean forward to hear. Meanwhile, the research team behaves badly, bickers, has the audacity to ask when they'll get paid.

The Japanese don't seem to mind. On the contrary, they appear delighted. They have received exactly what their money was intended to buy. They have purchased bizarre and brilliant Californians who can behave any way they like. The odd behavior reassures them: Ah! These must be real top-rate engineers!

VI.

We are attending conventions. Here is our itinerary: we will be traveling closer and closer to the machine. Our journey will be like crossing borders formed by mountain ranges. On the other side, people will be very different.

We begin "high," at a conference of computer trainers and technical writers. Women are everywhere. There is a great deal of nail polish, deep red, and briefcases of excellent leathers. In the cold, conditioned air of the conference hall drifts a faint, sweet cloud of perfume.

Next we travel to Washington, D.C., to an applications development conference, the Federal Systems Office Expo. It is a model of cultural diversity. Men, women, whites, blacks, Asians—all qualified applicants are welcome. Applications development ("high-level," low-status, and relatively low-paying) is the civil service of computing.

Now we move west and lower. We are in California to attend a meeting of SIGGRAPH, the graphics special-interest group of the Association for Computing Machinery (ACM). African Americans have virtually disappeared. Young white men predominate, with many Asians among them. There are still some women. This is the indication—the presence of just a few women—that we are getting ever closer to the heart of the machine.

From here we descend rapidly into the deep, low valleys of programming. We go first to an operating-systems interest group of the ACM. Then, getting ever closer to hardware, we attend a convention of chip designers. Not a female person in clear sight. If you look closely, however, you might see a few young Chinese women sitting alone—quiet, plainly dressed, succeeding at making themselves invisible. For these are gatherings of young men. This is the land of tee shirts and jeans, the country of perpetual graduate-studenthood.

Later, at a software-vendor developers conference, company engineers proudly call themselves "barbarians" (although they are not really as "low" as they think they are). In slides projected onto huge screens, they represent themselves in beards and animal skins, holding spears and clubs. Except for the public-relations women (the scent of Chanel N° 5 rising from the sidelines), there is only one woman (me).

A senior engineer once asked me why I left full-time engineering for consulting. At the time, I had never really addressed the question, and I was surprised by my own answer. I muttered something about feeling out of place. "Excuse me," I found myself saying, "but I'm afraid I find the engineering culture very teen-age boy puerile."

This engineer was a brilliant man, good-hearted, and unusually literate for a programmer. I had great respect for him, and I really did not mean to offend him. "That's too bad," he answered as if he meant it, "because we obviously lose talent that way."

I felt immense gratitude at this unexpected opening. I opened my mouth to go on, to explore the reasons for the cult of the boy engineer.

But immediately we were interrupted. The company was about to have an interdivisional water-balloon fight. For weeks, the entire organization had been engaged in the design of intricate devices for the delivery of rubberized inflatable containers filled with fluid. Work had all but stopped; all "spare brain cycles" were involved in preparations for war.

The friendly colleague joined the planning with great enthusiasm. The last I saw of him, he was covering a paper napkin with a sketch of a water-balloon catapult.

Here is a suggested letter home from our journey closer to the machine: Software engineering is a meritocracy. Anyone with the talents and abilities can join the club. However, if rollerblading, Frisbee playing, and water-balloon wars are not your idea of fun—if you have friends you would like to see often, children you would like to raise—you are not likely to stay long.

VII.

I once designed a graphical user interface with a man who wouldn't speak to me. My boss hired this man without letting anyone else sit in on the interview; my boss lived to regret it.

I was asked to brief my new colleague, and, with a third member of the team, we went into a conference room. There we covered two whiteboards with lines, boxes, circles, and arrows in four marker colors. After about half an hour, I noticed that the new hire had become very agitated.

"Are we going too fast?" I asked him.

"Too much for the first day?" said the third.

"No," said our new man, "I just can't do it like this."

"Do what?" I asked. "Like what?"

His hands were deep in his pockets. He gestured with his elbows. "Like this," he said.

"You mean design?" I asked.

"You mean in a meeting?" asked the third.

No answer from our new colleague. A shrug. Another elbow gesture.

Something terrible was beginning to occur to me. "You mean talking?" I asked.

"Yeah, talking," he said. "I can't do it by talking."

By this time in my career, I had met many strange engineers. But here was the first one who wouldn't talk at all. Besides, this incident took place before the existence of standard user interfaces like Windows and Motif, so we had a lot of design work to do. Not talking was certainly going to make things difficult.

"So how can you do it?" I asked.

"Mail," he said immediately, "send me email."

So, given no choice, we designed a graphical user interface by email.

Corporations across North America and Europe are still using a system designed by three people who sent email, one of whom barely spoke at all.

VIII.

Pretty graphical interfaces are commonly called "user friendly." But they are not really your friends. Underlying every user-friendly interface is a terrific human contempt.

The basic idea of a graphical interface is that it does not allow anything alarming to happen. You can pound on the mouse button all you want, and the system should prevent you from doing anything stupid. A monkey can pound on the keyboard, your cat can run across it, your baby can bang it with a fist, but the system should not crash.

To build such a crash-resistant system, the designer must be able to imagine—and disallow—the dumbest action. He or she cannot simply rely on the user's intelligence: who knows who will be on the other side of the program? Besides, the user's intelligence is not quantifiable; it's not programmable; it cannot protect the system. The real task is to forget about the intelligent person on the other side and think of every single stupid thing anyone might possibly do.

In the designer's mind, gradually, over months and years, there is created a vision of the user as imbecile. The imbecile vision is mandatory. No good, crash-resistant system can be built except if it's done for an idiot. The prettier the user interface, and the fewer odd replies the system allows you to make, the dumber you once appeared in the mind of the designer.

The designer's contempt for your intelligence is mostly hidden deep in the code. But, now and then, the disdain surfaces. Here's a small example: You're trying to do something simple, like back up files on your Mac. The program proceeds for a while, then encounters an error. Your disk is defective, says a message, and below the message is a single button. You absolutely must click this button. If you don't click it, the program hangs there indefinitely. So—your disk is defective, your files may be bolloxed up, and the designer leaves you only one possible reply: You must say, "OK."

IX.

The computer is about to enter our lives like blood into the capillaries. Soon, everywhere we look, we will see pretty, idiot-proof interfaces designed to make us say, "OK."

A vast delivery system for retail computing is about to come into being. The system goes by the name "interactivity." The very word—interactivity—implies something good and wonderful. Surely a response, a reply, an answer is a positive thing. Certainly it signifies an advance over something else, something bad, something that doesn't respond, reply, or answer. There is only one problem: what we will be interacting with is a machine.

Interactive services are supposed to be delivered "on demand." What an aura of power—demand! See a movie, order seats to a basketball game, make hotel reservations, send a card to Mother—all services waiting for us on our telephones, televisions, computers. Midnight, dawn, or day. Sleep or order a pizza: it no longer matters exactly what we do when. We don't need to involve anyone else in the satisfaction of our needs. We don't even have to talk. We get our services when we want them, free from the obligations of regularly scheduled time. We can all live closer to the machine.

"Interactivity" is misnamed. It should be called "asynchrony": the engineering culture coming to everyday life.

In the workplace, home office, sales floor, we will be "talking" to programs that are beginning to look surprisingly alike: all full of animated little pictures we are supposed to pick, like push buttons on a toddler's toy. The toy is supposed to please us. Somehow, it is supposed to replace the satisfactions of transacting meaning with a mature human being, in the confusion of a natural language, together, in a room, at a touching distance.

As the computer's pretty, helpfully waiting face (and contemptuous underlying code) penetrates deeply into daily life, the cult of the boy engineer comes with it. The engineer's assumptions and presumptions are in the code. That's the purpose of the program, after all: to sum up the intelligence and intentions of all the engineers who worked on the system over time, tens and hundreds of people who have learned an odd and highly specific way of doing things. The system contains them. It reproduces and re-enacts life as engineers know it. Soon we may all be living the programming life: alone, floating in mind-time, disdainful of anyone far from the machine.

Come in, CQ

1996

When I was growing up, the boy next door was a ham radio operator. His name was Eugene. He was overweight, went to the Bronx High School of Science to study engineering, and sat evenings in the basement, beaming his signal off into the atmosphere. The heart of Eugene's world was the radio room: a dim box filled with equipment, all of it furnished with dials and toggles and switches. It was there he spent his Saturday nights, alone in the dark, lit only by small red lights and a flex-arm lamp bent low over his operator's guide.

I grew up in the shadow of Eugene's radio. Over time, his antenna became more and more elaborate, and my family kept giving him permission to add anchors to the roof of our house. From a simple T-bar arrangement, the antenna sprouted new masts and crossbeams, finally a wide circular thing that could be positioned with a motor. This whole complicated structure whirred when the motor was engaged, vibrated in the wind, was twice reduced to dangling pieces by hurricanes. Mostly, it just sat there and cast an electronic shadow over our house, which is how I came to know everything about Eugene's secret life in the basement.

On Saturday nights, when my parents and sister were out, I could hear Eugene's voice and "see" him on the wire. There was Nat King Cole singing on the TV set, when, suddenly, Eugene's ham radio hijacked our television signal—invaded the set with the loud white noise of electronic snow. Through the snow came slashed-through static and a pattern like the oscilloscope on *The Outer Limits*, which I came to think of as the true physical presence of Eugene, the real Eugene, the one he was meant to be, under and beyond his given body. He always seemed to be broadcasting the same message. "CQ, CQ. Come in, CQ." Seek you. I seek you. "This is K3URS calling CQ. Come in, CQ." K3URS were his call letters, his license number, his handle. "Come in, CQ": Anyone out there, anyone at all, if you're there, please respond. To this day, nothing reminds me of engineering loneliness so much as that voice calling CQ through the snow.

Sometimes Eugene actually made contact, particularly on cold nights when signals flowed more cleanly through the atmosphere. Breaking through the television signal came both sides of their "conversation." What they did, it seemed, was compare radios. All those massive structures rising over neighborhoods, all that searching the night sky for another soul on the air, and they talked about . . . equipment. One talked—my amp, my mike, over. Then the other—my filter, my voltage regulator, over. This "talk" seemed to make them happy. I could see them laughing: a tight, saw-toothed pattern, a crash of jagged electrons on the screen. If CQ was the representation of loneliness, then this pattern was the look of engineering fulfillment.

It reassured the boys in the basement: All that hardware has a purpose, it said. It can indeed bring you company.

Thirty-five years later, when I had forgotten all about Eugene, there came a night when I had insomnia. Down the hall, in the study, my three computers were sleeping. Not sure what I was looking for, I went to wake them up.

The Mac PowerBook was really sleeping. Some hours ago, I had put it in "sleep mode," and now its small green light was blinking as steadily as a baby's breathing. The second was a PC on the floor. It had a twenty-one-inch screen that took up too much room on the desk and needed coaxing to go to sleep and wake up.

And then there was the Voyager, a thirteen-pound portable Sun UNIX workstation, a loaner I got from the project I was working on as a contractor, an ingenious machine designed to fold up for carrying then unfold on the desk like a delicate work of origami. It had put itself to sleep after having been idle for thirty minutes, and now, at the touch of a key, it came back to life. Its high-resolution, color LCD screen showed a graphical interface more beautiful than the Mac's, its colors glowing like pearls in the delicate dark of the room. A small window opened to show a clock. I knew the clock was digital, but for some reason, I was glad it had been given a face, a big hand and a little hand and a second-hand sweep, all of which said it was 3:05 a.m., Pacific Standard Time.

The PC's modem screeched as it dialed up the internet. Its screen gave off a flickering light. Still, despite insomnia and screech and flicker, I admitted to myself that I was happy. I liked sitting in a darkened room surrounded by fine machinery.

I got on a Bulletin Board I'd joined a year ago. It was full of jabber that was drifting off into puns and bad jokes, then to talk extolling the virtues of Macs over PCs and arguments about who had the brightest screens, the most hardy modems.

And suddenly—maybe it was the modems—I remembered Eugene and his laughing sine waves on my TV. We on the Bulletin Board were the new ham radio operators, I thought, the descendants of Eugene: we were scattered across the globe; we found communion through the love of our machines.

The memory made me jittery. I did not want to remember the childhood Saturday nights when I was left alone with the television. But it was too late. By simply recalling those times, I had forever woven them into my experiences on the Bulletin Board, experiences that I knew would never be the same. I signed off.

I turned to a digital connection wholly within the span of my adult life, the Well, the Whole Earth 'Lectronic Link, started in 1985. The conversation there was the opposite of the one on the Bulletin Board. The discussion was intense, intellectually contentious, more than I could bear in my insomniac state.

I started sending emails but got no replies, which was what I should have expected. Only the barest percentage of humans on earth was connected to the internet, and even those were not continuously logged on to email. Computer scientists were there, engineers and pro-grammers: the group leading the way to nearly continuous lives on the wire, the programming life that awaited us all.

But then I did get a near-real-time reply. I'd sent a work-related message to Karl, a team member on the consulting project that had loaned me the Voyager. And he wrote back almost immediately. "What are you doing on at 3 a.m.?" he asked.

What was I doing on at 3 a.m.? The screen seemed to dim. The whine of a disk drive set my teeth on edge. All unbidden came the thought that I was no longer the girl who thought she was better than Eugene, that sad, lonely guy. Somehow, over the years, I had become a Eugene. What was I doing? I was sitting in the dark, wanting to call out, "I'm alone; I'm awake; come in, CQ." And so did Karl, I thought. His workstation had the same clock with a face as mine did. What was I doing? "Same as you," I replied.

The next morning, we sat across from each other at a team meeting. Before that email encounter of the night before, I had never taken much notice of Karl. He was just another engineer in the group of five men, respected researchers at the company, just someone else I'd have to be wary around lest I make a mistake and be castigated as a stupid girl and a useless consultant—and why the hell did anyone hire an outsider contractor anyway? the team had complained. Now I saw that Karl was handsome. Black, thick hair, aquiline nose, a strong chin, leading-man handsome except for a fortunate flaw, small eyes too close together, which saved his looks from being insipid.

The meeting began, and the usual mind-fight ensued, technical arguments wielded like clubs, heedless of anyone's pride. In the midst of it, I tuned my attention to Karl's voice, a resonant baritone, which was steady and reasonable. I wondered about his mind, if it was spare and precise like his body; if it was gentling and calming like his voice. I looked across to see if his eyes were as bleary as mine, but I couldn't tell. And I wondered if we could talk about our brief encounter online last night. I wanted to say it was fun running into each other. I wanted to ask, How are you? Did you get some rest? He sat inches from me, but in what way was I permitted to know him?

This craze for the internet: a frenzy because of the web. The pretty point-and-click navigators. The pictures and sound. A Rolling Stones live broadcast. The web is turning the internet into television—TV for the ostensibly intelligent. It may not be acceptable to say you have been up all night, roaming through the weird cable channels selling costume jewelry. But somehow it's fine—impressive even—to say that you clicked around for hours on the web.

The web has a pretty face. But Karl and I saw what was behind it: the tangle of machines and networks and software, emails crossing boundaries, handed off from one location to another on its way to the recipient. It's all there to see in the header.

From jim@janeway.Eng.Neo.COM Thu Apr 27 11:22:45 1995

Return-Path: jim@janeway.Eng.Neo.COM

Received: from Neo.COM by netcom11.netcom.com (8.6.12/ Netcom)

   id KAA15536; Thu, 27 Apr 1995 10:55:59 -0700

Received: from Eng.Neo.COM (engmail2.Eng.Neo.COM) by Neo .COM (komara.Neo.COM)

   id AA15711; Thu, 27 Apr 95 10:43:37 PDT

Received: from janeway.Eng.Neo.COM (janeway-20.Eng.Neo.COM) by Eng.Neo.COM (5.x-5.3)

   id AA29170; Thu, 27 Apr 1995 10:42:06 -0700

Received: from hubris.Eng.Neo.COM by hubris.Eng.Neo.COM (5.0 -SVR4)

   id AA13690; Thu, 27 Apr 1995 10:42:05 +0800

Received: by hubris.Eng.Neo.COM (5.0-SVR4)

   id AA10391; Thu, 27 Apr 1995 10:42:04 +0800

From: jim@janeway.Eng.Neo.COM (Jim Marlin)

Message-Id: 9504271742.AA10391@hubris.Eng.Neo.COM

Subject: Design notes due

To: dev-team@hubris.Eng.Neo.COM

Date: Thu, 27 Apr 1995 10:42:04 -0800 (PDT)

X-Mailer: ELM [version 2.4 PL21]

Content-Type: text

Status: R

Without the covers, the internet was still the same old fusty network of networks deployed by the Department of Defense, developed further at the University of California, Berkeley. And it retained its original motive: a place for the Eugenes of the world to exchange information about, say, rocket designs or caching algorithms. Now it's where the daily work of engineering takes place, in the impatient, quirky UNIX operating system, where the shortest possible command is always preferred, like "ls" for "list" and "cd" for "change directory" and "elm" for "electronic mail," prompting the creation of an alternate tool named "pine," which stands for nothing except for the fact that it is a tree.

Two months went by, and I saw Karl in person only four times, at the much dreaded but inevitable group meetings. On each occasion I found myself growing more curious about him. My thoughts about who he was remained imaginary, however. His demeanor never changed. There were none of those sudden changes in temper that cut open a slice that lets you see a flash of another person's complexities. And his body offered no clues: no signs of weariness, no baggy eyes, no slouching of his upright posture. He never looked directly at me; he never mentioned our brief stumble into each other's insomniac lives. I wanted to think there was some emotion behind that avoidance, a suppressed interest in me, but most likely he was as incurious about me as I had originally been about him.

Otherwise I knew him the way I knew the other team members, through email. Each of us had to create a particular electronic persona, and that creation had to be flexible. We had to tune it depending upon the people on the other side of the email conversation. For my part, I played a tough character to the team; a responsible contractor to the team's boss, who had hired me; an intelligent interlocutor between the group and teams on related projects—or so I tried to be. I had to achieve comfort and skill at creating the right online persona, a prerequisite for working in a computing profession. Everything happens there: design, technical argument, professional visibility; in short, one's working life.

My electronic life on that project was a struggle, however. The company's email system was clunky. Even on the Sun workstations, there was nothing pretty about it. The email was text-based, and the editor was so bothersome that we rarely used it. Indeed it became the fashion and then the norm: type it out, leave in misspellings, missed words, and typos: send.

Their system also had a new feature I hadn't used before: the creation of aliases. The feature grouped a particular set of senders or recipients under one email name, which should have been simple and effective, if the aliases were clearly named. But on this project, the names seemed to have been assigned haphazardly, so it was never exactly clear whom I was talking to. The aliases included ever-widening circles of recipients, from the developers and project leads, to senior managers, to heads of other departments, and so on out to the world. One alias connected programmers and managers from California with managers in New Jersey; after that, other aliases disappeared into more distant time zones in Europe, Japan, India. Once, I slipped on the "To" line and inadvertently told a product manager just what I thought of his ideas. The others on the team— not reading the header, and assuming from the content that we were "alone"—jumped right in with a fine round of character assassination. "Those who can't do become product managers" was the nicest thing said.

Our group alias was not an especially friendly place. Being on the project distribution list was akin to being the object of a communist criticism/self-criticism session. The others had learned to exert technical influence by ferociously attacking your work while vehemently defending their own. It was a place purposely constructed to be a shooting gallery without apologies. What occurred there was a technical battle fought in the arena of technology—a tightening circle of machine reference. In a McLuhanesque way, cyberspace carries its own message back to the engineer: We are mind and machine mediated through mind and machine. A typical posting: "You are running in tautologies. Your whole way of thinking is a tautology. Or else you are stupid."

In this online battle, there is no sight of the victim's defensive posture, of course, no expression of fear and dismay; the wire gives off no smell of a human under attack. The object of attack must tough it out or quit. Shedding virtual blood on the screen is like trying to run from a grizzly: it only makes the bear want to chase you. As one project leader put it, "We try to encourage arrogance."

The only recourse is humor. It is acceptable to designate yourself "the goat of the week." It is fine to say something like "I agree to hold goatship for seven days, or until someone else commits an error of greater or equal stupidity, whichever comes first." But under no circumstances may you ask for compassion. For such sentiments, you must go to personal email, point-to-point—perhaps some middle-of-the-night search for company, which must be refuted by day.

The group's offices were like those of so many other technical companies. It had an elaborate campus right off a freeway exit, with green lawns between each of the buildings and flowering bushes that softened the edges of the acres-wide parking lot. It comforted its inhabitants with plashing fountains, faux waterfalls, and fake lagoons where actual ducks sometimes took up residence. The offices were neat and planned and organized, a perfect suburbia. It was nothing if not a physical and mental Levittown. The occupants were supposed to be comforted with the computerized equivalent of the washer-dryer and all-electric kitchen: workstations, network connections, teleconferencing cameras—*appliances.*

There, in that presumed paradise, the engineers were stranded in the company of an infantile mentality. They created artificial smartness, made a simulacrum of intelligence. But what they talked to all day was little more than a mechanism that read bits off a disk drive. If a comma in the code was out of place, it complained like a kid who won't tolerate a pea touching the mashed potatoes. And, exhausted though the programmer may be, the machine was like an uncanny child that never got tired. There was Karl and the rest of the team, fitting the general definition of the modern software engineer: a man left alone all day with a cranky, illiterate thing, which he must somehow make grow up. It was an odd and satisfying gender revenge.

Is it any surprise that these isolated men need relief, seek company, hook up to the net? Cyberspace: the latest form of phone yakking. The internet: Mother's little helper for the male engineer.

It took me a while to understand why most women engineers I've known tried to avoid fighting their technical battles online. We knew it was simply easier to walk down the hall to someone's office, close the door, and have a talk. We "code switched"—changed modes of communication—as we found it necessary. We might take someone out to lunch, arrange a meeting, drop in for a chat. Not all women can code switch. I've known some who never left their office; one bragged she had no interest whatsoever in physical existence and, as evidence, told us her home was not permitted to contain a single decorative object. But, being women as well as engineers, many of us can communicate on multiple channels. We use the internet as a tool, like the phone, a way to transmit news and make appointments. Online messages constitute one means of communication among many, one type of relationship among many.

This is not to say that women are not capable of engineering's male-like isolation. Until I became a programmer, I didn't thoroughly understand the usefulness of such isolation: the silence, the reduction of life to thought and form; for example, going off to a dark room to work on a program when relations with people get difficult. I'm perfectly capable of this isolation. I first noticed it during the visit of a particularly tiresome guest. All I could think was: There's that bug waiting for me, I really should go find that bug.

Women are supposed to prefer talking. I've been told that women have trouble as engineers because we'd rather relate to people than to machines. This is a thorough misconception. The fact that I can talk to people in no way obviates my desire (yes, desire) to handle a fine machine. I drive a fast car with a big engine. An old Leica camera—miracle of graceful glass and velvety metal—sits in my palm as if part of me. I tried piloting a plane just to touch it: taking the yoke into my hands and banking into a turn gave me the indescribable pleasure of holding a powerful machine while it held me. I'm an engineer for the same reason anyone is an engineer: a certain love for the intricate lives of things, a belief in a functional definition of reality. I do believe that the operational definition of a thing—how it works—is its most eloquent self-expression.

Ironically, those of us who most believe in physical, operational eloquence are the very ones most cut off from the body. To build the working thing that is a program, we perform "labor" that is sedentary to the point of near immobility, and we must give ourselves up almost entirely to language. Believers in the functional, nonverbal worth of things, we live in a world where waving one's arms accomplishes nothing, and where we must write, write, write in odd programming languages and email. Software engineering is an oxymoron. We are engineers but we don't build anything in the physical sense of the word. We think. We type. It's all grammar.

Cut off from real working things, we construct a substitute object: the program. We treat it as if it could be specified like machinery and assembled out of standard parts. We say we "engineered" it; when we put the pieces of code together, we call it "a build." And, cut off from the real body, we construct a substitute body: ourselves on-line. We treat it as if it were our actual self, our real life. Over time, it does indeed become our life.

Two more months on the project went by, and I still had no better idea of who Karl was. His email persona was as practiced and controlled as his physical presence. I decided, despite his good looks, that he was dull. I stopped thinking about him in any particular way. I clocked my hours, I submitted invoices, I got paid.

Then came another night of my sitting by the light of computer screens doing email. Suddenly there appeared a new posting on the group alias: one more insult being hurled at me. The thread had been going on for weeks. Three of the team members vied for being the most nasty, sarcastic, and vicious. My work was the object of their scorn. I say "my work," but they made no nice distinction between "me" and "my work." One wrote, "Wrong, wrong, wrong, wrong! You are completely dumb!" Another said, "What's the objective? Just to produce some piece of shit to satisfy your contract?" Tonight's new one: "Be very very afraid to show up at another group meeting. Things will not go well for you."

I had been working around people like this for years. I tried to remind myself that they treated each other this way. But the threat was one step too far.

But then immediately came another posting.

It was from Karl.

He wrote about a time he made a bad cut-and-paste error and therefore became "the official project whipping boy." He described how it felt to be the object of ridicule and ended with the report of yet another stupid mistake he had just made. I watched this posting roll up my screen in amazement. In all my experience, no engineer I had worked with had posted such a message to his colleagues. And here was Karl, my erstwhile middle-of-the-night companion.

To the group alias, I sent the following reply:

> Thank you, Karl, for sharing the whipping energies with me. Your company at the post is much appreciated.

Even as I typed a period at the beginning of a clear line and hit "Return"—sending this mail off to the entire project group—I was aware of a faint whiff of exhibitionism. His reply only enhanced the thrill:

> Delighted to meet you there. Any time.

Then we abandoned the group alias.

What followed were months of email that rode back and forth between us with increasing speed. Once a day, twice a day, hourly. We described our lives, interests, favorite writers, past work projects, and, finally, past lovers. Once we got to lovers, the deed was done. It was inevitable that we would have to go out, *see* each other. Yet we delayed. We wanted to stay where we were: in the overwhelming sensation of words, machine, imagination.

It's tempting to think of these email exchanges as just another epistolary romance—*The Sorrows of Young Werther* with phone lines. But the "mail" in electronic mail is just a linguistic artifact. Lasers can be described in terms of candle power, but there's no flicker, no slow, hot drip of wax, in laser light; and there's not much "mail" left in email. I had in my desk drawer a piece of paper on which Karl had written the title and author of a book he had recommended. There was his writing: precise and printlike, standing straight upward, as lean and spare as his body. Having this piece of paper, I knew what the email lacked: the evidence of his flesh, the work of his hand.

Although we seemed to be delaying, prolonging the time of imagination, the email was only rushing us. I read a message. The prompt then sat there, the cursor blinking. It was waiting for me to type "r" for "reply." The whole system is designed for it, is pressing me, is pulsing, insisting: Reply. Reply right now. Even though I meant to hold the message awhile, even though I wanted to treat it as if it were indeed a "letter"—something to hold in my hand, read again, mull over—I cannot resist the voice of the software, which was murmuring, murmuring: Go ahead. You know you want to. Reply right now.

What was missing then was geography. There was no delightful time of imagination as my letter crossed mountains and oceans. In the world of paper mail, I would be hearing my words in my lover's mind, envisioning the receipt of the envelope, his feelings at seeing the return address, the opening, the reading. But my email was already there. And my electronic lover had the same pressures to type "r" as I did. Before I knew it, the reply was back. "Re:" the same subject. Even though we were both done with the subject and hadn't mentioned it for weeks, the subject heading lingered on, back and forth, marker of where this thread of messages began.

Still, Karl and I did manage to forge a relationship out of this environment designed for information exchange. He meticulously typed out passages from Borges, which we only admired, never analyzed. We shared our passion about punctuation. He sent me descriptions of his dreams. I sent him selections from articles I was working on. An electronic couple, a "we," began to evolve: "We think that way," he wrote once. "You and I feel that way," he said later. Suddenly we changed our "signatures." He ended his messages with "—K"; I responded as "—E." We were like adulterous corespondents who feared discovery then being sued for divorce.

But soon we came to the first communications problem of our relationship: interpolation. The clumsy email software copied the contents of the original message into the reply when you entered a terse, program-ish command. At the beginning of an empty line, the recipient entered "~m" and the machine answered, "interpolating message number *nnn*."

For example, my original message said:

> There's something in this team's working process that's really broken. I think it's because they evaluate the messenger, not the ideas. I mean, when someone makes a suggestion, the immediate reaction is not to consider the idea but to decide if the person is worthy to be commenting on their work. I've never seen such a ruthless development team.

Which came back with Karl's interpolation:

> I couldn't agree more.
> Each one tries to be more vicious than the last. It's as if they believe they'll get more prestige the more obnoxious they are. [I had written.]
> > Interesting. I've felt alienated for a long time, but perhaps it takes an outsider to see exactly what's making us so dysfunctional. [He wrote back.]
> I've never seen such a ruthless development team. [I had written.]
> > It's the sort of thing that makes me wonder what I'm doing in the profession. [He wrote back.]

At first it seemed like an attentive gesture—he was responding to my every line—but soon I felt as though I was living with an echo.

Not only did I get a response back in a hurry, but what I got back were my own words! I would rather have seen what he remembered of my mail. I would have liked to know the flow of his mind, how it leapt from one paragraph to the next. Instead, I got interpolations. I didn't feel answered; I felt commented on. I got irritated, should have said something, as one should in any relationship. But I let it go. I just broke a thread (didn't type "r," dropping his subject on the "Re:" line) to signal my displeasure. Slowly, without our ever talking about it, we learned how to use the subtleties of interpolation.

I wrote to thank him for recommending a book.

> Thanks again, Karl. I don't want to finish it.
>> My pleasure.
> I like having it by my bedside.
>> My pleasure.
> —E
>> —K

Meanwhile, our daylight life continued on a separate, parallel track. When we "spoke " in the group alias, it was without overtones. I even reported a bug in Karl's code as I would have in anyone's. When I had to write to him about some work matter, I always "cc'ed" the lead engineer. The "cc" was the signal: Watch out, pretend you know nothing.

Only once did our fleshly world intersect with our work. I had to get a technical particular from Karl; mail would be too slow, so I used the phone. I said my name, and our voices dropped to a soft, low tone. I was talking about a program—"so it becomes 'root' then calls 'setuid' to get read/write/execute permissions on the file"—but I was murmuring. In my mouth, "root" and "call" and "permissions" became honeyed words. He responded slowly. "Yes. That's what it does." Pause. Low talk: "All permissions. Yes."

The email subject heading for the past month had been "Dinner?" and somehow we both knew we couldn't keep writing messages under that topic and never actually have dinner. Perhaps it was simply the way words had power over our software-engineered lives: the dinner date sat there as a mail header, and we had no choice but to obey it. There were real and good reasons why we should have resisted the header. We worked together. Both of us were just out of long-term relationships. Still, there was a momentum by now, a critical mass of declared "we-ness," which was hurtling us toward each other. It must be done: We will have dinner.

We arranged to meet at a restaurant in the Haight-Ashbury neighborhood near where I lived. I arrived on time; he was late. A half an hour went by, and my body parts began to go numb—one foot, the other, a pinky—as the time for his actual presence grew closer. Or maybe he won't come at all, I thought, which might be for the better. Panic: We will have to speak. We will have to know when to talk and when to listen. We have no practice in this. All we know is we must type "r" and reply, reply right now. Without the press of the system, how will we find the auditory, physical rhythm of speech?

He arrived. "Traffic. I'm sorry," was all he said.

I should not have worried. We barely spoke. The menu came. We ordered. The food came. And then: our conversation had an all too familiar feel. One talked, stopped; the other replied, stopped. An hour later, we were still in this same rhythm. One: stop. The other: stop. With a shock, I realized that we had finally gone out to dinner only to . . . exchange email. I could see the subject headings flying back and forth, even the interpolations. "About what you said about . . ."

His face was the one thing I had imagined during all those past months when I had sat staring into screens, the same serious attention, deep voice, earnest manner with an occasional smile or tease. But it was as if his face were not there at all, so little effect did it have on the flow of "talk." I looked at our hands lying near each other's on the table: they might as well have been typing.

We closed the restaurant—they had to vacuum around us. It was nearing one o'clock in the morning on a Tuesday, and Karl gave off none of the cues of a man interested in going home. He said, "Yes, the beach," before I could even get to the alternatives of the Marina, the new pier at the Embarcadero, a South of Market club. Yes, the beach.

A storm was coming in off the Pacific. The air was almost palpable, about to burst with rain. The wind had whipped up the ocean, and breakers were glowing far out from the beach. The world was conspiring around us. All things physical insisted we pay attention. The steady rush of the ocean. The damp sand, the tide pushing in to make us scuttle up from the advancing edge. The birds pecking for dinners on the uncovered sand. The smell of salt, of air that had traveled across the water all the way from Japan. The feel of continent's end, a gritty beach at the western edge of the city.

Yet he talked, talked, talked. My turn, over; your turn. He walked briskly, never adjusting his pace to mine. Finally, I couldn't stand it. I stood still. I put my hands in my pockets, faced the ocean, and watched the waves setting up in the dark. I felt my whole body saying, "Touch me. Put your arm around me. Only brush my shoulder. Even just stand next to me, your hands in your pockets, but let our jacket sleeves graze each other."

Yet he kept marching up and down the beach. Clearly he didn't want to leave. He was determined to stay, talk, talk, talk, walk at that relentless, never-adjusting pace. Which should I have believed:

this body-absent talk or his staying with me on this deserted stormy beach?

Across the road was an old windmill that didn't turn anymore. He was interested; he wanted to go there, walk, see everything. I told him I thought the windmill once worked, something about an aquifer under the park and the windmill pumping up water. We looked up and thought it over. It was consoling, this technical talk, this artifact of a thing that once might have done actually useful labor, handiwork of the Progressive Era, great age of engineering.

Surrounding the windmill were tulips, white, and a bench. I wanted to sit quietly on the bench, let my eyes adjust to the dark until the tulips glowed like the breakers. I imagined us sitting there, silent, in the lee of a windmill that didn't turn in the wind.

But I looked up to the top of the mill, and I couldn't help myself from saying: "A dish!"

There was what appeared to be a small satellite dish perched near the top.

He looked up. "Signal repeater," he said.

"Not a dish?"

"No, signal repeater."

He was probably right. It was kind of small for a dish. "I wonder what signal it's repeating," I said.

We were finally quiet for a moment, as we looked up and thought about the signal being repeated from somewhere to somewhere across the ocean.

"Navigation aid?" I hazarded. "Marine weather?"

"Depends," he said. "You know, signal strength, receiving station location."

Specter of hardware. World of Eugenes. Clear broadcasts on cold nights. Bits and protocols on air and wire. Machines sleeping in the dark. A voice calling CQ through electric snow. "Yeah," I said, "signal strength," giving up on the night.

For a few hours the next morning, I let myself feel the disappointment. Then, before noon, the email from Karl resumed.

His subject heading was "Thank you!" He was grateful for the "lovely, wonderful" evening, he wrote. "Before going to bed, I started reading the essay you gave me," he went on to say. He wanted to call me in the morning but didn't get to sleep until 4:00 a.m., woke up late, then rushed from meeting to meeting.

I wrote back to thank him in turn. I said that when we walked on the beach I could smell and feel the storm heading for us across the Pacific. How, when the rain's ruckus woke me up in the night, I didn't mind; how I fell back to sleep thinking: Rain, I was expecting you.

Immediately the body in the machine had returned us to each other. In this interchange there is the memory of the beach, its feel and smell, mentions of beds and sleep. "Bed," a word we would never say in actual presence, a kind of touch by word we could only do with our machines. Karl was who he was, a man who came alive through words on a screen. There was no use expecting more of him. The facts of our "real" lives—all the years before we met in the group alias—meant we would never touch on deserted shorelines or across dinner tables. Our public selves would have to go on talking about programs and users and file permissions. So we were lucky for the email. It gave us a channel to reach each other, at least—an odd intimacy, but intimacy nonetheless.

He ended his note with "We should do it again soon . . ." "Would love to," I replied. *Love to*: a formality by now in our emails, a habit forged in code. Below I left the interpolated signatures:

—K

—E

———————

Two months later, my contract came to an end. Karl and I exchanged messages for a while, then, without our making any agreements about it, we stopped.

As time went by, I no longer thought about Karl. Then one day I came across an old article from *The New York Times*. The Coast Guard was turning off its Morse code equipment. At 7:19 p.m. on Friday, March 31, 1995, stations in Norfolk, Boston, Miami, New Orleans, San Francisco, Honolulu, and Kodiak, Alaska, made their final transmissions and simultaneously signed off.

"Radiomen" would henceforth be called "telecommunications technicians." The dots and dashes of S-O-S would no longer be the universal message of disaster. Ships at sea would now hear about storms and relay distress signals via the Global Maritime Distress and Safety System, which includes "a satellite-relayed signal giving the ship's location." Signal repeater: just as Karl had thought on the beach that night. I thought about writing to tell him, but no, I told myself to forget about Karl and nights and beaches.

Veteran radiomen gathered to mourn the passing of the Morse code. "Dots and dashes are probably the easiest things to detect bouncing off the atmosphere," said one. And I remembered the stormy nights, when Eugene's antenna could not penetrate the cloud cover. He would have to resort to code, which he liked to say aloud as he transmitted: "Dit-dit-dah, dit-dah-dah."

One ten-year radioman, Petty Officer Tony Turner, talked about losing the feel of the sender. The transmission came "through the air, into another man's ear," he said. The code had a personality to it, a signature in the touch and rhythm on the key. For Turner, the signature's origin was no mystery: "It's coming from a person's hand."

The Dumbing Down of Programming

SOME THOUGHTS ON PROGRAMMING, KNOWING, AND
THE NATURE OF "EASY"

1998

I.

Last month I committed an act of technical rebellion: I bought
one operating system instead of another. On the surface, this may
not seem like much, since an operating system is something that
can seem inevitable. It is there when you get your machine, some
software from Microsoft, an Ur-condition that can be upgraded but
not undone. Yet the world is filled with operating systems, it turns
out. And since I have always felt that a computer system is a significant statement about our relationship to the world—how we organize our understanding of it, how we want to interact with what we

know, how we wish to project the whole notion of intelligence—I suddenly did not feel like giving in to the inevitable.

My intention had been to buy the latest commercial version of Windows NT, which was a sensible thing to do. In my work as a software consultant, I need a home computer that tracks my clients' programs as they evolve. My clients' systems ran on NT; the decision to buy the system was therefore correct, the professional's platform of choice in a world where Microsoft systems are everywhere.

But somehow I left the store carrying a box of Linux. It was an impulse buy; there was no practical reason for me to install that operating system. Yet there was no resisting it. Linux represented a revolution in computer programming and, indeed, a change in the ways society could use computing technology.

Before the availability of operating systems like Linux, programmers were kept at a remove from the system internals. The code came to them in a form they could use and run; they could write code that interacted with the system's core; but the internals were invisible to them. The "source code," the original programming statements, were locked inside sealed black boxes, were corporate assets: secrets.

Linux gave away its secrets. Its code was "open source," allowing programmers to read the actual, internal programs. Anyone curious could converse electronically with experienced software engineers, see how operating systems were constructed, suggest changes, find bugs, propose ways to fix them.

My particular Linux installation was from a company called Slackware. Alternatively, I might have ordered an open-source system from a company called Red Hat or GNU (like the wildebeest but pronounced with a hard "G": *GU-new*). Slackers, hats, ungulates—names that may explain the countercultural world I was about to bring into my home.

However, impulsive act or not, buying Linux was no mistake. For the mere act of installing the system—stripping down the machine to its components, then rebuilding its capabilities one by one—led me to think about what has happened to the profession of programming, and to consider how the notion of technical expertise has changed. I began to wonder about the wages, both personal and social, of spending so much time with a machine that has slowly absorbed into itself as many complications as possible, so as to present us with a façade that says everything can and should be "easy."

I came of technical age working with an operating system called UNIX, a successor to a series of platforms developed at Bell Laboratories in the 1970s. The operating system was written in the C programming language, which was created by Dennis Ritchie. In 1978, Brian Kernighan and Ritchie released a book titled *The C Programming Language* (Kernighan was the lead author). It was from this book that I learned C and the basic tenets of UNIX.

UNIX was an early instance of a relatively open-source system. Bell Laboratories granted a source-code license to the University of California, Berkeley, for student use, and in 1986, I worked for a company that had, in turn, licensed the system from Berkeley. Thus I had the opportunity to look inside and see what a system was made of.

There is a continuing controversy over who should be named the originator of open-source systems. In 1983, Richard Stallman, a graduate student at MIT, had proposed the creation of a UNIX-compatible open-source system that did not have to be licensed from Bell. In 1991, the same idea was put forward by Linus Torvalds, a Finnish-American computer-science student. The question was whether or not Torvalds had copied UNIX code, whereas the system internals of Stallman's GNU operating system were said to be completely original. Torvalds seems to have prevailed, at least on the issue of naming: Linus plus UNIX equals Linux.

But on that day when I brought home my box of Slackware, I was happily unaware of the contentious history. I knew only that Linux was a child of UNIX, where I had learned my craft; therefore, the anticipation of installing Linux had the feeling of a homecoming.

I began by ridding my system of Microsoft, which should have been simple but was not.

I had been using beta releases of Windows NT. I subscribed to the Microsoft Developer Network; the company sent out folders full of CD-ROMs, relentlessly, with every incremental change to the system. I had not kept up. I installed some releases but not others, some tools but not all, and my computer therefore was a wreck of incompatible modules. The betas were interesting for the peculiar ways in which they failed—interesting to a programmer, I mean—a study in the meandering minds of software designers, the twisting trails through which systems get made.

What I received on those beta CDs was binary code, programs already compiled into machine-executable form. I could not read the source code that Stallman, Torvalds, and others were determined I should be able to see. Without the source, I was at the mercy of Microsoft. I could install the versions as they came, write code that interacted with them, run the resulting programs; that was all. I couldn't fix the bugs that surely were inside the test version of the operating system. Therefore, there was no way of knowing if bugs came from my side or NT's. The beta gives you an early look at changes to come in the final release. But I came to hate the system—Microsoft meant for it to be a UNIX-killer. It was as if the company was determined to destroy my childhood home. I installed their CDs when I felt like it. My rebellion, I suppose, was that I did not obey the call for relentless upgrades—I was a bad member of the Developer Network.

In UNIX, I learned with power-greedy pleasure that you could kill a system right out from under yourself with a single command. This power was almost the first thing anyone teaches you not to do, then, with a devilish glee, tells you exactly how to: run as the user with complete systems permissions, go to the root level of the disk directory, then type in

   rm -rf *

And then, at the stroke of the ENTER key, gone are all the files and directories, recursively, each directory deleting itself once its files have been deleted, right down to the very directory from which you entered the command: the snake swallowing its tail. Just the knowledge that one might do such great destruction is heady. It is the technical equivalent of suicide, yet UNIX lets you do it anyhow. UNIX presumes you know what you're doing. You're the human being, after all, and it is a mere operating system. Maybe you *want* to kill off your system.

There is an equivalent suicide method in the regular, home-system version of Windows. You insert a system floppy disk into drive A and enter:

   format C:

But DOS is not sure you know what you are doing. It's always checking up on you. It responds:

   Warning: All data on removable disk drive C: will be lost!
   Proceed with format (Y/N)?

Yes, yes, I know that.

Getting rid of NT should have been nearly as simple, just two extra steps, which I performed as instructed. Then I sat back to wait for removal of the Microsoft system.

But no.

Error: Cannot reformat active partition.

Change some settings, try again:

Cannot reformat active partition.

Try other settings:

Cannot reformat active partition.

Then, over and over, slamming down the ENTER key:

Cannot reformat active partition.
Cannot reformat active partition.
Cannot reformat active partition.

I feared for the health of my ENTER key. I looked for manuals: found none. Searched for help disks: hiding somewhere in the mass of CDs Microsoft had relentlessly sent me. Two hours of pawing through stacks of disks. Horns of rush-hour traffic. Light fading from the sky. Disks tumbling to the floor.

Now full night settled in. I picked up disks and floppies, threw them back to the floor like the litter they were. The crash of plastic was loud against the quiet outside. A demonic determination drove me through the hours. No hardware or software was going to get the better of me. Grit your teeth in the face of failure! I told myself.

It was half past midnight when I found the right setup disk. I followed the instructions.

Done.

Gone were all the layers of operating systems. The original disk operating system (DOS), with its plain white text on a black screen. Windows 95, its colorful graphical interface overlaying the old DOS text commands. Then at the top was Windows NT reaching down to layers below, using code from Windows 95 over DOS. Down and down to the naked machine, to the microcode residing deep inside chips and circuit boards.

Goodbye to everything pretty. Goodbye to video and sound, to wallpaper and fonts and colors and styles; goodbye to windows and icons and menus and buttons and dialogues. All the lovely graphical skins turned to so much bitwise detritus. This was not at all like Keir Dullea's turning off the keys to HAL's memory core in the film *2001*, each key turn removing a "higher" function while HAL's voice descended into babyish pleading. I felt I was performing an exactly opposite process: I was making my system not dumber but smarter. Now everything on the system would be something *put there by me*, and in the end the system itself would be cleaner, clearer, more knowable—everything I associate with the idea of "intelligent."

There, now: I had a bare machine. Just to see what would happen, I turned on the computer. It powered up as usual, gave two long beeps, then put up a message in large letters on the screen:

NO ROM BASIC, system halted

What? Had I somehow killed off the ROM, my read-only memory? It doesn't matter that you tell yourself you're game for whatever happens. There is a moment of panic when things seem to go horribly wrong. I stared at the message for a while, then calmed down. The machine had no operating system. What in the world did I think would happen except something weird?

I might have left it at that; it was two in the morning; my whole body ached. But, having gotten through all the prior problems, I wasn't going to give up now. A mystery! Something weird! What something weird exactly? There was nothing on the disk. How could the machine do anything in the face of this nothing?

I searched the net, found hundreds of how-to FAQs about installing Linux, thousands about uninstalling operating systems—endless pages of obscure factoids, strange procedures, good advice and bad. I followed trails of links that led to interesting bits of information, currently useless to me. Long trails that ended in missing pages, dead ends.

Then, sometime around 3 a.m., there appeared my solution:

Why do I get NO ROM BASIC, system halted?

And the answer:

"This should get a prize for the PC compatible's most obscure error message."

The FAQ described the very earliest IBM-compatible PCs, which had, built into the machine, the ability to write and run programs written in the BASIC coding language. That coding facility resided in the read-only portion of memory, the ROM.

"Needless to say," the answer continued, "there's no such thing as a BASIC ROM in today's [PC] compatibles."

No operating system. Look for BASIC! The least and smallest thing the machine could do in the absence of all else, its one last imperative. The machine had no instructions, no idea what to "boot," what to do, what to read, what to ask you to enter. Yet it reached for something: the ability to run BASIC, a small and compact language, easy to learn, the novice's entry into the programming world.

I had not seen a PC with built-in BASIC in sixteen years, yet here it still was, a vestigial trace. It seemed I had happened upon some primitive survival response, a low-level bit of hardwiring, like the mysterious built-in knowledge that lets a blind little mouseling, newborn and helpless, find its way to the teat. The discovery of this trace of BASIC was somehow thrilling—an ancient potsherd found by accident in the rubble of a demolition.

Now I returned to the FAQs, lost myself in digging, passed another hour in a delirium of trivia. I learned that my basic input/output system (BIOS) was no longer supported. At one moment after midnight on December 31, 1999, it would reset my system clock to . . . 1980. *What?* Why 1980 and not zero? Then I remembered: 1980 was the year IBM programmers finished building the first PC; 1980 was Year One in PC time.

The computer was suddenly revealed as palimpsest. The machine that is everywhere hailed as the very incarnation of the new had revealed itself to be not so new after all, but a series of skins, layer on layer, winding around the messy, evolving idea of the computing machine. Under Windows was DOS; under DOS, BASIC; and under them both the date of its origins recorded like a birth memory. Here was the very opposite of the authoritative, all-knowing system with its pretty screens full of icons. The mere impulse toward Linux had led me into an act of desktop archaeology. And down under all those piles of stuff, the secret was written: we build our computers the way we build our cities—over time, without a plan, on top of ruins.

II.

"My Computer." This is the face of the machine offered to us by Microsoft. "My Computer." "My Documents." Baby names. My world, mine, mine, mine. "Network Neighborhood," just like Mr. Rogers's.

I looked over at my Linux machine, which I'd managed to get booted from the Slackware setup. It sat there at a log-in prompt, plain white characters on a black background. I thought of the banished Windows NT system, its little colored icons on soothing green wallpaper, the programming tools now missing from the screen: Microsoft Visual C++, Sybase PowerBuilder, Microsoft Access, Microsoft Visual Basic, and others, on and on. Then I could stop wondering what the user-friendly NT system had been protecting me from, because the answer was written on the technical catalogues and software boxes all around me:

Developers get the benefit of visual layout without the hassle of having to remember HTML code. —*reviewers' guide to Microsoft J++*

Templates, Wizards and JavaBeans Libraries Make Development Fast. —*box for Symantec Visual Café for Java*

Simplify application and applet development with numerous wizards. —*ad for Borland JBuilder in Programmers' Paradise catalogue*

Thanks to IntelliSense, the Table Wizard designs the structure of your business and personal databases for you. —*box for Microsoft Access*

Developers will benefit by being able to create DHTML components without having to manually code, or even learn, the markup language. —*review of J++ 6.0 in PC Week*

Has custom controls for all the major internet protocols (Windows Sockets, FTP, Telnet, Firewall, Socks 5.0, SMPT,

POP, MIME, NNTP, Rcommands, HTTP, etc.) And you know what? You really don't need to understand any of them to include the functionality they offer in your program. —*ad for Visual Internet Toolkit in the Components Paradise catalogue*

My programming tools were full of wizards. Little dialogue boxes waiting for me to click "Next" and "Next" and "Finish." Click and drag, and—shazzam—thousands of lines of working code. No need to get into the "hassle" of remembering the language. No need even to *learn* it. It is a powerful siren-song lure: You can make your program do all these wonderful and complicated things, and *you don't really need to understand.*

The Microsoft C++ AppWizard allows a programmer to create an entire application skeleton in six clicks of a mouse. At the final click, the program immediately processes the code and builds the framework. Up pops a main and a secondary window, both of them furnished with default menus, icons and dialogues for printing, finding, cutting and pasting, saving, and so forth. The process takes three minutes.

Of course, I could look at the code that the Wizard has generated—all the functionality AppWizard has just slurped into my program, none of it trivial.

But everything in the environment urges me not to. The best approach is to look for the "TODO" comments in the generated code—"to do," like a list of errands attached with magnets to the refrigerator door—and do some filling in with little pieces of C++.

In this programming world, the writing of code has moved away from being the central task to become a set of appendages to the entire Microsoft system structure. I'm a scrivener here, a filler-in of forms, a setter of properties. Why study the technical underbelly, since it's already working—since my deadline is pressing, since the marketplace is not interested in programs that do not work well in the entire Microsoft structure, which AppWizard has so conveniently prebuilt for me?

This not-knowing is a seduction. I feel myself drifting up, away from the core of what I've known programming to be: text that talks to the system and its other software, talk that depends upon knowing the system as deeply as possible. What a sweet temptation it is to succumb: Wizard, dazzle me.

My programming tools had become like "My Computer." The same impulse that went into the Windows user interface—the desire to encapsulate complexity behind a simplified set of visual representations—now inhabited the way I wrote programs. What had started out as the annoying, cloying face of a consumer-oriented system for a naïve user had somehow found its way into C++. Dumbing down was trickling down. Not content with infantilizing the end user, the purveyors of point-and-click seem determined to infantilize the programmer as well.

I once worked on a project in which a software product originally written for UNIX was being redesigned and implemented on Windows NT. Most of the programming team consisted of programmers who had great facility with Windows and Microsoft Visual C++. In no time at all, it seemed, they had generated many screens full of windows and toolbars and dialogues, all with connections to networks and data sources, thousands and thousands of lines of code. But when the inevitable difficulties of debugging came, they seemed at sea. In the face of the usual weird and unexplainable outcomes, they stood agog. It was left to the UNIX-trained programmers to fix things. The UNIX team members were accustomed to not knowing. Their view of programming as language-as-text gave them the patience to look slowly through the code. In the end, the overall "productivity" of the system, the fact that it came into being at all, was not the handiwork of tools that sought to make programming seem easy, but the work of engineers who had no fear of "hard."

No wizard can possibly banish all the difficulties. Programming is still a tinkery art. The technical environment has become very complex—we expect sections of programs running anywhere to communicate with programs running anywhere else—and it is impossible for any one individual to have deep and detailed knowledge about every niche. So a certain degree of specialization has always been needed. A certain amount of complexity-hiding is useful and inevitable.

Yet, when we allow complexity to be hidden and handled for us, we should at least notice what we are giving up. We risk becoming users of components, handlers of black boxes that do not open or don't seem worth opening. We risk becoming people who cannot really fix things, who can only swap components, work with mechanisms we can use but do not understand in crucial ways. This not-knowing is fine while everything works as we expected. But when something breaks or goes wrong or needs fundamental change, what will we do except stand helpless in the face of our own creations?

III.

I used to pass by a large computer system with the feeling that it represented the summed-up knowledge of human beings. It reassured me to think of all those programs as a kind of library in which our understanding of the world was recorded in intricate and exquisite detail. I managed to hold on to this comforting belief even in the face of years in the programming business, where I learned from the beginning what a hard time we programmers have in maintaining our own code, let alone understanding programs written and modified over years by untold numbers of other programmers. Programmers come and go; the core group that once understood the issues has written its code and moved on; new programmers have come, left their bit of understanding in the code, and moved on in turn. Eventually, no one individual or group knows the full range of the problem behind the program, the solutions we chose, the ones we rejected, and why.

Over time, the only representation of the original knowledge becomes the code itself, which by now is something we can run but not exactly understand. It has become a process, something we can operate but no longer rethink deeply. When knowledge passes into code, it changes state; like water turned to ice, it becomes a new thing, with new properties. We *use* it; but in a human sense we no longer *know* it.

The year-2000 problem is an example on a vast scale of knowledge disappearing into code. And the soon-to-fail national air-traffic control system is but one stark instance of how computerized expertise can be lost. In March 1998, *The New York Times* reported that IBM had told the Federal Aviation Administration that, come the millennium, the existing system would stop functioning reliably. IBM's advice was to replace the system completely, because, they said, there was "no one left who understands the inner workings of the host computer."

No one left who understands. Air-traffic control systems, book-keeping, drafting, circuit design, spelling, assembly lines, ordering systems, network communications, rocket launchers, atom-bomb silos, electric generators, operating systems, fuel injectors, CAT scans—an exploding list of subjects, objects, and processes rushing into code, which eventually will be left running without anyone left who understands them. A world floating atop a sea of programs we've come to rely on but no longer truly control. Code and forget, code and forget: programming as a collective exercise in incremental forgetting.

Linux won't recognize my CD-ROM drive. The operating system is supposed to handle drives like mine, but no. I try various commands;

still nothing. Finally, I'm driven back to the how-to FAQs and realize I should have started there. In just a few minutes, I find one that describes my problem in thorough and knowledgeable detail.

The problem is the way the CD-ROM is connected, and as I reach for the screwdriver and take the cover off the machine, I realize that this is exactly what I came for: to take off the covers. Now I get to know this machine to the metal. I have battled Microsoft's consumerization of the computer, its cutesying and dumbing down and bulletproofing behind dialogue boxes. I realize that Linux has taken me back to UNIX before it was owned by corporations, released in unreadable binary form, so easy to install, so hard to uninstall.

This sudden movement to Linux is our desire to revisit the idea that a professional engineer can and should be able to do the one thing that is most basic to our work: examine the code, the actual program, the real and unvarnished representation of the system. I exaggerate only a little if I say it is a reassertion of our dignity as humans working with mere machines; a return, quite literally, to the source.

IV.

Once my installation of Linux was working, I felt myself qualified, as a bona-fide Linux user, to attend a meeting of the Silicon Valley Linux Users Group. Linus Torvalds is the scheduled speaker. The meeting was to take place in a building on the sprawling campus of Cisco Systems, in San Jose. I was early; I took a seat in a nearly empty room that held exactly two hundred chairs. By the time Torvalds arrived, half an hour later, more than twice that many people had crowded in.

Torvalds is a witty and engaging speaker, but it was not his clever jokes that held the audience; he did not cheerlead or sell or sloganize. What he did was a sort of engineering design review. Immediately he made it clear that he wanted to talk about the problem he was just then working on: how to write an operating system that runs on multiple processing chips ("a symmetrical multiprocessing kernel for Linux").

For an hour and a half, the audience sat rapt as he outlined the trade-offs. The need to isolate programs from one another—to lock system resources—so that one program does not interfere with another's processing space. How many locks would be a good number, not so few as to risk having one program step on the memory of another, not so many as to make programs wait too long for the system. What speed of processor should you test on, since faster processors would tend to cloak the slowing effects of lock contention. And so on, through the many countervailing and contradictory demands on the operating system, all valid, no one solution addressing them all.

An immense calm settled over the room. We were reminded that software engineering was not about right and wrong but only better and worse, solutions that solved some problems while ignoring or exacerbating others. That the machine the world wants to see as possessing some supreme power and intelligence was indeed intelligent, but only as we humans are: full of hedge and error, brilliance and backtrack and compromise.

The next month, the speaker at the Silicon Valley Linux Users Group is Marc Andreessen, cofounder of Netscape. The day before, the source code for Netscape's browser was released on the internet—all the code for all to see—and Andreessen is here as part of the general celebration. The mood tonight is not cerebral. Andreessen is expansive, talks about the release as "a return to our roots on a personal level."

The next speaker is Tom Paquin, manager of Mozilla, the organization that will coordinate the changes to the Netscape code. He is unabashed in his belief that free and open source, and armies of programmer contributors, can compete with the juggernaut of Microsoft, with the giant of Oracle. "Technologists drive this industry," he says, bravely, whistling in the dark, I think. "The conventional wisdom is it's all marketing, but it's not."

Outside, a bus is waiting to take the attendees up to San Francisco, where a big party is being held in a South of Market club called the Sound Factory. There is a long line waiting to get in, backed up almost to the roadway of the Bay Bridge. Andreessen enters, and he is followed around by lights and cameras like a rock star. Strobes flash, a band's guitar screeches, and engineers, mostly men, stand around holding beer bottles.

Above us, projected onto a screen no one is looking at, is the Netscape browser source code. I stare at it: it's blurry from the projector's unfocused red-blue-green guns, unreadable as it scrolls frantically down. There is something foreboding in this blur and hurry. The mood feels forced. Despite the band and the lights and Andreessen's triumphant pass through the room, I cannot convince myself that technologists truly do drive computing, that it is not all marketing; cannot convince myself that, if we only get the source code into the hands of people who understand it, we will redeem our human souls.

I live around the corner from the Sound Factory, and I walk home. I log on to the web and look through some routines in the Linux open source, then join a Usenet forum where suggestions for code changes have come in from programmers all around the world. I am not in the group alias here; I am in the midst of a worldwide design review. From expert to novice; the brash pronouncements of the young; the old hands who know the errors of the past; the frightened and the fierce; the braggarts and the ones who are grateful to be in the room with better minds. All this, too, is what brought me to Linux, I realize. Not just the machines but the people: the society of programmers, talking.

What We Were Afraid of As We Feared Y2K

1999–2000

Today is February 12, 1999. In ten months and nineteen days, the world's computers will face the prospect of failing due to the "year-2000 bug," otherwise known as Y2K.

The problem can be summarized as follows: Computers have been handling dates with the years represented by two digits: 98 for 1998, 99 for 1999, and so on. Which brings us to 2000, when machines will see the year as 00. From the dawn of the modern computer era to this day, digital systems have never seen a "today's date" in which the year was not in the range of 40 to 99. What will happen when they encounter 00? No one precisely knows.

There are dire predictions of airplanes falling out of the sky, the collapse of the world banking system, the world being plunged into primordial darkness; a belief that this zero-zero, this running out of countable years, prefigures the end of days.

Until recently, technical people seemed to be keeping their wits about them. They understood there are real year-2000 problems. Countless programs, written over decades, assumed that a year could and should be stored as two digits. But no matter. Ten months and nineteen days is a long time. Programmers would develop search tools; the tools would locate the most critically affected pieces of code; then the programmers would change the code. Testers would test. Deployment teams would install provisional versions. Then the usual round-and-round would ensue—programmers fixing problems, testers retesting, deployment teams redeploying—until things were going pretty well. It would be crazy; the result would not be perfect but good enough. Systems fail all the time. Technical people go to work and bring them back up: normal technical life.

And yet, and yet . . . Something happens to everyone who spends time really thinking about Y2K. A deep fear begins to overtake them, some sort of an animal insecurity, as if they're sniffing something scary upwind. It is happening to most of the programmers I talk to, to the analysts, the consultants, and the year-2000 project managers; and it is happening to me.

I first heard the fear two months ago. It was close to midnight. The phone rang. I had been staring into a screen for most of six hours, trying to make sense of some beta code. I was experiencing that peculiar disappointment when I'm trying to travel into another programmer's mind and I fail. Sometimes you get a glimpse of the person on the other side: something sleek in the design; something funny or clever; something generous in the code's clarity. But that night: no one. I suppose that's why I picked up the phone on one ring.

"You should write about Y2K," said a man's voice.

He identified himself as a programmer but otherwise wanted to remain anonymous. He was glad my phone was listed, he said, so he could find me. Then he advised me to delist it. "It won't be safe, you know," he said.

In a low, emphatic, yet oddly hysterical tone, he went on to describe the collapse of global telecommunication systems, the complete failure of the North American electrical grid, crippled railroads, grounded airplanes, stranded trucks, food shortages, riots, marauding gangs, mayhem, death. "Water won't flow, you understand. Water!"

Survivalism was going around like the flu. Men were buying guns and lanterns and camp stoves and stockpiles of propane cylinders—guns, especially guns—getting ready to repair to the hills. I took him for one of those.

At the time of that phone call, I was rather enjoying the whole fuss over Y2K. The public was getting a glimpse of the real guts of digital systems, computers in their physical existence, metal and wires, hardware and software, creations of mortal human beings. Although I had deep sympathy with the social distress, I was almost gleeful that the secret was out: computers fail, sometimes spectacularly. It also gave me particular pleasure that Y2K was poking a stick in the eyes of technical true-believers such as Kevin Kelly and John Perry Barlow, both of whom I respect but deeply disagree with. They had promoted technology with religious ardor. We would become digital creatures; computers would free us from the confines of our decaying bodies; we would float in the ether of that exhaustively invoked cyberspace. It all spoke of resurrection.

I thought it was funny. Computers were expected to save us, whether before or after Y2K. We would transcend the physicality of life and live forever in digital form (pre-Y2K belief). Or, by dying at the end of days, we would ascend to heaven, our souls thereby attaining immortality (post-Y2K). Now it seemed the dying might come first.

The "millennium bug," as Y2K is also called, is misnamed on two accounts. First, it is not occurring at the turn of the millennium. We start counting our years at one, not zero. The math is simple: The first millennium runs from the end of year $1+1000$ years$=1001$. And the second, still in progress, runs from $1001+1000$ years$=2001$. But never mind. The human imagination finds something quasi-mystical in round numbers. And it is appropriate that millennial trembling comes in the fear of retribution from our secular higher power: the digital machine.

Second, the "millennium bug" is not a bug.

A bug is a piece of code that causes a program to behave not as intended. The decision to handle years as two-digit numbers was intentional, conscious, and utterly rational.

Two-digit years were designed to maximize the use of scarce resources. Long-term storage on tapes and disks was highly limited. Space available in "core memory"—the memory programs use while running—was even more confined. From the beginning of the digital age until this very moment, every single program that had ever been written was designed to run in years beginning with "19." It made no sense to waste valuable space for those redundant, useless nineteens.

Why, when this scarce resource became no longer scarce, did the two-digit years live on? When tapes were abandoned, and disks had capacities of gigabytes (trending toward terabytes), and physical working memory grew to megabytes (heading for gigabytes, and more), why weren't the programs rewritten to keep pace with the great march of technology? The answers go to the heart of how computer systems are invented and evolve.

It is early March. I am visiting a brokerage firm where a quality-assurance manager I'll call Lawrence Bell oversees the testing of what the company calls its Y2K remediation efforts. Bell is not his real name. So far, I have not found a computer professional who is authorized to speak publicly about Y2K.

The company's system is a classic journey back through technical time: New programs running over the internet. Desktops with 1990s interfaces connected to sturdy databases of the 1980s. UNIX servers running on an operating system written in the 1970s. All the way back to a mainframe computer of a late-1960s vintage, which is running programs that have never been formally tested, that "nobody thinks about," but that "have to run or we're in trouble," says Bell.

At this juncture, it is obvious that the company should have rewritten the mainframe code; should have replaced the 1980s databases. But their needs for computing could not stand still. They could not survive as a business if they did not fulfill the needs of their brokers and analysts: to let them sift through masses of data, give them connections to vast networks. If they did not give their investors twenty-four-hour internet access to market and account information. If they could not compete with other brokerages offering complex investment-analysis tools. Impossible to divert resources from the demands of new technologies to rewrite forty-year-old programs.

Even if they had decided to rewrite the systems, how could they peel back the years? Layers of code are now wrapped around layers of code like new skin growing over old, integrated, to become a single organ.

And then there would be the problem of finding programmers willing to work on the code of a bygone era. Young programmers want to be at the forefront, feel themselves to be the inventors of the world. It's an illusion, since each generation builds upon the work of prior ones, but it is a necessary illusion. There are millions of lines of code yet to be written, and armies of programmers who must devote most of their waking hours to writing them. Mainframes: shades of a dimly remembered time before there was something called the internet.

The old code then achieves a sort of immortality. It runs. Leave it alone. *Don't think about it.*

If not for the coming of the year 2000, as long as the dark programs kept doing their jobs, they might have lived on in whatever counts as forever in the computing age. Yet now new programmers must search out their forebears, the authors of the old systems, who are in their fifties and sixties. The young are forced to recognize their desperate need for Papa's knowledge and Mama's wisdom; to learn from them, and quickly, before their elders leave them without passing on their secrets.

Two more weeks go by, and I'm on the phone with Jim Fuller (not his real name). He has been programming for more than thirty years, most of it spent as a systems programmer at the Federal Reserve. He is now working on their Y2K project. Fuller laughs and tells me he is fixing code he probably wrote himself. "Hell," he says, "I couldn't have fathomed that it would be running thirty-plus years later."

We talk about that for a while, how most of the veteran programmers are amazed to learn that their ancient code is still working somewhere. They were sure someone would replace it. All those new machines. The luxuries of expanded memory and storage space. The wonderful programming tools. Translators that can take the intermediate form of code called "assembler"—the machine instructions readable by human beings—and turn it into higher-level source code, into COBOL, the language that was originally used to create the programs. "I never imagined anyone would ever see this code again," he says. And I think once more about the tendency of code to become immortal.

I ask him how the project is going. "Better than the magazines say it is," he says.

His voice is steady. The Y2K remediation process he describes is precise, orderly. They started with an inventory, contacting all the vendors of the software the bank relies on. Then they got their operating systems in order. Next they wrote programs to look for key phrases in their software, code-scanning routines that automated the process of finding date-related sections of their programs. Before fixing the code, changing the handling of years from two digits to four, they had to be sure that the source code they were looking at was indeed the binary code running on the machine, the machine-readable zeros and ones. "This took time, but wasn't difficult," Fuller says. Even the disaster of disasters—source code missing altogether, no way to scan the program for date-handling keywords—was being managed. Fuller called their method "superzap." What they did was turn the binary code into the intermediate-level code of assembler, which they could then read and manipulate. "It works," says Fuller, "if you're careful enough."

As he goes on to describe fixing the code and testing it—machines set forward and back in time, programs to create virtual time environments—a calm washes over me. I'm not going to lose all my money on January 1, I think. The United States banking system is not going to collapse. The reports of disaster are just stories written by nontechnical people who have never before looked into the cubicles where code gets written. Good, solid, dedicated programmers like Jim Fuller would do just what I'd expected they'd do: Be resourceful. Make tools. Fix. Test. Fix. Test. Make it work "if you're careful enough."

Then Fuller says, "I read an article about how the Federal Reserve would crash everything if our work went bad. It was the first time in my life I understood everything the Federal Reserve did." He laughs uneasily. "I discovered we were kind of important."

Thirty years at the Federal Reserve, I think, and this is the first time he knows what it really does. A nice, competent programmer used to thinking about his work in terms of source code and assembler looks over the top of his cubicle. I hear the fear in his voice. Y2K is forcing him to learn what his code does in the world.

"People I work with are very caught up in this," he says. "At group meetings they all say, 'I'm not going to make it.'"

He pauses.

"Fixes. They think they can't do the fixes in time."

There comes a longer pause.

"They're out there looking for shotguns."

Shotguns? He had just described a disciplined series of steps that "worked" and were "not difficult." Superzapped—no problem.

"Our own system is under control," Fuller says. "It's everyone else I worry about. I'm worried how few companies are doing what we're doing. I'm worried about the banks, because I don't know anything about them. If I knew, I'd probably think they're doing okay. But nobody's talking about it."

Nobody's talking about it. One organization will not disclose to another what it is doing about Y2K. Their systems are interconnected—but what is on the other side? Companies are sending out Y2K questionnaires to anyone their systems interact with, trying to understand the other companies' state of readiness. Congress has passed a law limiting the liability for Y2K-related failures, which, by bringing up the issue of liability, is having the perverse effect of scaring everyone. The questionnaires go unanswered.

This is the great darkness outside, I realize. Who is out there? What are they doing? Can you trust them to help you? Get a tent, flashlights, lanterns, canned goods, guns and ammo.

"Will the Federal Reserve stay up?" I ask him.

"I don't know," he says.

Something bad is going to happen. I can't shake the feeling. It has been another long day spent squinting into code. The room has gotten dark around me without my noticing that the sun has disappeared behind the tall building at the corner. It's that time of day when people outside think it's twilight and people inside call it night. Three weeks have gone by since my talk with Jim Fuller, but I can't get his voice out of my head.

All that old code. Millions (billions?) of computers. Running billions (trillions? quadrillions?) of programs. In those programs an unimaginable number of statements comparing this year to last. All those mainframes. All that COBOL code no one has looked at in thirty years.

```
IF NEW-YEAR LESS THAN OR EQUAL TO CURRENT-
YEAR THEN CALL "ABEND" BY CONTENT
ERROR-MESSAGE
END-IF.
```

The machine's internal view of years consists of two numbers.

The current year is 1999; the software's internal picture is 99.

The new year is 2000; the software's internal picture will be 00.

At midnight plus one machine-cycle on January 1, the code, roughly expressed in English, will read something like this:

> If 00 is less than or equal to 99 (as it is), send an
> error message to "ABEND," a routine that stops the
> program with an abnormal end.

ABEND. That is, crash.

There is no escaping the digital juncture we have come to. Any code statement of the above form will always bring us to failure. Any year expressed as its last two digits, from now to the end of time (2000, 2099, 3000, 3099 . . . 10,099), will always and forever be less than or equal to ninety-nine.

And this is just one statement in one subroutine in one program. Surely another program is waiting to hear from this one. And others are waiting upon that one, and others, on and on, failures flowing downward and outward to cells, veins, capillaries. An epidemic of infection: the whole massively interlinked organism succumbing to sepsis.

Something in me is being shaken. I've always known systems have their peril, but I've also known their beauty. At the heart of me is a love for what the machines can do, the wonders they can achieve in the hands of dedicated human beings; a deep connection to the art of programming, the elegance of thought that can be at the core of it—thought that makes things, thought that works.

And now there is the prospect of a great not-working. I don't want to believe the harbingers of doom. And yet, and yet. Y2K is breaking a bond. Beauty is giving way to peril.

"No more programmers working without adult supervision!" declaims Edward Yardeni, chief economist for Deutsche Morgan Grenfell and celebrity stock-market analyst.

We are in a crowded hotel ballroom atop San Francisco's Nob Hill. It is the opening day of the Year 2000 Symposium. With cameras from *60 Minutes* rolling, Yardeni tells the audience that all that Y2K code cannot possibly be fixed in time. The millennium bug, proliferating through the economy, will bring on a world recession on the order of the 1973–74 downturn, after which came a decade of limping growth. All this will occur, he says, because the world's systems "were put together over thirty, forty years without any adult supervision whatsoever."

The crowd applauds. It is just what they want to hear. They are like spurned lovers. All those boys we coddled with big salaries, in their tee shirts and cool eyewear, whom we fetishized for their brilliance—we left them alone to play with their machines and screens and keyboards and they have betrayed us.

No Q&A follows. Even if there were one, I know I would not participate. I am too angry. No one likes an angry questioner at fancy keynote speeches, especially not an angry woman. So I sit in my seat and fume. Programmers do not decide which new systems should be built and which should be abandoned. Programmers do not allocate company resources to one project or another. Programmers are the resources. Managers make those decisions. Corporate officers make those decisions. Venture capitalists decide which new technologies shall be funded and which shall not. It is precisely the adult supervision Yardeni should be mad at.

As the morning session wears on, a popular theme emerges: the technical world has been "shortsighted." Speaking of the advent of the four-digit year, one presenter exclaims, "How could they not see it coming!" The "they" is not exactly specified. It is a general "they" somewhere out there, hiding in cubicles—another exhortation greeted by enthusiastic applause.

Here I almost give in to my anger. I want to stand up and shout that some of the most successful and groundbreaking technologies did not "see it coming." The designers of the IBM PC assumed there would be only one user who would never run more than one program, which would never be larger than 640K. The original internet protocol afforded what seemed a very large number of server addresses at the time, but then had to handle the explosion of the web. The internet itself was designed so that circles of colleagues could converse with trust, a calm community digitally unprepared for the invasions of thieving hordes.

These systems did not see "it" coming because the future comes step-by-step. One day we are amazed that we can keep a general ledger without papers and pens, the next we want all financial data always available; then, in no time, we want to query great masses of data. We start with joy that a single person can experiment with a computer. Soon we want to connect that computer to another, and another, and another, until we are perpetually and ubiquitously connected. The human reaction to the technology itself—our using it, imagining what else we can do with it—determines what the future will be. Technology is not the driver of change; what drives technology is human desire.

Programmers are not shortsighted; in fact, they are in a constant encounter with the future. They must somehow coerce today's tools to enact the next desire—desire as defined and constantly redefined by those managers, corporate officers, and venture capitalists. What is available today—disk space, memory, chip speed—is never adequate to get to the following step easily. Scarcity of machine resources is a permanent state in computing. Invention after invention tries to squeeze the last capability out of what is there: Store years in two digits. Break up email messages into packets, send them over the available channel, reassemble them on the receiving side. Turn plain copper phone wire designed for the analogue sway of voices into discreet bits on a Digital Subscriber Line.

The scarcity of our time is bandwidth: how to send billions of bits through pipes constructed for millions of bits; then trillions down pipes redesigned for millions; and so on, as hunger grows for what can be sent over the internet. Satisfying that hunger falls to programmers. They must squirrel around until the code becomes tangled, loses the elegance a programmer strives for. One day, when we devise new ways to push bits, we will look back at that old code and see that untangling it will make fixing Y2K look easy.

In the afternoon of the Year 2000 Symposium, there are a variety of workshops to help attendees understand Y2K and its effects. The year-2000 problem has engendered a whole new set of technical specialists—Y2K remediation consultants, code renovation experts, givers of tutorials, workshops, and advice—who are taking advantage of frightened companies, in my opinion. My main comfort is the hope that, once January 1 has come and gone, these new experts will have to find a new line of work.

I'm attending a workshop about creating a "time machine," a virtual time environment to test "fixed" Y2K programs, like the one Jim Fuller talked about. Carl Gehr of the Edge Information Group is patiently explaining that, when designing the test environment, "you have to specify an upper limit" for the year. While everyone scribbles notes, an awful thought occurs to me.

"But what upper limit?" I find myself saying out loud. "Should we be worrying about the year 9000? Or 10,001?"

Carl Gehr stops talking; attendees' heads come up from their notes; the room goes quiet. It seems that this is the first time, in all the rush to fix their systems, that the attendees have been able to stop, reflect, think about a faraway future.

Finally, from the back of the room comes a voice. "Good question."

The presenter glances over at his colleague Marilyn Frankel, who is waiting to talk about temporary "fixes" for Y2K-affected code. "Marilyn will address that later, I'm sure," Carl says.

Marilyn does not.

My favorite approach to Y2K comes from two attendees who work for a railroad company. The men describe their system as a network of sensors and controllers with code embedded in the hardware. It is a "real-time" system. It has to know what is happening right now: what time, what train, what car, what container. The company cannot rewrite the code; there is no time to replace and test all the sensors and controllers.

The two men then tell us of an ingenious temporary solution: lying to the system about today's date.

The company decided to reset the internal clocks of the network to 1972. They chose that year because the days of the week in 1972 are the same as those in 2000. In 1972, January 1 fell on a Saturday. New Year's Day in 2000 will fall on a Saturday. Given that adjustment, they say there is no problem with a year being expressed as just two digits.

I don't understand their system well enough to know how this fixes things. But they have tried it. It works. It literally buys them time.

I find it thrilling. Their solution reveals the deeper truth: computers have no idea what goes on outside of them except what humans tell them. I thought fondly of their machines running bravely forward into a false future, a fake "new year" already comfortably old.

I am in New Orleans, where I've been invited by Texaco to watch a Y2K test of their system. The invitation came from Jay Abshier, Texaco's year-2000 project manager. With him are Robert Martin and Fred Cook. These are their real names. Abshier is the only Y2K professional I found who would talk on the record. He thought long and hard about going public, he says. "I want to clear up the hype," he said on the phone while extending the invitation. "I want to show that Y2K is not a hoax."

The Texaco system, like that of the railroad company, works in "real time." It consists of a network of devices with embedded code; each device reports what is happening right now in a range of processes from drilling to pipeline deliveries. Abshier, Martin, and Cook are veteran technical people. Abshier has worked for Texaco for eighteen years, as has Martin; Cook tops them with nineteen. Like Jim Fuller at the Federal Reserve, they know the code very well. Martin laughs and says, "Oh yeah, we understand it. We wrote most of it ourselves."

(On Abshier's desk is a foot-high golden-toned cross, reminding me I am not in San Francisco anymore.)

They are showing me a test of a remote terminal unit, or RTU, one of the real-time reporting devices. They have done the test before; it is being run for my benefit, so I can see what they are up against.

The RTU is not an impressive-looking thing, just a metal box about the size of a paperback book, mounted on the wall. Inside the box are several integrated-circuit boards, Fred Cook tells me, each board containing chips with embedded logic, the hardwired code they themselves have written. The RTU is fairly primitive: it does one task. It measures the flow of liquids or gases through a pipeline, the instantaneous flow rate, the flow at this moment. It stamps the flow with a date and time, stores it temporarily in its internal memory, then sends the data to their centralized computer: the Supervisory Control and Data Acquisition system, or SCADA. I imagine that SCADA's heart resides on some mammoth mainframe. It turns out to be on the little PC on the other side of the room.

Fred Cook attaches a laptop to the RTU, and here we go with the test.

He resets the date and time on the unit:

12/31/99 23:59:50

We watch the RTU's display as the seconds count up to midnight:

50, 51, 52, 53, 54, 55, 56, 57, 58, 59

Then the date rolls over:

01/01/:0

"Colon zero," says Cook. "It's, like, what is *that*?"
Then he resets the date and time to:

01/01/00 23:59:45

And again we watch the count-up to midnight, until the RTU displays:

01/01/:1

"I'm guessing it's not just a display problem," I say.
Cook takes me over to the SCADA console across the room and enters the command to retrieve the machine's idea of the date and time. The console screen replies:

01/01/101

Then he enters the command to retrieve the data sent to SCADA by the RTU. And SCADA answers:

Meter Data Not Available - Contract Hour Not Current

"Not current." CURRENT. All the COBOL code in the world comes back at me.

IF NEW-YEAR LESS THAN OR EQUAL TO CURRENT-YEAR THEN . . .

Crash.

This is just one device, I think. How much damage can it do? Cook, Martin, and Abshier patiently explain that the RTU is a small data-collection point in a wider universe of intelligent devices. Via microwave, hardwire, and radio—there are thousands of devices, code embedded in each of them, all constantly sending data to SCADA. Thirty thousand points of data.

If the RTUs fail, Texaco has no idea how much oil is running through their pipelines. Their systems keep running, but they are running amok. Texaco can't analyze production, can't bill their customers, cannot know what is or is not flowing down the line—can't function as a company. By law, if they lose contact with their field devices and can't re-establish communication within four hours, Texaco has to shut down their wells. And then no oil flows to Texaco's customers, and the customers can't function as companies. And the companies who rely on those customers can't function, rolling outward to the last consumer. Here is the systemic infection I feared, spreading without remedy through the massively interlinked organism that is technology.

Yet, after the demonstration is over, the three men exude optimism. They have tested a host of other devices in their networks. They're finding problems but no "showstoppers," according to Abshier. He reminds me that his motive in going public is to show that Y2K is not a hoax (I am convinced); that the problems are real and may indeed be locally severe; and also that hard work, engineering good sense, and intercompany cooperation can minimize the effects and the damage. Abshier, Cook, and Martin are a comforting presence. They have the plainspoken confidence of systems veterans. Says Abshier, "Engineers know all these systems are not going to fail. Engineers are not stupid."

After the test, we go to the control room of Texaco's "Stormac" center. Stormac monitors Texaco's thirty-two offshore platforms in the Gulf of Mexico. The center's name is an acronym for "Systems for Texaco's Operational Remote Monitor and Control," but since watching the weather is a critical function of the system, one suspects all those words are just an excuse to call it Stormac.

The atmosphere in the Stormac control room is uncertain. The room is about the size of a small lecture hall. The lighting is dim. It has the padded quiet of a recording studio where you can hear your ears ring. Five large consoles show data readings from offshore platform transmissions. Suspended from the ceiling is a muted television set permanently tuned to the Weather Channel. It seems that, despite the hot, hazy sunshine outside, there is a tropical depression developing in the Gulf. Robert Martin, who would have to supervise any personnel evacuated from the platforms, keeps sliding his eyes over to the TV screen. "We're waiting to see if it's named," he says, meaning they were waiting to see if the depression is becoming a tropical storm.

Maybe it's the potential storm or the sense of vulnerability it is inducing, but Abshier suddenly gets jumpy. He starts talking about the nitrogen vendors he depends on. The other four hundred critical suppliers. The subsidiaries in South America and Indonesia. The big customers. Airlines, other oil companies, utilities, outside pipeline operators, the automobile industry ("every car off the assembly line has oil in it"): What will happen if they succumb to Y2K and stop working, supplying, buying? Abshier's composure wavers as he lets himself consider all the possible points of failure. "I'm aware of the interdependencies," he said, "the cascading effect. One pipeline going down—what's the cascade effect?" He may be able to keep his own systems running, but "it's everyone else I worry about," he says. The former relationships of trust. The suppliers and customers who were partners in the enterprise of capitalism: suddenly become strangers.

The sensible guy in him has a "high confidence level in the utilities," he says. Then again . . . Then again . . . He is planning to take Texaco's data center off the grid before the year is out and place it on its own generators. He tries not to make too much of the generator decision. "Might as well do it just to be safe," he says.

Before the day is out, I ask Abshier about the religious fervor Y2K is stirring up, the millennial expectation of apocalypse. "I'm religious," Abshier answers, "and a lot of people on my team are, too. I have a couple emails asking me, 'Is this the end of time?' Well, if you subscribe to the Christian belief that there is an end of time, it also says that no one knows when it's going to happen. So I say no, Y2K can't be the end of time—it's too obvious."

The months go by. The celebrity economist Ed Yardeni is still out there predicting doom. He has become a sought-after conference speaker, a source in every publication's digital Rolodex. On October 12, he tells *Fortune* magazine, "The approach we're using now to fix Y2K is virtually guaranteed to create failure." His predictions have not changed. We are fated to slog once more through the sludge economy of the mid-1970s. No growth, languishing stock market, what then president Jimmy Carter described in 1979 as the nation's general "malaise."

Yet I work to retain a more optimistic thought about the 1970s. I think of the railroad systems analysts, their machines humming through those years of economic and social strife. Meanwhile, Lawrence Bell tells me he thinks that nothing critical in his system will fail. Whom to believe in the general cacophony of doomsayers? The media reports become more hysterical as the end of the year approaches. Deaths by the hundreds of thousands, by the millions, black death by a new and more lethal bug.

It is December 31, 1999, 7:30 p.m., Pacific Standard Time. I am hosting a New Year's Eve party. In a crowd of friends, there usually is someone who does a Thanksgiving dinner or Christmas celebration, and I'm the designated New Year's Eve giver. The tradition for me is to get dressed up in a long gown, makeup, jewelry, as if we're holding the party in the 1930s. Martinis and champagne. Smoked salmon and pâté and caviar. I'm nervous not because I truly think the world will come to an end—though that adds a certain tension—but because I'm always nervous when all the food and drinks are out and no one is there yet.

The layout is a little different this year. In addition to the glassware and dishes and flowers are eight squat twenty-four-hour candles. They rather ruin the look of the table—their glass is frosted like a bathroom window—but I've put them out because of some advice I'd gotten in New Orleans from Fred Cook. "Get your supplies," he'd said. "Fill up your car. Plan for your local disaster."

Your local disaster. San Francisco sits on top of a great big earthquake fault, and no calendar on earth can suggest when a quake will come. I should have gotten together my earthquake-preparedness kit long ago. Flashlights and batteries. Solenoid hand-crank radio.

Water. Canned goods. Cash in small denominations. Medications. First-aid kits. Insurance papers. Bank statements. Hammers and crowbars, in case you have to break your way out. We'll be on our own for three days, everyone tells us. No lights, no heat. Most of all, no one coming to help. A person tends to put off thinking about things like this. Y2K seemed a good time to think about it.

It is getting near eight o'clock, and people start trickling in. Minutes later, somehow, the place is packed, the music starts, and we're on our way.

There is a roof deck on the building, and another tradition is for us to go up and watch the New Year's fireworks exploding on the Embarcadero. It's fifteen minutes to midnight. The elevator is packed with people who don't live in the building: kids from the nearby clubs, young women drenched in perfume wearing terrifyingly high heels. We take our champagne and have to go up in shifts. It's seven minutes to midnight by the time we're all there.

There's barely any room left on the deck. Everyone is shouting, drinking, many already are very, very drunk: a Walpurgis Night before the end of civilization. We count down: ten, nine, eight . . . one! The fireworks explode. We scream and fill our glasses. And then . . . the fireworks keep going off. The streetlights stay on. Girls keep screaming. Boys whoop. The screaming and whooping and drinking go on. We leave.

We take the stairs, just in case, and try to keep up the good cheer, but the mood is subdued, deflated. The whole thing is silly, really, and we know it. During the party, we'd had on the muted TV as midnight swept across the globe. Kiritimati, the Christmas Island, went first. Then New Zealand, the South Pole, Fiji. Russia, Australia. Japan. Korea. China. Hours later, television networks got to Europe and the Eastern United States. Crowds in Paris drinking and going wild. New Yorkers in Times Square reveling as the ball goes down. The world spinning through time zone after time zone, human constructs of dates and years we describe to computers, and yet . . . nothing particular happens. Chicago, Denver . . . The new year finally descends upon us in San Francisco. Nothing. Nothing special to report.

All the same, we're aware of being disappointed. The party ends earlier than usual. The twenty-four-hour emergency candles sit unlit. There's a lot of food left over. I put the excess smoked salmon away and go to wash my hands. And I remember the guy who called me at midnight so many months ago to warn me about the end of days. Water won't flow. Water!

I think of all the good programmers and testers. Jim Fuller, Lawrence Bell, the guys from the railroad, Jay Abshier, Robert Martin, Fred Cook, my colleagues and friends, all the technical people blamed for the looming end of time.

I am glad for the coming of the year 2000, almost sorry for the lack of a failure tonight. The outside world may not understand what peril we were under and what my colleagues have done to keep us from it. Yet I know, as the next weeks and months unfold, there will be some problems that are "locally severe," in Abshier's words. By then I hope society will remember its fear, and its relief, and feel a little fear again, and know that the danger was real.

I go to the sink and turn on the tap. I am not the least bit worried about the water. Like all those systems across the globe, it runs.

The Rise and First Fall of the Internet

The Museum of Me

1998

Years ago, before the internet as we know it had come into existence—
I think it was around Christmas, in 1990—I was at a friend's house,
where her nine-year-old son and his friend were playing the video
game that was the state of the art at the time, *Sonic the Hedgehog*. They
jumped around in front of the TV and gave off the sort of rude noises
boys tend to make when they're shooting at things in a video game,
and after about half an hour they stopped and tried to talk about what
they'd just been doing. The dialogue went something like this:

"I wiped out at that part with the ladders."

"Ladders? What ladders?"

"You know, after the rooms."

"Oh, you mean the stairs?"

"No, I think they were ladders. I remember because I died there twice."

"I never killed you around any stairs or ladders. I killed you where you jump down off this wall."

"Wall? You mean by the gates of the city?"

"Are there gates around the city? I always called it the castle."

Had the boys been playing the same video game? Were there gates or castles? Stairs or ladders? How to explain where one fired his weapon and the other died? The boys muddled along for several more minutes, making themselves more confused as they went. Finally, they gave up trying to talk about their time with Sonic the Hedgehog. They just looked at each other and shrugged.

I didn't think about the two boys and Sonic again until I watched my clients try out the World Wide Web. By then it was 1995, the internet as we know it was beginning to exist, but the two women who worked for my client, whom I'd just helped get online, had never before connected to the internet or surfed the web. They took to it instantly, each disappearing into nearly an hour of obsessive clicking. After which they tried to talk about it:

"It was great! I clicked that thing and went to this place. I don't remember its name."

"Yeah. It was a link. I clicked here and went there."

"Oh, I'm not sure it was a link. The thing I clicked was a picture of the library."

"Was it the library? I thought it was a picture of City Hall."

"Oh no, it was the library. I'm sure it was the library."

"No, City Hall. I'm sure because of the dome."

"Dome? Was there a dome?"

Right then I remembered Sonic and the two boys. Like the boys, my clients had experienced something pleasurable and engaging, and they very much wanted to talk about it—talking being one of the primary ways human beings augment their pleasure. But what had happened to them, each in her own electronic world, resisted description. Like the boys, the two women fell into verbal confusion. How could they speak coherently about a world full of little wordless pictograms, about trails that led off in all directions, of idle visits to virtual places chosen on a whim-click?

Following hyperlinks on the web is like the synaptic drift of dreams, a loosening of intention, the mind associating freely, an experience that can be compelling or baffling or unsettling, or all of those things at once. And, like dreams, the experience of the web is intensely private, charged with immanent meaning for the person inside the experience, but often confusing or irrelevant to someone else.

At the time, I had my reservations about the web, but not so much about the private, dreamlike state it offered. Web surfing seemed to me not so much antisocial as asocial, an adventure like a video game or pinball, entertaining, sometimes interesting, sometimes a trivial waste of time; but in a social sense it seemed harmless, since only the person engaged in the activity was affected.

Something changed, however, not in me but in the internet and the web and in the world, and the change was written out in person-high letters on a billboard at the corner of Howard and New Montgomery Streets in San Francisco. It was the fall of 1998. I was walking toward Market Street one afternoon when I saw it, a background of brilliant sky blue, with writing on it in airy white letters that said: "now the world really does revolve around you." The letters were lowercase, soft-edged, spaced irregularly, as if they'd been skywritten over a hot August beach and were already drifting off into the air. The message they left behind was a child's secret wish, the ultimate baby-world narcissism we are all supposed to abandon when we grow up:

the world really does revolve around me.

What was this billboard advertising? Perfume? A resort? There was nothing else on it but the airy white letters, and I had to walk right up to it to see a URL written at the bottom; it was the name of a company that makes semiconductor equipment, machinery used by companies like Intel and AMD to manufacture integrated circuits. Oh, chips, I thought. Computers. Of course. What other subject produces such hyperbole? Who else but someone in the computer industry could make such a shameless appeal to individualism?

The billboard loomed over the corner for the next couple of weeks. Every time I passed it, its message irritated me more. It bothered me the way the "My Computer" icon bothers me on the Windows desktop, baby names like "My Yahoo" and "My Snap"— my, my, my; two-year-old talk; infantilizing and condescending.

But there was something more disturbing about this billboard, and I tried to figure out why, since it simply was doing what every other piece of advertising does: whispering in your ear that there is no one like you in the entire world, and what we are offering is for you, special you, and you alone. What came to me was this: Toyota, for example, sells the idea of a special, individual buyer (It's not for everyone; it's just for you), but chip makers, through the medium of the internet and the World Wide Web, are creating the actual infrastructure of an individualized marketplace.

What had happened between 1995, when I could still think of the internet as a private dream, and the appearance of that billboard in 1998, was the growing commercialization of the web, a slow, creeping invasion, probably unstoppable. And that commercialization is proceeding in a very particular and single-minded way: by attempting to isolate the individual within a sea of economic activity. Through a process known as "disintermediation," producers are removing the expert intermediaries, the agents, brokers, middlemen, who until now have influenced our interactions with the commercial world. What bothered me about the billboard, then, was that its message was not merely hype but the reflection of a process that was already under way: an attempt to convince the individual that a change currently being visited upon him or her is a good thing, the purest form of self, the equivalent of freedom. The world really does revolve around you.

In Silicon Valley; in Redmond, Washington, the home of Microsoft; and in the smaller Silicon Alleys of San Francisco and New York, "disintermediation" is a word so common that people shrug when you try to talk to them about it. Oh, disintermediation, that old thing. Everyone already knows about that. It has become accepted wisdom, a process considered inevitable, irrefutable, good.

I have long believed that the ideas embedded in technology have a way of percolating up and outward into the nontechnical world at large, and that technology is made by people with intentions and, as such, is not neutral. In the case of disintermediation, an explicit and purposeful change is being visited upon the structure of the global marketplace. And in a world so dominated by markets, I don't think I go too far in saying that this will affect the very structure of reality, for the net is no longer simply a zone of personal freedoms, a pleasant diversion from what we used to call "real life"; it has become an actual marketplace that is changing the nature of real life itself.

Removal of the intermediary. All those who stand in the middle of a transaction, whether financial or intellectual: out! Brokers and agents and middlemen of every description: goodbye! Travel agents, real-estate agents, insurance agents, stockbrokers, mortgage brokers, consolidators, and jobbers—all the scrappy percentniks who troll the bywaters of capitalist exchange—who needs you? All those hard-striving immigrants climbing their way into the lower middle class through the penny-ante deals of capitalism, the transfer points too small for the big guys to worry about—find yourself some other way to make a living. Small retailers and store clerks, salespeople of every kind—a hindrance, idiots, not to be trusted. Even the professional handlers of intellectual goods, anyone who sifts through information, books, paintings, knowledge, selecting and summing up—librarians, book reviewers, curators, disk jockeys, teachers, editors, analysts—why trust anyone but yourself to make judgments about what is more or less interesting, valuable, authentic, or worthy of your attention? No one, no professional interloper, is supposed to come between you and your desires, which, according to this idea, are nuanced, difficult to communicate, irreducible, and, most of all, unique.

The web did not cause disintermediation, but it is what we call an "enabling technology": a technical breakthrough that takes a difficult task and makes it suddenly doable, easy; it opens the door to change, which then comes in an unconsidered, breathless rush.

We are living through an amazing experiment: an attempt to construct a capitalism without salespeople, to take a system founded upon the need to sell ever-greater numbers of goods to ever-growing numbers of people, and to do this without the aid of professional distribution channels—without relying on sidewalks, shops, luncheonettes, street vendors, buses, trams, taxis, other women in the fitting room to tell you how you look in something and to help you make up your mind, without street people panhandling, Santas ringing bells at Christmas, shop women with their perfect makeup and elegant clothes, fashionable men and women strolling by to show you the latest look—in short, an attempt to remove the necessity of the city, in all its messy stimulation, in favor of home and hearth, where it is safe and everything can be controlled. The city, the downtown, the agora, the displays in the windows and aisles of the shops have become advertising media, representations of goods seen on a browser, front ends to websites, outdoor excursions for otherwise homebound customers on the internet.

The first task in this newly structured capitalism is to convince consumers that the services formerly performed by myriad intermediaries are useless or worse, that those commissioned brokers and agents are incompetent, out for themselves, dishonest. And the next task is to glorify the notion of self-service. Whereas companies once vied for your business by telling you about their courteous people and how well they would serve you, their job now is to make you believe that only you can take care of yourself. The lure of personal service that was dangled before the middle classes, momentarily making us all feel almost as lucky as the rich, is being withdrawn. In the internet age, under the pressure of globalized capitalism and its slimmed-down profit margins, only the very wealthy will be served by actual human beings. The rest of us must make do with web pages, and feel happy about it.

There are several illusions about the web, foremost of which is that it makes you more powerful, releasing you from controlling forces. But the web also weakens your control over digital life. Consider the computer on your desk or on your lap. It has a powerful chip, a large disk for storage, upon which, best of all, you may install your own software. The code is yours; if you like the version you have, you don't have to upgrade it. Over time you can gain expertise, become a "power user," an Excel master.

Now to the web. The software has moved off the desk and onto a server somewhere far away. You can't buy a web program, learn to use it, gain confidence over time. When you log on to a website, you never know what's going to happen. Buttons move, icons disappear, forms are rearranged, procedures are scrambled. Overnight, whole areas of functionality vanish, and strange new ones appear. Yesterday you were an expert user; today you're a beginner and a fool. On the web, the commercial world does not really revolve around you; it twirls you around.

And then there is the illusion of endless choice. The idea is that the web opens access to an unprecedented range of goods and services from which you can select the one thing that will please you the most, and from that choice comes happiness.

Yet maybe something like this has happened to you: One day, the faucet in my downstairs bathroom started to leak. After a handyman twice failed to fix it, I had to accept the fact that I needed a new one. In the past, I would have called a plumber. Or, more likely, I would have removed the old faucet, taken it in to a good plumbing-supplier, looked at a selection of, say, six or eight appropriate replacements, chosen one, taken it home, and installed it. One day: job done.

But now, having succumbed to the lure of the electronic marketplace, I instead turned to the web. On Google, I typed in "faucet," and thence began to browse. I began after lunch and started out on an endless trail of dot-coms: faucetdepot, faucetdirect, faucetbay. I looked up and it was night: faucets r us, deltafaucet, chicagofaucets, peerlessfaucet. The next day: brizo, faucetline, faucetsupply. A kind of fever came over me. Never before had a single-hole, single-handle faucet seemed such an exquisite object of desire. I looked at hundreds, possibly thousands of faucets. The set of all faucets in the universe had expanded to infinity, it seemed. Day three: elkay, grohe, moen, homedepot, lowes, bedbathandbeyond, faucetone, faucetcentral, faucetchoice.

Faucetchoice! By then I had bookmarked tens of websites, had printed out a stack of paper, had learned about spout reach and deck width and valves, but the perfect faucet eluded me. I was vaguely aware that the choices began to repeat; this site then another offered the same units. But, in my fever, the faucets seemed ever new, ever different, ever unique.

Days went by, then weeks. I still did not have a faucet.

People who have no choice are generally unhappy. But people with too many choices are almost as unhappy as those who have no choice at all.

And that was the state of unhappiness into which the web had lured me. I had cut myself off from the plumbers, contractors, and plumbing-supply salespeople who would have helped me see the world of faucets in its true form—a rather small one, where maybe eight or ten quality units in my price range would have really worked for me. Instead, on the web, I was alone, adrift in a sea of empty, illusory, misery-inducing choice.

I fear for the world the internet is creating. Before the advent of the web, if you wanted to sustain a belief in far-fetched ideas, you had to go out into the desert, or live on a compound in the mountains, or move from one badly furnished room to another in a series of safe houses. Physical reality—the discomfort and difficulty of abandoning one's normal life—put a natural break on the formation of cults, separatist colonies, underground groups, apocalyptic churches, and extreme political parties.

But now, without leaving home, from the comfort of your easy chair, you can divorce yourself from the consensus on what constitutes "truth." Each person can live in a private thought bubble, reading only those websites that reinforce his or her desired beliefs, joining only those online groups that give sustenance when the believer's courage flags.

It's possible to believe that evolution is just another mythical creation story (evolutionlie.faithweb.com); that Jews, through secret cabals, really do control the world (jewwatch.com); that the white race is superior to all others (cofcc.org); that every American citizen is on an evil crusade to crush Islam (alneda.com); that Saddam Hussein's weapons of mass destruction still lie beneath the sands of Iraq, awaiting discovery (jihadwatch.org); or, along with all 501 members of the National Organization for Anti-Feminism, that women should go back into the kitchen (groups.yahoo.com/group/Anti-feminism).

From the well-designed sites with their own domain names to the many-slashed URLs of the little groups on yahoo; from sites attracting thousands of eyeballs to those visited by a few hundred diehards: something for everyone.

A democracy, indeed a culture, needs some sustaining common mythos. Yet, in a world where "truth" is a variable concept—where any belief can find its adherents—how can a consensus be formed? How can we arrive at the compromises that must underlie the workings of any successful society?

One evening, while I was watching television, I looked up to see a commercial that seemed to me to be the most explicit statement of our fracturing society. I gaped at it, because usually such statements are kept implicit, hidden behind symbols. But this commercial was like the sky-blue billboard: a shameless and naked expression of the web world, a glorification of the self, at home, alone.

It begins with a drone, a footstep in a puddle, then a ragged band pulling a dead car through the mud—road warriors with bandanas around their foreheads, carrying braziers. Now we see rafts of survivors floating before the ruins of a city, the sky dark, red-tinged, as if fires were burning all around us, just over the horizon. Next we are outside the dead city's library, where stone lions, now coated in gold and come to life, rear up in despair. Inside the library, red-coated fascist-like guards encircle the readers at the table. A young girl turns a page, loudly, and the guards say "Shush!" in time to their march-step. We see the title of the book the girl is reading: *Paradise Lost.* The bank, too, is a scene of ruin. A long line snakes outside it in a dreary rain. Inside, the teller is a man with a white, spectral face, who gazes upon the black spider that is slowly crawling up his window. A young woman's face ages right before us, and in response, in ridicule, the bank guard laughs. The camera now takes us up over the roofs of this post-apocalyptic city. Lightning crashes in the dark, red-tinged sky. On a telephone pole, where the insulators should be, are skulls.

Cut to a cartoon of emerald-green grass, hills, a Victorian house with a white picket fence and no neighbors. A butterfly flaps above it. What a relief this house is after the dreary, dangerous, ruined city. The door to this charming house opens, and we go in to see a chair before a computer screen. Yes, we want to go sit in that chair, in that room with candy-orange walls. On the computer screen, running by in teasing succession, are pleasant virtual reflections of the world outside: written text, a bank check, a telephone pole, our connection to the internet. The camera pans back to show a window as its curtain swings in the breeze, and our sense of calm is complete. The computer company's name fills the screen. Then cut to the legend: "Wouldn't you rather be at home?"

In sixty seconds, this commercial communicates a worldview that reflects the ultimate suburbanization of existence: a retreat from the friction of the social space for the supposed idyll of private ease. It is a view that depends on the idea that desire is not social, not stimulated by what others want, but generated internally, and that the satisfaction of desires is not dependent upon other persons, organizations, structures, or governments. It is a profoundly libertarian vision, and it is the message that underlies all the mythologizing about the web: the idea that the civic space is dead, useless, dangerous, and the only place of pleasure and satisfaction is your home. You, home, family; beyond that, the world. From the intensely private to the global, with little in between but an Intel processor and a search engine.

In this sense, the ideal of the internet represents the very opposite of democracy, which is a method for resolving difference in a relatively orderly manner through the mediation of unavoidable civil associations. Yet there can be no notion of resolving differences in a world where each person is entitled to get exactly what he or she wants. Here all needs and desires are equally valid and equally powerful. I'll get mine and you'll get yours; there is no need for compromise and discussion. I don't have to tolerate you, and you don't have to tolerate me. No need to care for my neighbor next door when I can stay with my chosen neighbors in the ether, my email friends and the visitors to sites I visit, people who think as I do, who want what I want. No need for messy debate and the whole rigmarole of government with all its creaky, bothersome structures. There's no need for any of this, because now that we have the World Wide Web the problem of the pursuit of happiness has been solved! We'll each click for our individual joys, and our only dispute may come if something doesn't get delivered on time. Wouldn't you really rather be at home?

But who exactly gets to stay at home? Only a certain class of knowledge worker can stay home and click. On the other side of this ideal of work-anywhere freedom (if indeed it is freedom never to be away from work) is the reality that somebody had to make the thing you ordered with a click. Somebody had to put it in a box, do the paperwork, carry it to you. The reality is a world divided not only between the haves and have-nots but between the ones who get to stay home and everyone else, the ones who deliver the goods to them.

The internet ideal represents a retreat not only from political life but also from culture—from that tumultuous conversation in which we try to talk to one another about our shared experiences. As members of a culture, we see the same movie, read the same book, hear the same string quartet. Although it is enormously difficult for us to agree on what we might have seen, read, or heard, it is out of that difficult conversation that real culture arises. Whether or not we come to an agreement or understanding, even if some decide that understanding and meaning are impossible, we are still sitting around the same campfire.

But the web as it has evolved is based on the idea that we do not even want a shared experience. David Ross, the director of San Francisco's Museum of Modern Art, once told an audience that we no longer need a building to house works of art; we don't need to get dressed, go downtown, walk from room to room among crowds of other people. Digital images will do. Never mind losing the tactile sense of paint on canvas, the play of shadow and light as we circle a sculpture, the impression of scale, a work that fills a room you share with tens of others, or requires that you stand close, one person at a time—that intimacy.

Other people are annoying interlopers. They stand between you and your experience, which is special, unique, for you and only you. Now that we have the web, Ross asserted, we can look at anything we want whenever we want. We no longer need him or his curators. "You don't have to walk through my idea of what's interesting to look at," he said to a questioner in the audience named Bill. "On the web," said the director, "you can create the museum of Bill."

And so, by implication, there can be the museum of George and Mary and Helene. What, then, will this group have to say to one another about art? Let's say the museum of Bill is featuring early Dutch masters, the museum of Mary is playing video art, and the museum of Helene is displaying French tapestries. In this privatized world, what sort of "cultural" conversation can there be? What can one of us possibly say to another about our experience except "Today I visited the museum of me, and I liked it."

Fiber Optic Nights

Three Months in Early 1999

I can't get a drink and I can't get a seat and I can barely find a place to stand. I'm in a South of Market bar called Infusion. It's midnight on a Tuesday. Three drunk programmers, talking about back-end throughput, have jammed me behind the bar stool occupied by Ana Marie Cox, the blogger Wonkette. Ana and I try to talk, but she would have to spin her head around like a wooden dummy, so we give up. I'm trying to shout hello to a couple of people I know, but they can't hear me over the talk of page views and click-throughs and what to say to a venture capitalist. *Wired* writers and editors hang out here, since their office is a block away. I see a guy who hopes to be the magazine's next editor-in-chief. Various programming veterans. But mostly young, young, young men hungry to do a startup, take it public, get very rich.

Infusion is named for the big square glass jars of infused vodka stacked three high over the back bar. Thyme, ginger, rosemary, what have you. But mostly everyone drinks beer or plain old well vodka, martini after martini. Ana's got one already set up behind the one she's drinking. Miraculously, the stool next to her gets empty, she puts her hand on the seat to ward off a big man bearing down on it, and it's mine. I order a martini. Much better. Then another. Soon another. At this stage of inebriation, I can't resist the atmosphere of wild optimism. I let myself fall under the delicious cloud of dreams: the great global internet that will change human life—indeed, change humans themselves. It is a lucky coincidence that a psychic plies her trade in the flat upstairs, offering to read tarot cards and palms, and so divine the future.

One-forty-five a.m.: Last call. The brutality of the lights-on killing every illusion. You know San Francisco is really a hick town by the absurdly early bar closing times. The crowd has thinned by now anyway. Ana and I stumble out together. We'll make our own late night another time. She goes off on her Vespa. I worry that she might not get home okay.

Second Street is quiet and dark once the bar closes and the psychic unplugs the rope of Christmas bulbs around her door. A few lights show from the pre-quake wooden flats still standing. Dim lamps under the Bay Bridge overpass reveal the twirling carcasses of pigeons caught in the netting strung up to keep them away. Only four units show lights from my own building, the Clocktower—loft condominiums constructed inside the walls of a derelict printing factory—more evidence of the early-night-hick-ness of San Francisco. Otherwise, Second Street looks abandoned from Howard out to the edge of the Bay, which is now a pile of dirt and industrial waste but was once the docks for the boats that brought the mail to San Francisco. Here are the ghost-shells of the former warehouses and factories that were the industrial heart of the city. South of Market: SOMA. Formerly known as what lay south of the streetcar tracks on Market Street: South of the Slot.

They're out there again, right under my window. Two-thirty in the morning, a crew setting up klieg lights on tripods, the street lit like a night scene in a film. They've waited for the Bay Bridge traffic to thin and the bars to close. I don't suppose they actually wait for the bar closing, but it feels that way. The programmers and bloggers head home; the bar lights click off. It's still dark for a moment. Then: the movie lights blast on, the monster tractor of a machine grinds its gears, dangles its chains, hooks off the trench plates, clang-crashes them down across the street. It won't be long now, maybe half an hour: the jackhammering that cracks open the street and the night; a pause for the low men on the job to shovel away the dirt, the quiet interval feeding the hope that it's all over; then the jackhammers again; the pause; repeat; until first daylight.

Three weeks ago, I knew something like this was coming because of the markings on the pavement. First came the surveyors, then the men spraying the macadam and sidewalks with explosive Day-Glo colors. Orange, red, blue, yellow, a blinding white. Diamonds, squares, "Z"s, circles, arrows; straight lines, jagged lines, angled lines, wavy lines. Pacific Bell, Comcast, Pacific Gas and Electric, Department of Public Works. Water, electricity, sewers, phone, cable. All that lies beneath the street, the underground of civilization.

The markings start at Second and Bryant and run north two long blocks to Folsom, where stands the main switching station of the telecommunications colossus AT&T. The building is eight stories high, with a slim line of windows facing east on the sixth floor, another facing south, otherwise completely clad in aluminum-shiny metal plates, like the armor of a video-game warrior. Something deep inside it generates a perpetual Tesla-coil, high-voltage-warning hum that pervades the soundscape and makes you want to grind your teeth.

This noise and digging up, the cracking open of the order buried under the street, the trenches bearing down on a switching station that is routing millions of phone calls: I know all this must happen. The neighborhood must make way for the internet startups moving into the former factories and drab, unlovely offices—eGroups, salon .com, Organics.org, Soma Networks, CompuMentor. The energy of the neighborhood tells you this is just the beginning.

When I moved to SOMA, in 1996, there was a homeless man, slim, fair-haired, bearded, who did yoga every night under the bridge approach. He didn't bother anyone. He just sat in a full lotus and stared ahead. Some residents in my supposedly cool building kept calling the cops to chase him away—so much for their being urban pioneers. The yoga man always came back. Then the movie lights came on, and stayed on, and he disappeared. I don't think he'll come back this time.

There are still remnants of SOMA's past life. A small lithography factory. The photographers' supplier on Bryant. A sewing sweatshop, Chinese women doing piecework, trekking south from Market at 5:00 a.m., back north to Chinatown at 3:00 p.m. The hiring hall of the Marine Firemen's Union, three stories wrapped in marble. Above the entrance is a medallion, ten feet in diameter, with a bas-relief of a worker pulling a man-high lever in the bowels of a ship. He is surrounded by the gears of a great machine: a paean to physical labor, to the glory of the working class.

The union hall with its marble looks to stay; I hope it will. But the sweatshop, the lone lithographer must soon succumb to what will follow the hammering, the digging, the disruption of life in the old SOMA. Now come the startups with their works of the imagination, labor no more physically taxing than the lifting of a monitor.

The work below the window has been going on for three weeks. The crew doesn't look near done. I don't know when I'll sleep again.

Daylight, lunch hour, entrepreneurs and programmers gather in South Park, an oval of grass and trees between Second and Third Streets, once a needle park for junkies when the neighborhood declined in the 1970s, now a place to eat and picnic and talk on cell phones loudly enough that everyone can overhear everyone else's confidential business plans.

There are two white-tablecloth restaurants facing each other across the oval: Echo, and the South Park Cafe, both bustling. Wineglasses are filled with Sancerre and Bordeaux. Plates of fresh fish and skirt steak with red-wine sauce arrive at the tables. You need a reservation to get in. Oh, the exuberance! The joy of internet creation. The excitement of living exactly in the right time, in the center where everything is about to happen.

At the lower end of the oval, where the park slopes down toward Third, black men own the picnic table there and drink beverages wrapped in paper bags.

The horizon is broken by cranes in all directions, giving their fingers to the sky. They rose in just two months—how is that possible? Third Street, Brannan, Bryant, Townsend, King Street. Is this a bubble? I have devised a crane index: how many cranes makes for too many buildings? From my windows, I used to be able to see a slip of the Bay, the occasional slick of a freighter gliding through, the brick smokestack of an old but still-working power plant, the path of the smoke telling me the direction of the wind. Now the buildings rise and divide the skyline among themselves like it's loot.

Friends who haven't seen me for a while come to visit. Says one, "You're being walled in!"

Weeks go by, and the crews are still working. Every night, I achieve unconsciousness in short slices of time. Then come the workers who fill in the trenches, lay down macadam, give back the street. A few days of peace.

But tonight the lights are on again; no jackhammers, but my window shades are as white as movie-theater screens. A new set of workers are here, men in white jumpsuits who arrived in a white van. They cone off a lane of the street, stand in the blare of light, and surround an open manhole, one man down in the hole, two watching from above. Another vehicle arrives, a truck with cable wrapped around a spool about five feet in diameter. The spool moans, grinds to life; then winches cable down the hole. Two weeks of this.

One day, strangely, the men arrive in the morning: in daylight! They open the manhole again, one man down, two up. They leave and come back at irregular intervals—one day here, another not—in the mornings, in the afternoons. Each time they take off the cover, I think to myself, Ah! The manhole of mystery.

It's a Friday-night beer-and-wine party at eGroups, a startup founded by Carl Page, a good friend and Larry Page's brother. About eighty people are here, with the usual heavy quota of boys with beer bottles. Their space is in an old industrial wreck down the street from my building. Redbrick and timber, five stories, empty for about twenty years. Looks derelict until you make out lights shining in a window here and there, evidence of would-be internet-success dreamers nesting like starlings in an old barn.

The office furniture consists of cheap folding tables set next to each other, short end to short end, forming three lines that stretch about ten yards across the space. Gone is any notion of a cubicle or privacy; the programmers sit side by side, shoulder to shoulder. It's hot. The ventilation is as bad as it was for any past factory worker. Software assembly line, stale air: sweatshops are the new garage.

I wander around and say hello to the people I know and finally get to Carl to congratulate him for getting eGroups out of a sixties-style house way out in the nowhere of Diamond Heights and into this space in SOMA, where all good startups ought to be. We talk awhile, then I go off, the way you're supposed to do at stand-up parties, not stick yourself to the side of one person, which is what I dearly like to do. Nearby is a thick circle of young men surrounding someone. A few of them, seemingly unable to make contact with whoever is the object of their desire, move off, and it's like a drape opening to reveal exactly whom they want to be close to: Larry Page and Sergey Brin, the founders of Google.

I know Larry and Sergey through my friendship with Carl. Every time I have talked with Larry, I was aware of being in a presence beyond anything I have known in a human being. His intelligence quotient lies four standard deviations from the mean abilities of a regular person, at the far, far right end of the bell curve. Four sigmas away from the center. Five? No. Five sigmas represent a singularity, which I do not believe in. Nonetheless, with Larry . . .

I go over to say hello. We stand around without talking for thirty seconds or so.

Then Larry asks me, "What are you doing these days?"

What exactly am I doing? He means in software. Some consulting, I think to say, which is a boring subject, so I don't talk about it. What I'm doing of any substance is trying to educate myself about symmetrical multiprocessing. After I heard Linus Torvalds's talk at the Linux user-group meeting, the subject took hold of me, became an obsession. The problem seemed to combine mathematical theory, the physicality of performance on actual machines, and philosophical questions about how one discerns precedence, what should go first. Any serious software engineer would scoff at my dragging in philosophy, the fuzz of the humanities.

The pause in which I have had these thoughts must have seemed an eternity to the lightning-quick minds of Larry and Sergey. Finally, I say:

"I'm fooling around with symmetrical multiprocessing."

Their faces snap to eye-to-eye. I hear them inhale. Larry turns to me and says:

"Do you want a job?"

Do I want a job? Opportunity of a lifetime! Symmetrical multiprocessing is the key to blazing searches through massive amounts of data, enabler for the defining algorithm of our time.

But all I can think is that I'm a fraud and I don't know a damn thing. Curse of the self-taught: fear that you know only points here and there, islands of knowledge, and between them are chasms into which you will fall in humiliating failure, a fear that followed me from the first time I learned how to code. It does no good to tell myself that even MIT computer-science students don't know everything, yet they are confident and don't worry about the islands and the chasms.

But this time is different. This time my fear is not a physiological problem. The darkness is real; I don't have the mathematics, the foundation, to make a substantial contribution to symmetrical multiprocessing. To work for Google would force me beyond what I could do. Yet I know the same is true for anyone who works at Google. They work where the streets have been pulverized and the underground torn up and the old ideas plucked out to make possible what was not possible before.

I look around at the boys with beer bottles, the culture of very young men I had been pleased to leave.

I say to Larry, "Thanks, but I'm tired of programming."

Another night at Infusion; another night at last call and closing. I take a walk to try to get my senses in order. They don't get in order.

Home now. And of course the crew's there. One man down the manhole of mystery, two keeping guard. Several times over the past weeks, I've asked one of the men what they were doing. It was clear they were installing some cable—but for what? For Comcast? I got the begrudging reply of "street work" (hence the continuing mystery of the manhole).

Tonight one of the up-top guards is a guy I've seen working for months, a burly man I think of as Barbarossa, for his scraggly red beard. And I know he recognizes me. I'm still booze-loose, so I come right out and say, "Come on, Redbeard, you know me. It's time you told me what's going on."

He laughs and says, "I think of you as the girl with the weird glasses." (I do wear strange glasses.)

We're nickname friends, thinks my wet brain, so I ask again, "What's up?"

He turns to the other guy up top, as if wondering what he should say; then he finally turns to me and says:

"We're laying fiber."

"For AT&T."

"What else?"

Oh, fiber optic cable! Great giver of bandwidth! Data bits traveling not in the slow electricity of metal wires but as light shining through strands of glass. Poor old wires delivering 10 Mbits per second. Now comes the light: 100 Mbits per second. One hundred million zeros or ones every second.

"Wow" is all I can say, sounding stupid. At least I didn't say "Oh wow." I stay there for a few seconds, then say, "G'night, Red."

He laughs. "G'night, Weird Glasses Girl."

I go up to my place and look out the window at Red while he and his compadre keep an eye on the guy down the manhole of fiber, the man working on the glass-filled pipes through which the soon-to-explode internet will flow. What cannot be done with the hundred millions of bits? What limits can we not surpass? Then a shadow falls over those hopes, and the name of the shadow is AT&T, the metal-clad warrior, soon to possess and control the bits shining through glass.

But never mind for now. I think of the jammed restaurants in South Park; the cafés where you can overhear business plans and funding sources; the Friday-night beer parties where you might run into the founders of Google; the crowded bars, four-deep trying to order; everywhere you can see, hear, feel the madness of rebellion and the narcissism of self-congratulation, the crazy joy of believing that what we are doing here has never been done before. The neighborhood craves the bandwidth. SOMA can't wait for the fiber to be lit.

Off the High

2000

We should be celebrating. We're in Toronto, from April 7 to 9, at the tenth annual meeting of the Computers, Freedom, and Privacy Conference. The Canadian Parliament is in the process of passing a far-reaching data-protection and privacy law; the Canadians here are joyous. But otherwise the conference is subdued compared with the hot debates and irreverent fun of past years.

The strange brew of people who attend CFP usually makes for a crackling time. Cryptographers and lawyers and hackers. European privacy commissioners in their well-cut Italian suits. Noted academics giving research papers. Creators of key elements of the internet. A convicted cyber-felon turned reporter forbidden to touch the internet. The codirector of the ACLU. A company head with the job title "Evil Genius." One year a United States senator stopped by. As did the chief counsel of the NSA. Not to mention recruiters from the FBI. It's only a small exaggeration to say that nowhere else on earth could you meet a technology crowd like this all in one room.

But where is the bacchanal like the ones of the mid-1990s? When cypherpunks, the bad boys of crypto, whistled and laughed and heckled as a government regulator proposed weaker encryption standards. When programmers and technology editors broke all the pool regulations and floated until dawn while drinking forbidden beverages out of real, breakable glasses (also forbidden). When a person like myself, in one weekend, could become very close to the privacy commissioner of Bavaria, a long-haired cypherpunk, a media producer, and a graduate student using algorithms to research the environmental effects of suburban lawns. And there is no replacing the fizzy high we all felt when, in 1996, the BBC came with its lights and cameras to hunt for the essence of the internet, interviewing whomever. Ah! How could one resist succumbing to the belief that we were living through an unprecedented time, the years of the web's rising reach and power?

Maybe what has put the damper on this year's conference is that, after the Canadians pass their law, the United States will be the sole nation in the highly industrialized world without legal data-protections. Or maybe it's the fact of being in Canada, where everyone who is an American knows that, on crossing back into the United States, they will lose their constitutional right not to be subjected to unreasonable searches.

But the cause is deeper, as becomes clear when the conference unfolds. Four iconic members of the internet culture will give voice to, or cause, the anxiety that undercuts the celebratory mood: Neal Stephenson, the author of the novel *Snow Crash* and a cult figure among geeks everywhere. Phil Zimmermann, the creator of Pretty Good

Privacy (PGP), the most widely used email encryption tool in the world. Bailey Whitfield Diffie, better known as Whit, co-author of the Diffie-Hellman key exchange, the essential cryptographic protocol that allows computer users to communicate privately across insecure channels. And, not least, the man credited with inventing the World Wide Web itself, Tim Berners-Lee.

Competing ideologies: Which is best at keeping the internet free for individual exploration, meanwhile protecting it from overseeing eyes? The rule of law versus the rule of code. Civil society or cryptography. Parliaments or programmers. Privacy commissioners or small, private groups of coders.

On one side are the supporters of social policy and political activism, believers in legislation, in politics with all its messiness and confusions. Such a fortunate, successful mess had led up to the passage of the Canadian law, which had involved hundreds of people in battling groups. "Everyone fought," said one of the participants.

On the other side are the geeks, nerds, crypto-anarchists, and techno-libertarians who believe that government is the enemy (despite the fact that the technical basis for the internet was a free gift to the public from the United States Department of Defense), that regulations are anathema, and the best defense for the web is cryptography. There is only one way to keep the internet free and private: more technology. Technologists created the internet, goes this argument, and only technologists can save it. John Gilmore, a cofounder of the Electronic Frontier Foundation (EFF), an organization that fosters freedom of expression in online communications, and a respected member of the internet technical community, expressed this viewpoint perfectly when he said, "I want to guarantee [privacy] with physics and mathematics, not with laws."

In the nine previous years of panels and talks and workshops, the arguments had gone back and forth over the two belief systems, a respectful but deadly serious game of tug-of-war, the rope sliding left and right, finally averaging over time with the flag in the middle.

But this year it was as if a virus had passed through the conference, a Legionnaire's leftward-moving disease, the flag suddenly yanked over the line toward politics. Phil Zimmermann stepped gently over the divide. Neal Stephenson was subtle but clear in his leftward defection. Tim Berners-Lee went over the line sorrowfully, bemoaning what had happened to the web. And Whit Diffie leapt over like a man on fire.

Zimmermann's and Stephenson's conversions came at a dinner speech. Stephenson was giving the talk. His head is shaved. He has a reddish mustache that grows down and merges with his goatee.

Only by a stretch of the imagination could Stephenson's talk be called a presentation. There were no PowerPoint slides, not even a reading from one of Stephenson's books. He used plastic transparencies that were hand-drawn with something like Magic Markers, which he slipped in and out of an overhead projector he might have first seen in grade school. The talk was like his latest book: long (the recently published *Cryptonomicon* came in at over nine hundred pages) and hugely digressive (the book includes disquisitions on Bach's organ music and how to eat Cap'n Crunch).

After a series of slides, many turns of mind, and a deep mental stack of points and stories, Stephenson came to a clear statement that somehow followed from what had come before. He said: The best defense for one's privacy and personal integrity is not cryptography but "social structures."

This was a surprise. The threads that hold *Cryptonomicon* together are encryption and decryption; the book includes the code of a crypto-algorithm. Stephenson himself is a former programmer.

His works take place in the mathematical worlds of hackers, where, for instance, one character in the book compares even the ocean to an ideal computer. Whatever ambivalence Stephenson expressed in his books about hacker communities, nowhere does he call cryptography a false guarantor of personal privacy and integrity.

Stephenson showed a series of transparencies: at first small circles, then, slide by slide, circles that grew larger, merging with other enlarging circles, their Venn diagrams overlapping to create a wide, inclusive field.

Stephenson, oracular as always, said very little as the slides followed one another. Yet it was impossible not to understand the circles as the social structures he had called essential for privacy. He left it to the listener to define those structures, but they could only have been civic associations, where agreed-upon rules of behavior were accepted by larger and larger constituencies, perhaps voluntarily, perhaps with touches of law. His point was about code: Without a sociopolitical context, cryptography is not going to protect you.

"Relying on cryptography," Stephenson said, "is like having a fence with one high picket." The slide showed a single, tall picket, a bird considering it with bulging eyes.

Stephenson singled out PGP for criticism, which perhaps was brave, going after the email encryption tool most used in the world. But offering his criticism at that moment was also callous, given that Zimmermann was in the audience.

After the long talk was over, Stephenson opened up the floor for questions. Zimmermann raised his hand. He has the roundly soft body that is not unusual among the male chair-sitters of his profession. He wore a sports jacket over a tee shirt. He had never given up his 1970s aviator glasses.

Zimmermann had been nothing but a firm believer in the libertarian point of view that crypto is the solution to ensuring privacy. Anything else—law, regulation, "social structures"—amounts to forms of coercion. Zimmermann had gone so far as to risk being labeled a criminal by the federal government. The United States had declared strong encryption to be a weapon; as such, it could not be exported. PGP has strong encryption; it was exported. Zimmermann was investigated as possibly being a felon, although he was never charged.

The room went quiet as we waited to hear what Zimmermann would say. After some seconds, he said softly, "I never meant PGP to be the defense of the lone libertarian."

Leaving the question: What else would defend him?

The next one to cross the line was Tim Berners-Lee, and his move was not subtle. It came as he received the EFF Pioneer Award, which is given every year "to honor significant contributions to the advancement of rights and responsibilities in the Information Society," as it is described by the EFF.

Berners-Lee was the perfect recipient of the award. He embodies the libertarian ideal of the individual genius and anarchic creation—no one gave him the assignment to propose and invent hypertext and hypertext markup language (HTML), the essential foundations of the web. Yet his work belies the ultra-libertarian belief articulated by John Gilmore, who said at an earlier workshop, "Everything that works on the web was created by small groups working in isolation." Berners-Lee did not work in isolation. He created not only the World Wide Web but also the World Wide Web Consortium, which he founded as a place for technologists to offer proposals, suggest plans, and come to a consensus about guidelines and specifications.

Berners-Lee could not be at the conference. He sent a videotape, obviously knowing in advance that he would win.

Berners-Lee's expression is usually mild, friendly, and open, as it was when he spoke of feeling honored and grateful. But then a look of worry creased his face. He began talking about what had happened to the internet since the days when he had the vision of the web as a forum for individuals and groups to share thoughts and research and knowledge, a place for private and public exchanges among equals. He stressed that the web was built on egalitarian principles. But now, he said, that equality was being threatened.

He spoke about e-commerce, how the web was becoming a commercial selling machine controlled by large retailers.

And money: the massive infusions of venture capital, the rocket-ship rise of stock-market valuations.

And next a statement so unlike the usual technologist's viewpoint that he could not finish it:

"Libertarians are used to fighting the government," he said, "and not corporations . . ."

Berners-Lee was about to utter a heresy. According to the libertarian orthodoxy, unfettered business activity is an unalloyed good; the belief is in "free" markets, unregulated capitalism, the Ayn Rand view of a bounteous society. One does not "fight" a corporation. Any constraint of economic activity is *The Road to Serfdom*, as said in the title of the book by Friedrich Hayek, the canonical libertarian economist, who warned that government controls of any kind lead to a tyrannous state.

And then Berners-Lee went on to another unfinishable thought:

"I know we don't like regulation where we can avoid it, but . . ."

Regulation. Meaning laws, meaning government. Not only had Berners-Lee moved toward law in the divide between civics and code, he had taken a step on the road to a "tyrannous state."

His mood was sorrowful.

"We have to make sure that when people go to the internet, they get *the internet*," he went on to say, meaning the real net, the true one, the original—whatever that might mean to him, or to us. Somehow, even if it means laws and rules and governments, we must find our way back to the technologists' dream of the internet, the free exchanges among millions of equals; the following of links to links, unobserved, as we desire; the personal web pages we created, of our own designs, defeating the domination of Microsoft's and Apple's standard human interfaces. We must go back to that internet, even if it existed for only a flickering moment, or never existed except in idylls and nostalgia. We must route around the new bad corporate net; or create a superset of it; or an alternative. Or something.

"Everyone stop eating!" Whit Diffie shouted out as he started his dinner speech. He had to repeat it, clapping his hands, until the room went quiet.

Diffie looked the same as ever, impish in an excellent suit, his long, pointy goatee, and the gray-blond hair hanging down his back. Except for the suit (no shirt and tie), he is the consummate techno-libertarian, one of the handful of technologists who might rightly be called celebrity cryptographers, if such people can be said to exist.

Diffie began with a short history of cryptography, mentioning the Diffie-Hellman protocol that he and Martin Hellman had published in 1976, also other tools used along the way, and his faith in them as protections from governmental intrusions. "Crypto was a security technique that didn't require trusting anyone else," he said, which was certainly true of the D-H key exchange: the two people involved in the secure communication could very well be strangers. He told the crowd that he had always had a mathematical idea about the best way to authenticate the security of the communications.

So far, he seemed in tune with John Gilmore's belief in physics and mathematics as the best ways to maintain privacy. But Diffie's next sentence made clear his defection from the Gilmore camp.

"Now it turns out you have to trust other people," he said.

He went on to speak passionately, waving his arms, yelling as though he had no microphone, a man on a soapbox. He told the audience that software can reduce the amount of trust you need in human beings. As you move through the world, he went on, the sense of security, privacy, autonomy turns out to be "a function of social structures."

Here was the echo of Stephenson's dinner talk of the night before. Other people. Trust in human beings. Social structures. Bailey Whitfield Diffie: another renegade techno-libertarian, it seemed.

If Diffie had stopped there, his change of mind (or change of heart, for so it seemed, given the heat with which he spoke) would have been like the conversions of the sly Neal Stephenson, the reluctant Phil Zimmermann, the unhappy Tim Berners-Lee. But then Diffie paced back and forth and raised his voice to exhort us:

We were slaves to the mainframe! he said. Dumb terminals! That's all we had. We were powerless under the big machine's unyielding central control. Then we escaped to the personal computer, autonomous, powerful. Then networks. The PC was soon rendered to be nothing but a "thin client," just a browser with very little software residing on our personal machines, the code being on network servers, which are under the control of administrators. Now to the web, nothing but a thin, thin browser for us. All the intelligence out there, on the net, our machines having become dumb terminals again.

Now he paced more quickly, spoke yet more loudly:

Knowledge workers will lose their autonomy, he told us, they will be forced to use those slavish, dumb machines. They can become mere objects of surveillance by the companies they work for, as a result of "corporate imperialism over its workers."

("Corporate imperialism"—was there something wrong with the microphone?)

He said he could foresee a day when workers, doing their jobs from the "convenience" of their home, would be subject to "spot inspections" by their employers; a time when the home was effectively turned into a powerless, occupied zone under the control of "corporate properatarianism," as he put it, workers becoming the property of the companies they work for, mere objects of surveillance.

Here was a new, nightmarish dystopia, one rained down upon us by the supposed savior of humankind, the internet. Diffie's vision sounded like something out of *Brave New World*; except here the government is not the enemy, not the one watching you from the other side of the screen. Diffie had raised the specter of the evil corporation, its perpetual gaze, its imperialism over the human soul.

What shall we desperate knowledge workers do? Diffie asked the audience. "Organize!" he said. We need "the rise of labor again," said Whitfield Diffie, renowned cryptographer and former believer in the power of code. "We need to tighten up the relationships among knowledge workers," he said, "and bargain as a whole."

Organize! The rise of labor! Whit Diffie had come to CFP known as a devoted techno-libertarian. He was leaving as . . . a social activist.

There was something poignant in this conversion. The work he is most famous for had been published twenty-four years ago. Despite his shouts and manic pacing—perhaps because of his shouts and manic pacing—I had the sense of his dismay and sorrow at the loss of his youthful beliefs, and his desperate drive to find new ones, although I might have been projecting upon Diffie my own feelings of loss and dismay.

As the conference ended, I looked around and noted who was missing. For all the diversity of the CFP's attendees, the big corporate CEOs were not there. The venture capitalists were not there. The new millionaires the VCs had funded were not there. The great powers of Wall Street; the early, insider investors in the web; the young male venture capitalists in Palo Alto in their business-casual wear: not there. Those whose torrents of money had fostered the creation of a massive commercial web, their investing fury driving the technology-heavy Nasdaq index to manic heights—absent. Despite CFP's devoted cadre of social and technical defenders of the web, and their ten years of sophisticated debates, they were no match for the absentees.

A month before the conference, the Nasdaq had topped 5,000. Three days before CFP opened, the index suffered a fall of 29 percent. Then, while the conference continued, the Nasdaq bounced back up, almost erasing the losses. The public had accepted the popular wisdom promoted by market brokers and financial commentators: A fall in the prices of technology stocks makes them a bargain. A decline, they say, is a buying opportunity. This is not the end of the rocket ride! Here is your chance to climb aboard!

The public rushed right back in.

To Catch a Falling Knife

2002

*With the assistance of Clara Basile, Avalon Capital Management**

It's January 2000. I want to buy Webvan. All right, its market value is half of what it was three months ago. But that makes the stock a bargain, right? And it's back at its IPO price, so I better jump in now, before the big bounce-back, before everyone else buys on this downswing and drives up the price. Maybe to new heights?

The evidence of my own eyes drives me. I see their grocery delivery vans everywhere here in SOMA, parked in red zones, in front of hydrants, blocking driveways, double-parked. White and tan, on the

---

* Clara Basile contributed her knowledge of stock markets and their behaviors. However, the social, political, and literary interpretations do not necessarily reflect those of Clara Basile and/or Avalon Capital Management.

sides the image of an overflowing grocery bag enclosed in a green circle. The buyers order their groceries online, and the poor stock-pickers at the warehouse and the harried drivers must get the goods to them within a thirty-minute delivery window.

The most demanded delivery times, naturally, are after-work hours, so Monday through Friday the vans join the driver nightmare at the main approaches to the Bay Bridge, just below my window, engines idling in a cloud of pollution, radios blasting for the drivers who assert their control over the soundscape since mastering physical space is impossible; on the bad days, "motherfucker" prevails; on the very worst ones, guys get out of their cars and have fistfights.

I am impressed with the perseverance of the Webvan drivers traversing this mess. And I am struck by the ubiquity of the vans in SOMA. Which means, I think, that the cool new web generation is hooked on Webvan. This is the future.

I want to buy in. I want. I want. I want.

I don't believe in all of this web-stock madness; I know the game is rigged in favor of the VCs. My father, an accountant and small-time real-estate investor, gave me good middle-class advice when he warned me about the market: it's a crap shoot and you should put in only what you are prepared to lose. But there is no escaping one's guts. The air around me is drunken with greed. The rocketing technology stocks create a force field of desire. I am as intoxicated as I was in those fiber optic nights at Infusion, but crazier. I see the startup boys making millions. Why shouldn't I get into the game of betting on technology riches?

Intoxicated, as I said. One more martini, please.

I call Clara Basile, my longtime friend and financial adviser, and tell her of my desire. She answers soberly, "Do you know what the profit margins are in the grocery business? Three percent, maybe four. Would you buy Safeway?"

_____

Stock markets float in clouds of stories. Numbers and mathematical analysis may be the infrastructure, but narratives surround the market with words, tales, explanations, myths. The stories shape our thoughts and feelings about the great, mass, global economic behavior of billions of people who buy and sell stocks, bonds, funds, hedges, commodities, puts (a bet that a security will go down) and calls (a bet it will go up), and the complex financial instruments that recede from public view.

Narratives: For example, when making pitches to venture capitalists, would-be founders of startups describe what they're planning, why people will want what they're planning, their path to a bright future, and so on. This is called telling their story. The story must be at least plausible, at best alluring, appetite-whetting. The underlying realities of costs and revenue projections are understood to be inaccurate; similarly, the story is not exactly true. VCs expect that 90 percent of the startups they fund will fail. Yet narratives have a hold on all of us; our understanding of the past and present is a trail of stories and tales.

Each trading day, after the close of the U.S. markets, financial commentators tell stories about why the markets behaved as they did. On television, in newspaper reports and columns, on the web: one narrative after another. It was the snow in the Northeast that kept shoppers from the stores. It was the coup in an African oil-producing nation affecting supplies. It was the disappointing earnings in this or that stock (which met projections but did not satisfy the insiders' expected "whisper number"). The causes are politics, treaties, epidemics, hurricanes, job reports, rumors.

Some of the market explanations agree, some do not. Television "analysts" sometimes use exactly the same rationale for the market's movement both up and down. One day, the dollar goes up, and the market goes up, and the dollar's rise is the "reason" for the rising market. On another day, the dollar goes up, and the market goes down, and somehow the dollar's rise also "explains" the down movement.

(Clara adds that only movements in the long run, over years, may eventually reflect the "true story.")

But it doesn't matter that today's explanations are irrational. Wall Street needs the participation of the general public. Those owning "securities" (another fiction) want the value to climb, and this requires buyers to bid for their holdings. To society at large, trading must seem to make sense. When markets fall, the narratives must be as comforting as bedtime stories, supporting the soothing advice: Do not sell. Or, if traders are betting that a stock will fall, thereby profiting when it does fall, here come tales of company woes. The story says: Sell.

An almost irresistible narrative is the story of buying technology stocks on price dips, as I said earlier. It is so compelling a belief system that it takes great discipline (like Basile's) to escape it. Technology stocks will keep rising, goes the story; price drops are opportunities to get into the game. It was just this belief that overcame my good sense: Webvan is down; Webvan, like all of technology, surely will go up. The desire to join the herd is strong; if everyone is making this bet, so should I. (Basile saved me from that absurd buy; by 2001, Webvan had gone bankrupt.) Greed is the emotional undercurrent of this narrative: Do not hesitate. Yet more riches await you—buy.

During the internet boom, a special, untried, counterintuitive narrative was accepted not only by the general public but also by venture capitalists, stock-fund managers, trustees of inheritances, hedge-fund investors, financial consultants, overseers of pension funds, and market insiders of all stripes. This dream of the future said: Technology is different. The internet and the web are transforming society. A new economic order is dawning, a new reality of existence. The singularity of human/digital convergence approaches. In the new capitalism of technology, profits do not matter.

All right, maybe profits do matter, but not right now, maybe not for years. What determines if a startup or web company is succeeding is the number of eyeballs looking at the site, the count of unique visitors, of advertising click-throughs. The idea is to bring millions of viewers to the site. Once all those people are assembled, the companies will find a way to "monetize eyeballs"—that is, make money off the assembly and turn a profit.

In the meantime, a web company needs revenue, money to pay salaries and operating expenses. For the startup, the first revenue source is a round of financing from the venture capitalists; a year later, there may be a second round; yet a third after more time has gone by. But, eventually, the company will have to go out into the world and stand on its own.

I spoke with the founder of a startup. I asked him if he had a path to profitability; he did not. I asked if he had a revenue plan; he did. His answer was "Go IPO!" That is, have an initial public offering and reap the millions from the sale of the stock. Another way to look at this transaction is: Get the general public to finance a company with no known path to making money.

NASDAQ COMPOSITE INDEX

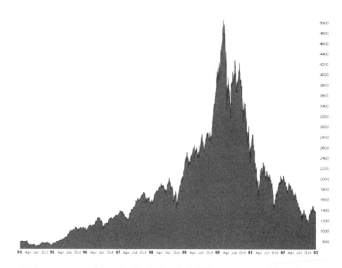

All charts courtesy of Clara Basile, Avalon Capital Management, and StockCharts.com

The market for technology stocks was not manic from the first. Between 1995 and 1998, the Nasdaq index rose at an approximately forty-five-degree angle, which Basile described as not irrational but as "an enthusiastic bull market." The Nasdaq, heavily populated by tech stocks, is our best gauge of financial and social interest in the overall values of technology.

The rise was not irrational because there was a reality underlying the climbing prices of technology stocks. Something new was indeed coming into the world. A vast online marketplace was truly coming into being; now the essentials (and frivolities) of everyday life could be acquired on demand at any hour of the day or night. As I had imagined and feared it would, the internet was penetrating the boundaries of economic, social, and personal life.

What brought the web to the millions, and the millions to the web, was a single class of programs: the browser. The period of the rising "enthusiastic" market closely follows the years during which the web browser was being created and widely deployed.

In the early 1990s, Tim Berners-Lee's releases of the web included what he called a browser-editor. However, it ran on only one operating system, NeXTStep, which was not a general-use consumer platform. The first browser to break through to the public was Mosaic, written by Marc Andreessen and Eric Bina, and released in 1993. It had graphical capabilities not available in Berners-Lee's—it could display images and text on the same page. Most important, Mosaic was ported to run on Windows, introducing the web to the rapidly growing population of personal-computer users. Andreessen went on to found Netscape. In 1994 the company released Navigator, another graphical browser that ran on Windows.

(A full history of the browser is beyond what I can discuss here. My apologies to the many creative researchers and programmers whose work contributed to the invention of browser interfaces to the web.)

Microsoft, as ever, was last in invention but first in its ability to out-market its rivals. The company licensed a browser from a company named Spyglass and reworked it as Microsoft Explorer. The company embedded Explorer in Windows 98 and made it the default browser, thereby literally driving competitors off the screen. Whatever one might think about Microsoft's anti-competitive "borrowing" of the creations of others, their incorporation of a browser into the prevailing operating environment of the time—theirs—effectively drove the rise of the web.

The world was now a bazaar. The number of computer users rose exponentially; and what they might see expanded exponentially. The choice of what we might see or read or buy seemed endless, as the supply of faucets had once seemed infinite to me. Advertising would help us find exactly what we wanted; meanwhile, advertisers, watching our every move on the web, would "suggest" what we "really" wanted.

There were financial factors that drove the start of the web mania, in 1998, as discussed below, but it can be no accident that the market madness was fueled in part by a true technological advance, the graphical browser, which now was in the hands of the millions.

The web was also a honeypot. What ignited an early explosion of the net was the seductive, vulgar, waggling finger of porn.

Just as wars over the centuries drove the invention of new machinery, the demand for porn was a driver of changes to the electronic medium of the web. We don't need catapults or Gatling guns or stealth bombers; we need to simulate the old in-and-out, the motions of tongues and fingers. Yet bandwidth was limited; downloads were slow; the network was built for exchanging text and small graphics. Porn sites then stretched the technical abilities of website interfaces by animating three or four still photographs in sequences that looped and looped, which worked just fine for, well, the illusion of in-and-out.

As the hundreds of millions across the globe craved more realistic views of sex, porn sites became the leading force in the push for more bandwidth, and more, and yet more. Higher bandwidth made for better visual content for all users. Also better ads (for the advertisers). And better porn (for the eager millions). Unlike all those startups not thinking about profits, the purveyors of porn made actual money.

In July through October 1998, there came a break in the upward movement of the Nasdaq. The index fell by 33 percent in eleven weeks.* The drop was not related to technology; it came in the wake of the spectacular failure of a hedge fund, Long-Term Capital Management. The financial factors are complex, but the fund's failure threatened a systemic collapse of financial institutions and world markets. In response, the United States Federal Reserve "flooded the market with liquidity," said Basile. That is, they made borrowing available at very low interest rates.

Sophisticated investors knew that, with the Federal Reserve supplying cheap, ready cash, markets would rise. With interest rates so low, returns would fall in the normally relatively safe investments that are tied to rates: bonds, savings accounts, money-market funds. Where else could one possibly make money? Only in the equities markets. The public would rush in to buy stocks; the demand for stocks would make their values rise; markets would go up. The Fed's money, therefore, had lowered the risks of investing in stocks. Now sophisticated market players could afford to make big, risky bets on technology startups. "The Fed had their backs," as Basile described it.

* The illustrations here show the overall and dramatic sweep of the technology boom and bust. The smaller movements over short periods may be harder to see within the full scope of the time period reflected in the charts.

And venture-capital money did indeed flood into startups, seemingly into any company whose name ended in dot-com. In 2000, VCs invested $105 billion in startups, 90 percent of it going to those related to technology—companies with dim prospects for making money.

With the markets down 33 percent in the wake of Long-Term Capital Management's failure, the public found the opportunity it had learned to wait for. Here was the perfect storm: simultaneously, both sophisticated and uninformed investors raced in to join the technology gold rush. The angle of the Nasdaq's rise inflected sharply upward. Between 1998 and 1999, the index doubled.

In October 1999, the mania for internet stocks began in earnest. From October 18, 1999, to March 10, 2000, in less than five months, the index *doubled yet again*, rising twenty-five hundred points. There were short dips along the way, but at each one, prices resumed their relentless climb. The mathematical shape of the rising market was approaching a parabolic curve, as Basile described it:

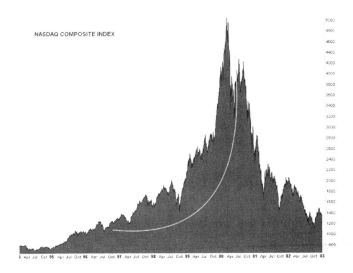

NASDAQ COMPOSITE INDEX

The boom was no longer about the nature and value of the web technologies being created. The deployment of the browser was no longer a critical factor; the flowering of individuals' web pages was not the driver of the value of internet stocks. What drove the mania was the *story* of the web. The internet had become not a celebration of computing but a stock-market event, as Tim Berners-Lee had feared it would. The Nasdaq was now a market reacting to itself: Stock prices rise; people buy because they want to get into the hot market; all that buying pressure causes stock prices to rise again. Then more people want a piece of the action; stock prices rise yet again. People buy; prices rise; etc. A sobered-up investor had to know this iteration could not continue to infinity.

Surely some insider investors were still buying stocks. But at this juncture, it was the unsophisticated general public that kept buying as the Nasdaq approached the very top, which it reached on March 10, 2000. The late buyers were people not in the know—people who had been seduced by the dreams of riches, who had invested parts of their paychecks, their savings, their retirement portfolios. The naïve public were the last ones into the manic market. They hear: Technology is rising! And they buy. Their buys are essential to keep the market climbing. In the internet boom, uninformed investors were the equivalent of the proverbial shoe-shine boys of the Great Depression. "Even shoeshine boys bought stocks," went the expression, meaning the dazzled masses who rushed in just as the market was about to crash in 1929.

And the crash of 2000 came. But even as the market fell precipitously, the story of buying on dips somehow endured: perhaps this was just a bigger dip. Both serious investors and the general public rushed in once more to buy technology stocks. The Nasdaq index bounced up about 30 percent, fell again briefly, then bounced back up once more. (This is the drop and bounce back that occurred during the CPF 2000 conference.) The index chart at this point looks like a cathedral on the highest point of a hill with two smaller spires below it, still rising into the sky. The third spire was the end. The index kept dropping. This was what Basile calls the falling knife: even if you think the market will turn up again—if more of the riches you dream of still lie ahead—you can't step in and buy. "The selling pressure is too fierce," said Basile; "the downdraft will skewer your greedy hand." The parabolic curve had broken. "When the curve breaks, you're dead," said Basile.

There were no more bargains to be had; there was no new capitalism of technology, as it turned out. Two market stories—always buy tech on dips, and profits do not matter—were revealed as lies. Said Basile, "The belief system was shattered." The index kept dropping until October 10, 2002, by which time it had fallen from the high more than four thousand points, or 78 percent.

I think of the boom and crash as a massive transfer of wealth from the bedazzled public to the venture capitalists and young men (yes, men) who sold their stock during the market's mania phase. Smart venture capitalists made fortunes by cashing out and selling to the general public. Certainly some VCs sold too late and lost a great deal of money. But one presumes that they and their investors were wealthy individuals and could afford their losses. In any case, they knew the risks, or should have known. Many founders and employees of startups discovered that their stock options were worthless. But few of them had invested their own money to begin with; they had been paid well while working at the startup; what they lost was not money but a dream of riches. The true, life-changing losses were borne by the middle class, and eventually the working class, the ones who had heard the call of technology late into the parabolic curve and were lured into the trap my father had warned me about. They lost what they could not afford to lose.

———

2002: SOMA has gone dark. Some startups survive—Organics, Salon, for instance—but otherwise the programmers and entrepreneurs have disappeared from South Park. No longer can you overhear the cell yells about eyeballs and revenue streams. Echo, one of the restaurants in the oval, has closed. Its opposite across the way, the South Park Cafe, no longer serves lunch. Gone are the white tablecloths, the glasses of Sancerre and Bordeaux, the plates of sea bass and steak garnished with slices of carrots cut into the shape of little flowers. On the downslope of the park, the black men drinking beverages out of paper bags still own their picnic table. The homeless man doing yoga never came back.

If not for the new Giants baseball park, where Second Street dead-ends at South Beach, SOMA might have gone back to its abandoned, hollowed-out days. New restaurants have opened to sell beer and hamburgers and hot dogs; there are no tablecloths. For the seven months of the lengthened baseball season, crowds dressed in the Giants' colors of black and orange march from Market Street to King Street and back, retracing the treks of the Chinese women who had toiled in the sweatshops and the programmers who had replaced them. Nights are filled with the sounds of fans hooting (the Giants won); later the howling of drunken stragglers; then the grumbling engines of cars inching toward the bridge, inebriated drivers swearing to do things to each other's anatomy.

I think of Barbarossa and his crew, of their lights and the orange cones that had blocked off the traffic. Do they remember those nights and days down the manhole of mystery? Does Redbeard still think of the girl in weird glasses?

No one goes down the manhole of mystery anymore. No need. Fifty percent of the fiber optic cable laid during the boom was never lit.

PART THREE PART THREE PART THREE **PART THREE**

Life, Artificial

Programming the Post-Human

COMPUTER SCIENCE REDEFINES "LIFE"

2002

There are times when you feel you are witnessing a precise moment in which science fiction crosses over into science. I don't mean the advent of voice-recognition software that lets us talk to computers, or even the prospect of space tourism, but a moment when one of the great, enduring conundrums of our speculative literature suddenly materializes as a problem in actual life. Perhaps the greatest of these is the problem of distinguishing humans from robots. What element, if any, separates us from machines?

This theme received its classic treatment by Isaac Asimov in his 1946 story "Evidence." In the story, a future society has forbidden the use of humanoid robots, since it is feared that the intelligent machines, identical in appearance to humans but with superior powers, will take over the world. A man named Stephen Byerley becomes the first "World Coordinator." Many years later, however, his humanity is still in doubt.

> "And the great Byerley was simply a robot."
> "Oh, there's no way of ever finding out. I think he was. But when he decided to die, he had himself atomized, so that there will never be any legal proof.—Besides, what difference would it make?"

What difference would it make? In January 2002, fifty-six years after the publication of Asimov's story, a group of computer scientists, cryptographers, mathematicians, and cognitive scientists gathered at "the first workshop on human interactive proofs." Their goal was the creation of a CAPTCHA, a "Completely Automated Probabilistic Public Turing Test to Tell Computers and Humans Apart."

In Asimov's story, distinguishing robots from humans was a matter of world-historical importance, a question of human dignity and worth. The problem for the scientists at the workshop appeared, on the surface, to be less consequential: the development of automated methods to prevent software robots, or "bots," from invading chat rooms and barraging email systems with spam. Yet their work had implications beyond the needs of commercial applications. We have become dependent upon electronic communications; we can no longer envision a future without computer-mediated interactions; so the issue for us has become as dire as it was for the inhabitants of Asimov's imagined world. Their problem is now ours: How do we tell a human from a machine?

What is interesting about this problem is that it is one we humans have brought upon ourselves. It is a consequence of a deeply human part of us, *Homo faber*, the toolmaker. We have imagined the existence of robots, and, now that we have dreamed them up, it's as if we feel compelled to build them, and to endow them with as much intelligence as we can. We can't help it, it seems; it's in our nature as fashioners of helpful objects. We can't resist taking up the dare: How far can we go in creating smart tools until our tools come to outsmart us, ceasing in crucial ways to be "ours"?

Underlying that dare is a philosophical shift in science's views about the role of human beings in the great project of life. Researchers in robotics and artificial life openly question the "specialness" of human life. Some call life as we know it on earth merely one of many "possible biologies" and see our reverence for humanity as something of a prejudice ("human chauvinism"). According to Rodney Brooks, director of MIT's Artificial Intelligence Lab, evolution spelled the end of our uniqueness in relationship to other living creatures by defining us as evolved animals; and robotics, in its quest to create a sentient machine, looks forward to ending the idea of our uniqueness in relation to the inanimate world. In what may reflect supreme humility (we are no better than the rocks or the apes) or astounding hubris (we can create life without the participation of either God or the natural forces of evolution), computer science has begun the debate over the coming of what has come to be called the "post-human": a nonbiological, sentient entity whose capabilities would exceed those of human beings.

According to this idea, the post-human's thoughts would not be limited by the slow speed of our own nervous systems. Unhampered by the messy wet chemistry of carbon-based life, loosed from the pressures of evolution, the post-human can be designed, consciously, to exceed our capabilities. Its memory can be practically limitless. It can have physical strength without bounds. And, freed from the senescence of the cells, it might live forever. If this sounds like Superman ("with powers far beyond those of mortal man"), consider another of those moments when science fiction passed over into science:

The date was April 1, 2000. The place was a lecture hall on the campus of Stanford University. Douglas Hofstadter, the computer scientist perhaps best known for his book *Gödel, Escher, Bach*, assembled a panel of roboticists, engineers, computer scientists, and technologists, and asked them to address the question: "Will spiritual robots replace humanity by 2100?"

Hofstadter began by saying, crankily, that he had "decided to eliminate naysayers" from the panel. He made his point with a cartoon of a fish that thinks it is ridiculous that life could exist on dry land (*gribbit, gribbit,* went the sound of a frog). "It is more amazing," he said, "that life could come from inert matter than from a change of substrate"—more amazing that life could arise from a soup of dead molecules than change its base from carbon to something else, such as silicon. Hofstadter looked into the future, and said, without nostalgia or regret: "I really wonder whether there will be human beings."

The room was filled to fire-marshal-alarming proportions. People jammed the doors, stood against the walls, sat in the aisles, on the steps in the steep balcony of the lecture hall, leaned dangerously against the balcony rails. The audience, young and old, students and veterans of the computing community of Silicon Valley, sat still and quiet, leaning forward, putting up with the crowding and the heat and Doug Hofstadter's grouchy refusal to use a microphone. From where I was sitting, high up in the balcony, the scene reminded me of nothing so much as those paintings of early medical dissections, crowds of men peering to where the cadaver lay slashed open in the operating theater below. On that day at Stanford, there was the same sense that some threshold, previously taboo to science, had been crossed. Computer science, which heretofore could have plausibly been said to serve humanity by creating its tools, was now considering another objective altogether: the creation of a nonbiological, "spiritual" being—sentient, intelligent, alive—who could surpass, and perhaps control, us.

This was not the first time that computer science seemed on the verge of creating a successor race of machines. When I was a young programmer, in the late 1970s and early 1980s, practitioners in a branch of computer science then called "artificial intelligence" believed they were close to creating an intelligent computer. Although AI would fail spectacularly in fulfilling its grand expectations at that time, the debate surrounding the field was alluring. I was then an in-the-trenches programmer, and, like many of my colleagues, I saw in AI the opportunity to explore the questions that had previously been in the province of the humanities. What are we? What makes a human intelligent? What is consciousness, knowledge, learning? How could these things be represented to a machine, and what would we learn about ourselves in the formation of that representation? It was soon clear that, in a secular society that had given up on the idea of God, we would be looking elsewhere for the answer to the question of what animates us; and that "elsewhere" would be the study of cybernetic intelligence, the engine of postmodern philosophical speculation.

It is for this reason that the question of the post-human is worth exploring. Whether or not we can build a "spiritual robot" by 2100, in asking what is "post"-human, we must first ask what is human. The ensuing debate inherits the questions that once belonged to philosophy and religion—and brings up the same ancient, deep-seated confusions.

Over the years, as I listened to the engineering give-and-take over the question of artificial life forms, I kept coming up against something obdurate inside myself, some stubborn resistance to the definition of "life" that was being promulgated. It seemed to me too mechanistic, too reductive of what we are. Even if I could not quite get myself to believe in God or the soul or the Tao, still, as I sat there high in the balcony of the Stanford lecture hall, listening to the cyberneticists' claims to be on the path toward creating a sentient being, I found myself muttering, "No, that's not right, we're not just mechanisms, you're missing something, there is something else, something more." And then I had to ask myself: What else could there be?

Over the last half-century, in addressing the question "What are humans?" cybernetics has come up with three answers. We are, in order of their occurrence in the debate, (1) computers, (2) ants, and (3) accidents.

The first, the co-identification of human sentience and the computer, appeared almost simultaneously with the appearance of computers. In 1950, only four years after the construction of ENIAC, generally regarded as the first digital computer, the mathematician Alan Turing famously proposed that digital machines could think. And by the time computers had come into general use, in the 1960s, the view of the human brain as an information processor was already firmly installed.

It is an odd view, if you consider it. ENIAC was conceived as a giant calculator: it was designed to compute the trajectory of artillery shells. Its role was understood as human complement, doing well what we do poorly (tedious computation, precise recall of lists of numbers and letters) and doing badly what we do well (intuitive thinking, acute perception, reactions involving the complex interplay of mental, physical, and emotional states). Yet, by 1969, when computers were still room-sized, heat-generating behemoths with block-letter-character screens, the computer scientist and Nobel Laureate in economics Herbert Simon felt no compunction about grouping computers and humans as related entities: "The computer is a member of an important family of artifacts called symbol systems . . . Another important member of the family (some of us think, anthropomorphically, it is the *most* important) is the human mind and brain." Simon went on to postulate "if computers are organized somewhat in the image of man"—without going on to question that "if." In existence barely twenty-five years, the machine that was designed to be our other—the not-human, accurate in a world where to be human is to err—had become the very analogue of human intelligence: the image of man.

Herbert Simon, along with his colleague Allen Newell, was a pioneer in the field of artificial intelligence. It is worthwhile now to give a close reading to Simon's groundbreaking book *The Sciences of the Artificial*, written in 1969. For here one can see the origins of the curious reasoning whereby the computer becomes a model for humanity.

Simon begins by discussing what on the surface might seem obvious: the difference between the natural and the artificial worlds. Natural objects have the authority of existence, he says; the "laws" of nature determine what must be. The artificial, in contrast, is designed or composed. "The engineer, and more generally the designer, is concerned with how things *ought* to be—how they ought to be in order to *attain goals*, and to *function*."

Then Simon's definition of an artifact becomes more complex. He describes it not as a thing in itself but as an interface. The artificial object is an interaction between "the substance and organization of the artifact itself, and an 'outer' environment, the surroundings in which it operates." The artifact, then, does not exist on its own. It is a bodiless, abstract process mediating between the article's substance and its existence in the world.

That is fair enough. Even a stone moves in reaction to a shifting environment. But then Simon's reasoning takes an odd turn. He goes on to say: "Notice that this way of viewing artifacts applies equally well to many things that are not man-made—to all things in fact that can be regarded as adapted to some situation; and in particular it applies to the living systems that have evolved through the forces of organic evolution." That is, it applies to all creatures—and, by extension, to us.

By the sixth page of Simon's book, where these statements appear, human beings have been removed from the realm of the "natural." Viewed as adaptable products of evolution, we have become hollow artifacts, interfaces to our environment, "systems" engineered by the processes of natural selection. It is a startling turnabout: what is being proposed here is not the possibility of creating artificial life but the redefinition of life itself as artificial.

Once you accept the definition of human life as artificial—designed, engineered—it is then an easy matter to say that the proper study of man is not man but some other engineered object, the machine. And this is indeed what Simon advocates: making the computer itself the object of study, as a phenomenon of a living system. "Since there are now many such devices in the world [computers], and since the properties that describe them also appear to be shared by the human central nervous system, nothing prevents us from developing a natural history of them. We can study them as we would rabbits or chipmunks and discover how they behave under different patterns of environmental stimulation." Standing amazed before this human-created machine, the computer scientist declares it to be our very identity; then, to learn who and what we are, he advises that we study . . . the machine.

This circular idea—the mind is like a computer; study the computer to learn about the mind—has infected decades of thinking in the computer and cognitive sciences. We find it in the work of Marvin Minsky, the influential figure in artificial intelligence, who, when asked if machines could think, famously answered: "Of course machines can think; we can think and we are 'meat machines.' " We see it in the writings of the cognitive scientist Daniel Dennett, whose book *Consciousness Explained* is suffused with conflations between human sentience and computers: "What counts as the 'program' when we talk of the virtual machine running on the brain's parallel hardware? . . . And how do these programs of millions of neural connection-strengths get installed on the brain's computer?" And we can read it in the extreme predictions made by the engineer Ray Kurzweil, inventor of the Kurzweil music synthesizer and of reading systems for the blind. Kurzweil sees the coming of "spiritual robots" almost entirely in the language of computer programming: calling memory "the mind file," which he will scan and "download" to a silicon substrate, analyzing it for its basic "algorithms," thereby creating a "backup copy" of the original human being, all without the aid of natural evolution, which he calls "a very inefficient programmer."

The limitations of this model of human intelligence should have become clear with the fading of that first naïve blush of optimism about the creation of sentient machines. In selecting the computer as the model of human thinking, AI researchers were addressing only one small portion of the mind: rational thought. They were, in essence, attempting a simulation of the neocortex—rule-based, conscious thinking—declaring that to be the essence of intelligence.

And AI did succeed in creating programs that relied upon rule-based thinking, creating so-called expert systems that codified narrow, specific, expert domains, such as oil exploration and chess playing.* But, as was pointed out by Hubert Dreyfus, the early critic of AI, the results of AI were disappointing, systems devoid of presence and awareness, a "disturbing failure to produce even the hint of a system with the flexibility of a six-month-old child."

Yet the idea of human being as computer lives on. Most troubling, even after becoming controversial in computer science, it has taken residence in the natural sciences. As Rodney Brooks put it in an article in *Nature*: "The current scientific view of living things is that they are machines whose components are biochemicals." The psychologist Steven Pinker, in the first pages of his classic book *How the Mind Works*, writes that problems of understanding the human "are both design specs for a robot and the subject matter of psychology." And this view shows up in surprising places—for instance, in an email I received from Lucia Jacobs, a professor of psychology who studies squirrel behavior at Berkeley: "I am an ethologist and know virtually nothing about computers, simulations, programming, mathematical concepts or logic. But the research is pulling me right into the middle of it."

Herbert Simon's views have come full circle; it is now standard scientific practice to study machine simulations as if they were indeed chipmunks, or squirrels: "What seems to be crystallizing, in short," wrote Jacobs of her work with robotic creatures, "is a powerful outlook on spatial navigation, from robots to human reasoning.

---

* Some observers of the 1997 chess rematch between Garry Kasparov and IBM's Deep Blue program, which Deep Blue won, saw the victory as evidence that an AI program could achieve something of the presence we associate with sentience. "Kasparov reported signs of a mind in the machine," wrote Hans Moravec, the noted roboticist. It seems there was indeed one game in which, due to some accidental combinatorial explosion, Deep Blue did not play like a machine, as Kasparov reported at the time. Kasparov then adjusted his play, looking for the strategies of that "mind," which failed to reappear. This put Kasparov off his game, and he played rather badly (for him). The point is that the program had not attained sentience; the human had projected sentience onto the machine, and had become flustered.

This is wonderful." Psychology and cognitive science—and, indeed, biology—are poised to become, in essence, branches of cybernetics.

However, the view of human biology as purely cybernetic may not endure indefinitely. In February 2001, the government-funded Human Genome Project and the private company Celera Genomics announced that they had succeeded in sequencing the full complement of human genes. What they found was shocking from a scientific point of view. "There are far fewer genes than we expected, only about 30,000 or so rather than the figure of 100,000 in the textbooks," said Dr. Eric Lander, who headed the Human Genome Project. "There is a lesson in humility in this. We only have twice as many genes as a fruit fly or a lowly nematode worm. What a comedown." And there went the simple mechanical view of one gene making one protein, and then—*chunk, chunk*—a machine processing all the proteins, and out comes one person.

Researchers are looking for other ways to explain the complexity of human physical and mental existence, said Lander. Perhaps the complexity comes from the way proteins are folded. Perhaps some proteins have multiple roles. Perhaps some genes are not "expressed," do not function in some circumstances. Perhaps there are some unknown relationships among the genes, tangles of interactions that will forever lead us down and down into the nature of matter itself. But one thing is clear: DNA is not "code." Now that we know the complete human genome, DNA has literally been *de*coded, stripped of its programming powers.

Failing to produce intelligence by modeling the "higher functions" of the cortex, cybernetics next turned to a model creature without any cortex at all: the ant. This seems like an odd place to look for human intelligence. Ants are not generally thought of as smart. But as a research model they provide one enormous advantage over the study of human brains: they yield an explanation of how apparent complexity can arise without an overseeing designer. A group of dumb ants produces the complexity of the ant colony—an example of organizational intelligence without recourse to the perennial difficulties of God or philosophy.

Again, the source for this key idea seems to be Herbert Simon. The third chapter of his book *The Sciences of the Artificial* opens by describing an ant making its way across a beach:

> We watch an ant make his laborious way across a wind- and wave-molded beach. He moves ahead, angles to the right to ease his climb up a steep dunelet, detours around a pebble, stops for a moment to exchange information with a compatriot. Thus he makes his weaving, halting way back to his home. So as not to anthropomorphize about his purposes, I sketch the path on a piece of paper. It is a sequence of irregular, angular segments—not quite a random walk, for it has an underlying sense of direction, of aiming toward a goal.
>
> I show the unlabeled sketch to a friend. Whose path is it? An expert skier, perhaps, slaloming down a steep and somewhat rocky slope. Or a sloop, beating upwind in a channel dotted with islands or shoals. Perhaps it is a path in a more abstract space: the course of search of a student seeking the proof of a theorem in geometry.

The ant leaves behind it a complex geometric pattern—how? The ant has not designed this geometry. Simon's revolutionary idea was to locate the source of the complexity not in the ant, which is quite simple "viewed as a behaving system," but in the ant's interaction with its environment: in the byplay of the ant's simple, unaware reactions to complications of pebble and sand. Simon then goes on to pronounce what will turn out to be inspirational words in the history of cybernetics:

In this chapter I should like to explore this hypothesis but with the word "human being" substituted for "ant."

With that, Simon introduces an idea that will reverberate for decades across the literature of robotics and artificial life. One can hardly read about the subject, or talk to a researcher, without coming upon the example of the ant—or the bee, or termite, or swarm, or some other such reference to the insect world. It is not clear if later adopters of "the ant idea" completely grasp the implications of Simon's view. They have concentrated upon the many low-level, dumb interactions of ants as they exchange pheromones, leaving out the difficulties of each creature's interplay with the environment. Yet what was distilled out of Simon's utterance has become an enduring model: organizational intricacy arises spontaneously out of the normal workings of the individual participants in a society or system.

This phenomenon, known as "emergence," produces outcomes that cannot be predicted from looking only at the underlying simple interactions. This is the key idea in fields known, variously, as "complexity theory," "chaos theory," and "cellular automata." It is also a foundation concept in robotics and "ALife," a branch of computer science that concerns itself with the creation of software exhibiting the properties of life. "Emergence" lets researchers attempt to create intelligence from the bottom up, as it were, starting not from any theory of the brain as a whole, but from the lowest levels of the body. The idea seems to be that, if you construct a sufficient number of low-level, atomic interactions ("automata"), what will eventually emerge is intelligence—an ant colony in the mind.

Sentience is not a thing, according to this view, but something that arises from the organization of matter itself. The roboticist Hans Moravec writes:

Ancient thinkers theorized that the animating principle that separated the living from the dead was a special kind of substance, a spirit. In the last century biology, mathematics, and related sciences have gathered powerful evidence that the animating principle is not a substance, but a very particular, very complex organization. Such organization was once found only in biological matter, but is now slowly appearing in our most complex machines.

In short, given enough computing power—which gets easier every year, as the computational abilities of chips increase exponentially—it's possible to build a robotic creature which crosses some critical threshold in the number of low-level organizational interactions it is able to sustain. Out of which will emerge—like Venus surfacing from the sea on the half shell—sentience.

There is a great flaw in this reasoning, however. Machines are indeed getting more and more powerful, as was predicted by the former Intel chairman Gordon Moore, in what has come to be known as Moore's Law. But computers are not just chips; they also need the instructions that tell the chips what to do: the software. And there is no Moore's Law for software. On the contrary, as systems increase in complexity, it becomes harder—very much harder—to write reliable code.

In a quest for robust systems, software engineers turned to working with what are called object-oriented methods. In this model, code is written in very small chunks, each performing the most minimal of tasks. The objects send small "messages" to one another, like ants rubbing antennas to communicate via pheromones. For example, when you ask a program to print a document, you first get a "dialog" object, which calls upon an "input characters" object and a "click button" object, another object that interacts with the printer, and so on. This is a highly simplified example. Something as mundane as printing evokes perhaps hundreds of objects, all of which run within a universe of tens of thousands of objects.

Roboticists foresee code that "evolves," objects that succeed in a process of Darwinian selection, eventually creating a self-sustaining system. The best of the objects are invoked for years; they are the hearty survivors. Weaker code is replaced and then must also stand up to the test of time. In this view, code objects are automata; as their numbers rise into the millions and billions, a self-organizing intelligence will emerge.

That thick cloud of interacting objects—that atmospheric mist of code—does indeed begin to run as if on its own. The complexity of the environment tends to move beyond the easy comprehension of an individual programmer. But what happens in this "running on its own" is a system soon running amok. It crashes, fails, succumbs to bugs. It is up to the human programmer to intervene: understand it, fix it, change it.

Darwinian selection, therefore, cannot be invoked as a rationale for the emergence of cybernetic life. Evolution is predicated upon the dire human imperatives to survive and reproduce. We are not abstract processes; we are not Simon's bodiless artifacts. We do not face survival pressures mindlessly. We know we are not ants. We know we are not code objects. We know we are going to die. In the quest to build humanoid robots, researchers may say they are building something—a mechanical object that simulates some aspects of human sentience. But it remains a simulation. The organizational principles of that mechanical object do not illuminate the real bases of human sentience. They do not tell us what we are.

The mistake in robotics is the same as that in AI: mistaking the tool for its builder. In particular, the error comes from mistaking the current methods of software writing as a paradigm for human mental organization. In the 1970s, a computer program was a centralized, monolithic thing, a small world unto itself, a set of instructions operating upon a set of data. It should be no surprise, then, that researchers at the time saw the human intelligence as a . . . centralized, monolithic, logical mind operating upon a set of data. By the 1990s, that monolithic paradigm of programming had been replaced by the object-oriented methods described above, with code written in discrete, atomic chunks that could be combined in a variety of ways. And—what do you know?—human sentience was hence seen as something emerging from the complex interaction of . . . discrete atomic chunks. Is cognitive science driving the science of computing, or is it the other way around?

There are signs that even the cyberneticists who promoted the concept of emergence as a paradigm for human sentience are sensing its limits. Christopher Langton, a key figure in ALife research, admitted there is the problem of "finding the automata"—deciding what indeed constitutes the lowest-level interactions that must be simulated in order to create life. How deep must one go: to interactions between cells? molecules? atoms? elementary particles of matter? Talking with me at a café in Linz, Austria, Langton looked up from a scribbled notebook and said with sincere worry: "Where's the bottom of physics?"

Meanwhile, the roboticist Rodney Brooks wondered about the "top" of the problem, the higher-level cognitive functions that are supposed to emerge from an organism's underlying complexity. After years spent creating robots that were like insects, Brooks recognized that something else is involved in the grand project of intelligence. He is now revisiting the problem that stumped AI researchers in the 1970s: how to give a cybernetic creature an awareness of its own state of being—its own needs, desires, intentions—and also an understanding that others have their own states of being—needs, desires, intentions—that are different from its own. In a discussion we held in March 2001, Brooks looked like a man who knew he was stepping off the brink when he said: "We're trying to introduce a theory of mind."

The bottom of physics. A theory of mind. And here we go again. Back we are drawn into the metaphysical thickets from which engineering hoped permanently to flee. The hope was to turn sentience into a problem not of philosophy but of engineering. "You don't have to understand thought to make a mind," said Douglas Hofstadter, wishfully, while introducing the spiritual-robot panel at Stanford. "The definition of life is hard," Rodney Brooks said to me. "You could spend five hundred years thinking about it or spend a few years doing it."

And here is the underlying motive of robotics: an anti-intellectualism in search of the intellect, a flight from introspection, the desire to banish the horrid muddle of all this "thinking about it," thousands of years of philosophical speculation about what animates us, without notable progress. "You can understand humans either by reverse engineering or through building," said Cynthia Breazeal, a former student of Brooks's. Don't think about it; build it—that's the hope. Equate programming with knowledge. Yet still we circle back to the old confusions, for conceptualization is as deep in our human nature as is tool building. *Homo faber* wrestles with *Homo sapiens*.

One way to get around the difficulties of human sentience is to declare humans all but irrelevant to the definition of life. This is the approach taken by ALife researchers, who see human beings—indeed, all life on earth—as "accidents," part of the "highly accidental set of entities that nature happened to leave around for us to study." As Christopher Langton writes in his introduction to *Artificial Life: An Overview*, "The set of biological entities provided to us by nature, broad and diverse as it is, is dominated by accident and historical contingency . . . We sense that the evolutionary trajectory that did in fact occur on earth is just one out of a vast ensemble of possible evolutionary trajectories . . ."

Based on the same foundations as modern robotics—emergence theory—ALife's goal is the creation of software programs that exhibit the properties of being alive, what is called "synthetic biology," the idea being that researchers can learn more about life "in principle" if they free themselves of the specific conditions that gave rise to it on earth. ALife research says farewell to the entire natural world, the what-must-be in Herbert Simon's formulation, with barely a backward glance (except occasionally to cite the example of ants).

"Life" in the context of ALife is defined very simply and abstractly. Here are two typical approaches: "My private list [of the properties of life] contains only two items: self-replication and open-ended evolution," writes Thomas S. Ray. And "life must have something to do with functional properties we call *adaptive*, even though we don't yet know what those are," writes Stevan Harnad. Bruce Blumberg, an MIT researcher who creates robotic dogs in software animations, describes the stance of ALife this way: "Work has been done without reference to the world. It's hard to get students to look at phenomena. It's artificial life, but people aren't looking at life."

What ALife researchers create are computer programs—not robots, not machines, only software. The cybernetic creatures in these programs ("agents" or "automata") go on to "reproduce" and "adapt." They thereby fulfill the basic requirements that allow them to be seen as living entities. So does the image of the computer as human paradigm, begun in the 1950s, come to its logical extreme: pure software, unsullied by exigencies of carbon atoms, bodies, fuel, gravity, heat, or any other messy concern of either soft-tissued or metal-bodied creatures. Again the image of the computer is conflated with the idea of being alive, until only the computer remains: life that exists only in the machine.

What these views of human sentience have in common, and why they fail to describe us, is a certain disdain for the body: the utter lack of a body in early AI and in later formulations like Kurzweil's (the lonely cortex, scanned and downloaded, a brain-in-a-jar); and the disregard for this body, this mammalian flesh, in robotics and ALife.

Early researchers were straightforward about discarding the flesh. "Meat machines," Marvin Minsky pronounced us to be. Said Herbert Simon: "Instead of trying to consider the 'whole person,' fully equipped with glands and viscera, I should like to limit the discussion to Homo sapiens, 'thinking person.'" Meat and glands and viscera—you can sense the corruption implied here, the body as butchery fodder, polluting the discussion of intelligence.

This suspicion of the flesh, this quest for a disembodied intelligence, persists today. Ray Kurzweil brushes aside the physical life as irrelevant to the project of building "spiritual" beings: "Mammalian neurons are marvelous creations, but we wouldn't build them the same way. Much of their complexity is devoted to supporting their own life processes, not to their information-handling abilities." In his view, "life" and "information-handling" are not synonymous; indeed, "life" gets in the way. He sees evolution as "a sloppy programmer," producing DNA that is mostly "useless" and "replete with redundancies."

And ALife researchers, seeing "life" in their computer programs, pay no attention at all to the body, imagining that the properties of life can somehow, like tissue specimens, be cut away from the dross of living. As Thomas Ray writes:

Whether we consider a system living because it exhibits some property that is unique to life amounts to a semantic issue. What is more important is that we recognize that it's possible to create *disembodied but genuine instances of specific properties of life in artificial systems.* This capability is a powerful research tool. By *separating the property of life that we choose to study from the many other complexities of natural living systems,* we make it easier to manipulate and observe the property of interest. [Emphasis added.]

One might think that robotics, having the imperative of creating some sort of physical container for intelligence, would have more regard for the human body. But the entire project of robotics—the engineering of intelligent machines—is predicated upon the belief that sentience is separable from its original substrate.

I had a talk with Cynthia Breazeal, who is now on the faculty of the MIT Media Lab. She is a most thoughtful researcher. Breazeal's work involves the creation of a creature that responds to human beings with simulated emotional reactions, and she shows a sincere regard for the emotional life. Yet even she revealed an underlying distaste for the body—a characterization she disagreed with. Growing impatient with me as I pressed her for a definition of "alive," she said: "Do you have to go to the bathroom and eat to be alive?"

The question stayed with me—Do you have to go to the bathroom and eat to be alive?—because it seemed to me that Breazeal's intent was to cite the most basic acts required by human bodily existence, and then see them as ridiculous, even humiliating.

But after a while I came to the conclusion: Maybe yes. Given the amount of time living creatures devote to food and its attendant states—food! the stuff that sustains us—I decided that, yes, there might be something crucial about the necessities of eating and eliminating that defines us. How much of our state of being is dependent upon being hungry, eating, having eaten, being full, shitting. Hunger! Our word for everything from nourishment to passionate desire. Satisfied! Meaning everything from well fed to sexually fulfilled to mentally soothed. Shit! Our word for human waste and an expletive of impatience. The more I thought about it, the more I decided that huge swaths of existence would be impenetrable—indescribable, unprogrammable, utterly unable to be represented—to a creature that did not eat or shit.

In this sense, artificial-life researchers are as body-loathing as any medieval theologian. They seek to separate the "principles" of life and sentience—the spirit—from the dirty muck from which it sprang. As Breazeal put it, they envision a "set of animate qualities that have nothing to do with reproduction and going to the bathroom," as if these messy experiences of alimentation and birth, these deepest biological imperatives—stay alive, eat, create others who will stay alive—were not the foundation, indeed, the source, of intelligence; as if intelligence were not simply one of the many strategies that evolved to serve the creatural striving for life. If sentience doesn't come from the body's desire to live (and not just from any physical body, but from this body's striving, this particular one), where else would it come from? To believe that sentience can arise from anywhere else—machines, software, things with no fear of death—is to believe, *ipso facto*, in the separability of mind and matter, flesh and spirit, body and soul.

Here is what I think: Sentience is the crest of the body, not its crown. It is integral to the substrate from which it arose, not something that can be taken off and placed elsewhere. We drag along inside us the brains of reptiles, the tails of tadpoles, the DNA of fungi and mice; our cells are permuted paramecia; our salty blood is what's left of our birth in the sea. Genetically, we are barely more than roundworms. Evolution, dismissed as a sloppy programmer, has seen fit to create us as a wild amalgam of everything that came before us: except for the realm of insects, the whole history of life on earth is inscribed within our bodies. And who is to say which piece of this history can be excised, separated, deemed "useless" as an essential part of our nature and being?

George Lakoff, the linguist, is perhaps the thinker most responsible for bringing the body back into the discussion of human intelligence. He and the philosopher Mark Johnson are the co-authors of two remarkable books (*Metaphors We Live By* and *Philosophy in the Flesh: The Embodied Mind and Its Challenge to Western Thought*) that outline the ways in which the body is integral to intelligence and human consciousness. Thinking is not logical and conscious, they argue, but metaphorical and mostly unconscious; that is, unavailable to rational introspection. And the source of most of these metaphors is the body itself. "The body provides the metaphors for the world," Lakoff said while speaking to a Berkeley group called the Philosophical Club. "This is not solipsistic, because we have evolved these bodies to interact with the world, as it is." Even formal logic itself has its source in physical existence: "The fact that we have muscles and use them to apply force in certain ways leads to the structure of our systems of causal concepts." Lakoff's most recent book (with Rafael Núñez, *Where Mathematics Comes From*) goes so far as to posit the idea that even mathematics, that branch of abstract thinking normally considered the polar opposite of the flesh, is also an extension of the body's "existence in space." As Lakoff and Johnson wrote in *Philosophy in the Flesh*:

> Reason is not disembodied, as the tradition has largely held, but arises from the nature of our brains, bodies, and bodily experience. This is not just the innocuous and obvious claim that we need a body to reason; rather, it is the striking claim that the very structure of reason itself comes from the details of our embodiment.

The details of our embodiment: the complex of tissues, fluids, sinew, and bone that we are made of. If we were made of something else—integrated circuits, for instance—we might have something called logic, but it would not necessarily be analogous to the ways human beings interpret the world—indeed, might not be anything we would recognize as intelligence at all. As Lakoff put it at the meeting, "What would be the logic of a bat? A jellyfish?"

Intelligence, then, is a consequence of our having this particular fleshly form, and what I mean by this particular form goes beyond that of human beings, or even primates. What I'm referring to is our existence as mammals. Oddly, in all the views of human intelligence promulgated by cyberneticists, this is the one rarely heralded: what we call sentience is a property of mammalian life.

Mammalian life is social and relational. What defines the mammalian class, physiologically, is not dependence upon the female mammary gland. What makes mammals different from other animals is the possession of a portion of the brain known as the limbic system. And it is the limbic system that allows us to do what other animals cannot: read the interior state of others of our kind.

To survive, we need to know our own inner state and those of others, quickly at a glance, deeply. This is the "something" we see in the eyes of another mammalian creature: it looks at us and knows, in its own way, that we have feelings, states, desires that are different from its own. We look at each other and know we are separate beings who nonetheless communicate. This is what people mean when they say they can talk to their dogs or cats, horses or bunnies: mammals reading each other. We don't go looking for this in ants or fish or reptiles; indeed, when we want to say that someone lacks that essential spark of life, we call them "reptilian." What we mean by this is that they lack emotions, the ability to relay and read the emotions of others; that they are, in short, robotic.

If sentience is a mammalian trait, and what distinguishes mammals is the capacity for social life, then sentience must have its root in the capacity for rich social and emotional interchange. That is: Sentience begins with social life, with the ability of two creatures to transact their inner states—needs, desires, motivations, fears, threats, contentment, suffering, what we call "the emotions." Moreover, the more avenues a creature has for understanding and expressing its emotional states, the more intelligent we say it is. Ants were not a good place to look for rich social interchange; the logical inference engines of early AI were a particularly poor choice of model; computer software running in the astringent purity of a machine won't find it. To get at the heart of intelligence, we should have started by looking at the part of human life ordinarily considered "irrational," the opposite of "logical," that perennial problem for computers: emotions.

The role of emotions in sentience can be seen in something as deceptively simple as a chair. Hubert Dreyfus pointed out the futility of trying to create a symbolic representation of a chair to an object that had neither body to sit in it nor a social context in which to use it: "What makes an object a *chair* is its function, and what makes possible its role as equipment for sitting is its place in the total practical context. This supposes certain facts about human beings (fatigue, the way the body bends) . . . Chairs would not be equipment for sitting if our knees bent backwards like those of flamingos, or if we had no tables, as in traditional Japan or the Australian bush."

The chair makes no sense without the emotions that accompany sitting down: relief for someone standing for a long while; boredom, edginess, anxiety for someone too long seated; feelings associated with what we are doing while sitting in the chair, hours at work on a deadline or the enervation of hours staring at a television. These and any number of other remembered and emotional states are part of our understanding of this object: schoolroom hard bench, mother's ugly armchair, dirty thing you retrieved from a curbside to take into your first apartment. We can construct an abstract idea of a chair—describe its use, say what it's made of, formulate its geometry, describe its relationship to other furniture; we can fashion a robot that moves its mechanical limbs in such a way that it "sits"—but none of this approaches the sheer richness of the sentient human experience that surrounds and suffuses this object, an experience simultaneously mental, tactile, physical, emotional, social, and cultural, each of these aspects so intertwined as to be inseparable.

Some roboticists are beginning an investigation into the ways in which a mechanical object can have, or appear to have, an emotional and social existence. "Most roboticists couldn't care less about emotions," says Cynthia Breazeal, one of the few who do care about emotions. Her "Kismet" robot, a very cute device with the face and floppy ears of a bunny rabbit, has simulated emotional states (expressed adorably, ears drooping piteously when it's sad); it is designed to interact with and learn from humans as would a child. "Social intelligence uses the whole brain," she says. "It is not devoid of motivation, not devoid of emotion. We're not cold inference machines. Emotions are critical to our rational thinking."

Rodney Brooks speaks of adding "an emotional model," of giving his new robot "an understanding of other people." Cynthia Breazeal's Kismet robot is designed to interact with humans and to "suffer" if it doesn't get attention. Bruce Blumberg, who "does dogs," as he puts it, understands that "you can't say you're modeling dogs without social behavior."

Of the three, however, only Blumberg seems to grasp the enormity of the problem they're undertaking: he is willing to admit that there is something ineffable about a living being's social and emotional existence. "My approach is to build computer devices to catch a spark of what's really there in the creature," he says, "to understand what makes dogs—and us—have a sort of magical quality." Then, perhaps embarrassed at this recourse to magic, he adds, "Ninety-nine percent of computer scientists would say you're no computer scientist if you were talking in terms of 'magical qualities.'"

Indeed, his colleague Breazeal has a pragmatic, somewhat cynical view of the emotions. Robots will need to have something like emotions, she says, because corporations are now investing heavily in robotic research, and "emotions become critical for people to interact with robots—or you won't sell many of them." The point seems to be to fool humans. About her robot Kismet she says, "We're trying to play the same game that human infants are playing. They learn because they solicit reactions from adults."

But an infant's need for attention is not simply a "game." There is a true, internal reality that precedes the child's interchange with an adult, an actual inner state that is being communicated. An infant's need for a mother's care is dire, a physical imperative, a question of life or death. It goes beyond the requirement for food; an infant must learn from adults to survive in the world. But without a body at risk, in a creature who cannot die, are the programming routines Breazeal has given Kismet even analogous to human emotions? Can a creature whose flesh can't hurt feel fear? Can it suffer?

Even if we leave aside the question of embodiment; even if we agree to sail away from the philosophical shoals of what it *really* means to have an emotion as opposed to just *appearing* to have one— the question remains: How close are these researchers to constructing even a rich simulation of mammalian emotional and social life?

Further away than they realize, I think. The more these researchers talked about their work, the longer grew the list of thorny questions they know they will have to address. "Is social behavior simply an elaboration of the individual?" asked Blumberg. "What does the personality really mean?" "We need a model of motivation and desires." "How much of life is like that—projection?" From Breazeal: "How do you build a system that builds its own mind through experience?" And this great conundrum: "A creature needs a self for social intelligence—what the hell is *that*?"

In turning to the emotions and social life, they have hit right up against what Breazeal calls the "limiting factor: big ideas"—theories of learning, brain development, the personality, social interaction, motivations, desires, the self—essentially, the whole of neurology, physiology, psychology, sociology, anthropology, and just a bit of philosophy. It all reminded me of the sweet engineering naiveté of Marvin Minsky, back in the early days of AI, when he offhandedly suggested the field would need to learn something about the nature of common sense. "We need a serious epistemological research effort in this area," he said, believing it would be accomplished shortly.

Of course, the biggest of the "big ideas" is that old bugaboo consciousness. Being difficult, fuzzy, unwilling to yield up its secrets despite thousands of years devoted to studying it, consciousness is something robotics researchers would rather not discuss. "In our group, we call it the C-word," said Rodney Brooks.

Brooks is an urbane and charming man, with a soft Australian accent. He seems genuinely interested in exchanging thoughts about arcane matters of human existence. It was early March 2001; outside was the beginning of a snowstorm that was predicted to shut down all of the Boston area. Brooks sat with me at a small conference table in his office at MIT, where photographs of his insectlike robots hung on the walls, and, piled in the corner among some books, was the robotic doll called "My Real Baby" he had made for the Hasbro toy company.

Consciousness, of course, is a problem for robots. Besides its being hard to simulate, the very idea of consciousness implies something unfathomably unique about each individual, that "magical quality" Bruce Blumberg was daring enough to mention. Brooks's impulse, like that of his former student Cynthia Breazeal, was to view the interior life rather cynically, as a game, a bunch of foolery designed to elicit a response.

I mentioned Breazeal's Kismet, told him I thought it was designed to play on human emotions. Then I asked him, "Are we just a set of tricks?"

He answered immediately. "I think so. I think you're a bunch of tricks and I'm just a bunch of tricks."

Trickery is deeply embedded in the fabric of computer science. The test of machine intelligence that Alan Turing proposed in 1950, now known as the Turing Test, was all about fooling the human. The idea was this: Have a human interact with what might be either a computer or another human being. Place a person behind a curtain, able to see the text of the responses but not who or what "said" them. If the person cannot tell if the response comes from another human being or from a machine, then the machine will be judged to be humanly intelligent. A circus stunt, if you will. A Wizard of Oz game. A trick.

Just then, sitting in Brooks's office, I didn't much feel like a bunch of tricks. I didn't want to think of myself as what Brooks had just described as "just molecules, positions, velocity, physics, properties—and nothing else." He would say this was my reluctance to give up my "specialness"; he would remind me that it was hard at first for humans to accept they descended from apes. He would not understand that I was not trying to define humans, as a species, as anything "special." Only that each individual human, ape, chimp, dog—any creature with a "theory of mind"—is special unto itself.

But I was aware of something else in me protesting this idea of the empty person, nothing but a set of mechanisms, a zombie process. It was the same sensation I'd had while at the spiritual-robot symposium hosted by Douglas Hofstadter, an internal round-and-round—the clicking, unbalanced ceiling-fan of doubt—that kept me thinking, No, no, no, that's not it, you're missing something.

I asked Brooks if he knew what consciousness was.

He answered, "I don't know. Do you know what consciousness is good for?"

And without hesitation, I told him yes, I knew what consciousness is good for. I told him we are born helpless and defenseless. Our only hope to survive is to make contact with other humans. We must learn to tell one individual from another, make alliances, immediately see on the face of another human being whether this is friend or foe, parent or stranger, kin or enemy. I told him I think human existence as a species is predicated on this web of social interactions, and for this we must learn to identify individuals. And out of that, the recognition of the identity of others, comes our own identity, the sense that we exist, ourselves, our self. Everything we call consciousness unwinds from that.

"It's not mystical," I told him. "It's an evolutionary imperative, a matter of life and death."

Brooks put his chin on his hand and stared at me for a moment.

Then he said: "Huh. None of our robots can recognize their own kind."

It took me several months, but after thinking about Rodney Brooks's remark about robots and their own kind, my round-and-round anxiety—that voice in me that kept protesting, No, no, you're missing something—finally stopped. For there it was, the answer I had been looking for, the missing something else: recognition of our own kind.

This is the "magical quality," mutual recognition, the moment when two creatures recognize each other from among all others. This is what we call "presence" in another creature: the fact that it knows us, and knows we know it in turn. If that other being were just a trick, just the product of a set of mechanisms, you would think that snakes could make this recognition, or paramecia, or lizards, or fish. Their bodies are full of marvelous mechanisms, reflexes, sensors to give them an awareness of the world around them. Ant pheromones should work. Robots with transponders beaming out their serial numbers should do the job. But we are, as Cynthia Breazeal said, creatures whose brains are formed by learning—that is, through experience and social interaction. We don't merely send out signals to identify ourselves; we create each other's identities.

It is true that identity, the idea of the human being as a unity, is not an entirely accurate concept. As Lakoff pointed out, most of our intelligence is unconscious, not available for introspection, having an independent existence, so to speak. And the body itself is not a unity, being instead a complicated colony of cells and symbiotic creatures. We can't live without bacteria in our gut; tiny creatures live on our skin and eyelids; viruses have incorporated themselves into our cells. We're walking zoos. Yet somehow, for our own survival (and pleasure), it is critical that we attain a unified view of ourselves, as unique selves.

This idea of being a unique self is not just some chauvinistic sense of specialness, some ego problem we have to let go of. Nature has gone to a great deal of trouble to make creatures within the same species distinct from one another. The chromosomes mix themselves up in the reproductive cells. Through the wonder of naturally recombinant DNA, nearly every human being on earth is distinct from every other. This recombining of the genetic material is usually thought of as creating diversity, but the corollary effect is the creation of uniqueness. Identical twins fascinate us for this reason: because they are rare, the only humans on earth (along with triplets, quintuplets, and other identical siblings) without their own faces. We're born distinct, and as our brains develop in the light of experience, we grow ever more different from one another. Mammalian life takes advantage of this fact, basing our survival on our ability to tell one from another, on forming societies based on those mutual recognitions. Uniqueness, individuality, specialness are inherent to our strategy for living.

AI researchers who are looking at social life are certainly on the right path in the search to understand sentience. But until they grasp the centrality of identity, I don't think they'll find what they're looking for. And then, of course, even supposing they grant there is something called an identity, a unique constellation of body and experience that somehow makes a creature a someone, a self—"What the hell is *that*?" said Cynthia Breazeal—even so, they will still have to find a way to program it.

Their task in simulating a self-identifying sentient creature will be like trying to simulate a hurricane. I thought about how weather simulations work. Unable to take into account all the complexity that goes into the production of weather (essentially, the whole world), simulations use some subset of that complexity and are able to do a fairly good job of predicting what will happen in the next hours or days. But as you move out in time, or at the extremes of weather, the model breaks down. At three days, the understanding gets chancy. Ten days out, the simulation doesn't work. The fiercer the storm, the less the simulation knows what it will do. Hurricanes are not something you predict; they're something you watch. And that's what human sentience is: a hurricane—too complex to understand fully by rational means, something you observe, marvel at, fear with a sense of awe, what finally we give up and call "an act of God."

Is Sadie the Cat a Trick?

2003

Photograph by Elliot Ross

When I returned from Boston, after talking with Rodney Brooks, I bought a robotic cat. It wasn't very advanced, just a cheap, vaguely cat-looking thing from Toys "R" Us. It was made of metallic plastic, nothing furry and fuzzy about it, nothing like a robotic toy Brooks would have made. I intended to have it around as joke fodder.

The "robot" was laughably unlike a cat to anyone who knows the real thing. It comes racing toward you when you call it, for instance, preposterous in a living cat. But one of its behaviors "worked." I left it on while I read, and after a time it began to make a pitiful noise. It seemed to "suffer" if I ignored it for some preprogrammed interval. Soon I found myself getting up to "pet" it—stroking an area on the plastic head that converts the whimpers into a soothing sound, not a purr but producing a similar effect. A cute trick, I thought, to get me to want to give it attention and "affection."

Sadie, my real cat, found the robot curious at first. She noticed its motion and sounds. Being nearsighted, like all cats, she went up close and sniffed it. Not finding any animal scent, she walked away and ignored it.

Then, about an hour later, Sadie came up to me, doing the things she always does when she wants attention: a slight scratching of my hand at half-claw, an intent look, a waving around of her tail, and, most of all, a rigidity in her entire body that always tells me without a doubt that she wants—no, needs—the attention we call petting. I gave her what she asked for. She started purring.

No one knows exactly what a cat means by purring. We may want to think it indicates something akin to happiness. But the source of purring, the physical instrument behind it, seems to be growling. I have read conjectures that purring/growling evolved in companion cats as a means to get humans to sit still and give them bodily warmth—a means to condition us, train us. In any case, whatever Sadie's "intent," it worked. She purred. I relaxed. I let her stay in my lap.

But then, as I sat enjoying the moment, my thoughts were invaded by Rodney Brooks. I remembered his saying that everything inside us is merely a set of "evolutionarily determined responses." And that the goal of those responses is to make us believe there is something essential in another being: we are built to fool one another. "I think you're a bunch of tricks," he'd said, "and I'm just a bunch of tricks."

I looked down at Sadie. Suddenly I could not help wondering if all this asking for and getting attention, this purring, wasn't just like the hardwired program in the plastic robot. Sadie at that time was nineteen years old, a wily and mature creature who would look me dead in the eye, and with whom I had a complicated relationship. Nevertheless, I was momentarily a little afraid of her. Was she nothing more than a mechanism, a cheap little program, an empty zombie? I looked into her eyes. And I asked aloud, "Are you just a trick?"

I had adopted Sadie from a shelter, a tiny cat, part Siamese, white with flame-point ears. A tag on the cage said she was two years old. An animal's age at a shelter is never certain. People who deposit a dog or cat or hamster usually lie, thinking their cast-off pet is more likely to get adopted if it's young. Their guilt-induced lie is correct.

My loft in the Clocktower Building has a thick wooden beam spanning the space. The beam is twenty feet above the floor, with trusses slanting up from it rising to the ceiling at an overall height of twenty-eight feet. To Sadie, it was a jungle gym, a superhighway, a paradise (I say this anthropomorphically, my human words for what I saw in her body). She flew up and down the beams at terrific speed, utterly fearless. What a creature! I thought. How unlike me, a wobble-footed biped afraid of heights.

There was a time in my twenties when everyone I knew had a cat, or cats, and conversations centered upon nothing else but their charms. Kitty Olympics in the hallway. Bodkin stalking the tub edge as one bathed. Oscar eating moths. Willa, who cawed like a crow. Wilcox, unmanned by the removal of his balls, becoming fat, a coward, but all the more lovable for it. There we were, in San Francisco, in 1973, a bunch of lesbian-separatists with short hair and lots of cats.

The talk of cats was inevitable, inescapable. But the point was, we needed our animal companions. We were fresh out of college, oversaturated with the proximity of other human bodies, drenched in human thought and language—deprived of the otherness and comfort of creatures who could not read or speak.

I didn't think of all this until after Sadie died. My husband, Elliot, and I were at a restaurant with a friend and her new girlfriend. This girlfriend was strange. I spoke of my recent loss: Twenty-one years of companionship. A lost love. Then this newly minted girlfriend fired me a disdainful look. "This cat didn't love you," she sneered. "That's just your idea of it, which has nothing to do with hers." First of all, how rude to sneer at a grieving cat-widow. Second, she'd never laid eyes on Sadie. How the hell did she know what Sadie thought of me?

Nonetheless, her disdain ate at me. What, indeed, was there between me and Sadie? Was there something "really" in her? Or was she simply enacting her own, physically engraved program, over which I had laid my human idea of relationship? A larger question emerged later, during my talks with Elliot: What kind of relationships can there be between human animals and other animals?

The last year of Sadie's life had been difficult. She was bone thin, her fur matted with concrete-hard clumps I could not cut even with scissors. As in most aged cats, her kidneys were shot. You're supposed to feed them this special low-protein diet when that happens, but Sadie wouldn't touch the stuff. And I thought, She's come this far, twenty-two at the time; let her eat what pleases her, else she'll die of starvation. She'd become severely arthritic, clearly in pain as she lowered herself with excruciating slowness onto the pillow next to the heater below my desk. She began side-winding, her hindquarters sliding out right or left from the vector in which she meant to be going. It was funny to look at; it was terrible to see. At one point, I had to hold her over her bowl so she could eat.

I woke up one morning to find her shit scattered on the stairs. Although she could barely walk, she had evidently tumbled down the stairs while trying to reach the litter box. I added a second box upstairs. There was a night when she lay on my bed while I read. I let myself believe for a moment that she was fine; we were fine; there would be more moments like this one. But then I felt something warm and wet soaking the blanket. Sadie was peeing. She looked up with an expression I can only call alarm. I say this because of what I saw in her body, head coming abruptly erect, feet scrambling over the side of the bed as she threw herself onto the floor to reach the box. Another day, I noticed the litter box was dry and she hadn't peed in a while. I carried her to the box, held her, and she urinated a hot stream between my hands. What an effort she had made not to pee on the floor! I thought. What a need to maintain a feeling of rightness in her body—what we humans might call dignity.

One day six months later, Sadie stepped out of her litter box and fell sideways. Elliot called out to me: "There's something wrong with Sadie." She was shaking all over, convulsing. I went over, held her, called her name, but I could see from her eyes she was no longer there. She had a very bad fifty seconds; then she was gone.

Elliot and I looked at each other, and we knew each other's immediate thought: We're free. We can live in New York for a while. We had not been able to be away for more than two weeks, shortened to one week, then two days, as Sadie approached her death. We had waited for the end; now here was the end. I held Sadie's emaciated, still-warm body until it was rigid and cold, feeling guilt, sadness, relief for Sadie's being released from pain, relief for our being released from caregiving. Elliot and I had fulfilled our obligations for two years, had given her fluids and pills and special foods, carried her up and down the stairs, had taken her to the vet and back, to the vet and

back. We performed the inescapable end-of-life duties awaiting anyone who has ever loved another being.

On the bookshelf, I set up a sort of shrine to Sadie: her ashes in a
wooden box, a note from the cat-sitter who had taken care of her
during my absences over the course of twenty-one years, a silly stone
tile someone had given me, which was engraved "Here Lives A Very
Fine Cat Indeed."

I also taped up a poem by Franz Wright that I had cut out from
The New Yorker, "On the Death of a Cat." I liked the fact that a well-
known poet was not ashamed to mourn a cat in print:

> In life, death
> was nothing
> to you: I am
>
> willing to wager
> my soul that it
> simply never occurred
>
> to your nightmareless
> mind, while sleep
> was everything
>
> (see it raised
> to an infinite
> power and perfection)—no death
>
> in you then, so now
> how even less. Dear stealth
> of innocence

licked polished
to an evil
lustre, little

milk fang, whiskered
night
friend—

go.

I read the poem over and over. I tried to tell myself that Wright wanted to console himself by believing his cat was not aware of death. Yet I knew it was probably more my hope than his.

I also hung up a picture of Sadie I'd taken before the decline of her last years. It's not at all an accomplished photograph. It was taken with a point-and-shoot camera, printed on a cheap inkjet printer, on copier paper. Nonetheless, there was something about it. Sadie had walked up very close to the lens, her face filling the frame. Her eyes look directly into the camera and, seemingly—seemingly— at me.

Elliot is a photographer, and he was particularly taken with the picture. He had not grown up with an animal companion of any sort. His first experience of it was when he came to live with me and Sadie—he was fifty-four at the time. When I was away one month, and he was taking care of her, he called me and said of Sadie, "I have fallen in love." Over time, he came to understand the complications of that statement.

After Sadie died, he kept gazing at her picture. He could not stop wondering: How can such a creature, so different from me, also share this thing called life?

Was Sadie a trick? Was all that life—from acrobat to purring companion to arthritic old lady to the trembling creature in her final bad fifty seconds—just part of her hardwiring? Perhaps Elliot and I needed to see Sadie as a sentient being for our own purposes. Perhaps it made us feel less alone to see her as a unique creature who grew, changed, aged; who knew all along what was happening to her, in her cat's way. Maybe Rodney Brooks and the nasty girlfriend were right: We're empty inside, fooling each other into believing there is more. Maybe there was nothing particular between me and Sadie, only the mutual advantage we derived from acting out our inborn responses.

Then again, I can't let go of the feeling that there was between us something you could indeed call "love."

Sadie provided companionship, of course. Before I met Elliot, she would sleep with me. Runt of the litter as tiny Sadie must have been, she liked to be crushed a little; everyone who ever held her noticed it. She would fall asleep in my arms, not minding—liking it?—if I lightly rolled over on her for a bit.

There was also familiarity, her coming to meet me at the door (even when her bowl was full, so it was not in the hope of getting dinner). There was the mutual recognition of ritual: I knew the time of day when she moved to her favorite chair to take the sun, so I anticipated it and raised the shade. She knew I wrote in the morning, and, before I got to the desk, she was lying on the pillow by the heater, which had not yet been turned on. If it were just warmth she'd wanted, she could have stayed in bed with Elliot, who was living with me by then. Instead, she decided she would wait for me by a cold heater. Companionship, familiarity, expectation, mutual recognition, bodily comfort: if this is not a definition of love between aging creatures, I don't know what is.

On the other hand, there was conflict. For twenty-one years, we had lived together in an open loft. We were always within earshot. The only place anyone could shut a door and be alone was a bathroom. This endless proximity would put a strain on any relationship, Elliot's and mine included. Add to this the fact that Sadie was a cat and I a human, and we were bound to engage in a certain amount of, well, fighting.

Like most cats, Sadie could not resist the appeal of certain chairs, especially those covered in a woven material, all the better to get the claws in. The smell of chicken drove her insane, and she would dump any trash can to get at the bones. She went through a very bad period (caused by thyroid problems discovered later) when she would attack me as I lay sleeping, biting my arm and tearing open the skin. On a more minor note, she was a white cat and I liked to wear black— don't come near me! I would scream—and it was impossible for me to fold clothes on the bed for all the cat hair. To this day I still find bits of her fur in my clothes.

To all this, I screamed "No!" and "Stop!" and "Sadie!" She never responded right away. For a moment she would look at me, standing rigid and still, as if searching deeply in her mind for whatever rule she had just broken. More cries from me of "No!" and "Stop!" and "Sadie!" and finally she'd whip her tail and walk away. She kept her ears bent backward, a sure sign of cat hostility. She would not meet me at the door for two days. When friends visited, they sometimes asked: Have you two been fighting? It was in the air, the discord, the ill-will.

And then, over hours, sometimes days, the ill-will dissipated. Fights went unresolved, just put behind us. The sources of conflict would arise again and again. And we went on.

This, too, is part of love.

There were parts of Sadie's life that had nothing to do with me. After finishing some apparently satisfying business in the litter box, she would come racing out, flying madly around the room, up and down the stairs, then around the room again. This was not behavior specific to Sadie; everyone who has a cat sees it. What does it mean? Why this furious energy? Do cats simply need to burn up energy? Or is it an "evolutionarily determined response," a survival necessity to get as far away as possible from a scent that gives away their location? Yet it was hard to think it was only a mechanism. I saw a creature at the peak of its power: the energy, the speed, what seemed to me, in my human words, the delirium of being alive.

There were also her violent moments, when she would rip apart a rug. This ripping was not the normal claw-sharpening but something so wild that no amount of my shouting could interrupt it. She would stand over a particular spot, trap it in her claws, and jump up, back arched, the rug flying up with her. The look in her eyes was like no other I had ever seen in her. She pounced again and again, body curved as into a "C," ripping into the weave and flying up with it.

To me there was no doubt what she was doing: standing over brought-down prey, ripping it apart, fighting to eat her share.

She had shed her human-given name. "Sadie" went the way of a molted snakeskin. She wielded her tail like a whip. Her lips were drawn back and revealed the threat of her little fang-teeth. She was not trying to "trick" me into anything; right then, I didn't exist. She was somewhere else, apparently deep into her evolutionary past, when humans and cats had no relationship except possibly being each other's food. It's said that, if you die alone in an empty room, a dog will sit beside your body until someone comes. A cat, on the other hand, sheds you completely. A cat eats you.

Yet, right then, Sadie was to me magnificent. I could only watch, marveling at the strength in that five-pound body, the agility, the ferocious energy, the focus, her escape from time.

It was like those moments in your most intimate relationships when you look over and are startled to remember: that other person is not you and is not yours to define. He or she suddenly seems to be some alien whom, inexplicably, you have decided to trust. Even as the two of you lie wrapped in each other's arms, you know that he or she can exist without you, and does just that now and again, in moments, and sometimes over longer stretches of time: sheds you. Yet you continue on, together. And that, too, I think, is an imperative of love.

Eventually, I took down the shrine to Sadie and put away her picture. I had to. I had left it up there so long that it had lost its emotional power. The robotic cat, however, is still on a shelf, just above the old laptops. I don't look at it much. It's useful as a bookend.

Memory and Megabytes

2003

In the summer of 2002, having finished a book I had been working on for five years, I decided to buy a new laptop computer. There should have been nothing remarkable in this decision. The words "new" and "computer" have a rapturous attraction for each other, while the phrase "old computer" carries within it a certain cultural stain. One day, right before I made the decision to buy the new computer, I sat in my car, stopped at a red light, and saw a collection of junked electronics on the sidewalk. A dead stereo, a cracked answering machine, a computer monitor trailing its cable like a dead snake—they seemed abashed, ashamed for us in our wastefulness, turning them out so soon after they had been shiny new. I'm sure their owner couldn't wait to get the stuff hauled away, to escape their forlorn looks, especially from the monitor, its face.

Like the former owner of the cast-off junk (who I imagined was right at that moment wiring up four speakers so huge they dominated his house), I wanted to play with my new machine right away, as soon as possible, to have it FedExed, overnight. I went home and called IBM, and the next day a brand new laptop was sitting on my desk. Processor an order of magnitude faster than my old one. Ten times the memory. Screen 33 percent larger. Twenty times the disk space—*billions* of characters waiting to be written and saved. If my new laptop were a car, we'd have to say this baby was loaded.

My old machine, meanwhile, had taken on the look of the junk at the curb. The screws holding the case together had worked themselves loose, and the little doors to various compartments were kept shut with masking tape. A couple of key caps were missing—torn off by me, actually, in a fit of rage against the "caps lock" key (don't get me started on the "caps lock" key, nasty relic of the mechanical typewriter, always in the way). The "N" key was worn completely bare— I think I say "No" very emphatically when software offers up stupid options. Some of the screen pixels were dead, leaving in scattered little white spots, upon which I had sometimes become fixated, blinded with hatred, unable to read what was on the display for their blank, empty whiteness.

Looking over at the old machine as it sat there kitty-corner to my brand-new one (whose screen was brilliantly, perfectly bright), I suddenly remembered a bad moment with my ex-husband, a man I'd made the mistake of marrying when I was nineteen. The marriage had lasted six months (if "lasted" is the right word in this context), and I hadn't heard from him in nine years when, one day, he called out of the blue. For a few minutes, the conversation seemed easy. We were joking around, laughing over all the things we'd felt compelled to buy as married people. Then I asked after his old car, one that I'd liked very much, a Nash Rambler, which would have been a classic by then. And, quite like old times, he put the knife to me: Oh, you know, he said. It's like your old girlfriend. She might get all fixed up, but you'd really rather have a new one.

At first, it made no sense to me that I would think of my old husband while looking at my old computer. Then I remembered there was more to the story of the out-of-the-blue phone call. A few weeks afterward, I received a letter from him, which I opened with trepidation. It turned out to be an announcement of his forthcoming remarriage. And then it was clear why he'd called: to reassure himself that he really would rather have a new one.

The versions of Microsoft Windows available now make it easy to copy everything over to your new computer. Just plug in a cable, run a little "wizard" program that guides you step-by-step through the transfer (this wizard is helpful, not a dumbed-down programming tool), and soon millions of information bits will be streaming from your old machine to your new one.

For all practical purposes, lack of space on the new machine is not a concern. Advances in the capacities of computer disk drives have been astronomical. In 1989, while the Berlin Wall was coming down, you could have expected about two megabytes, two million characters. Five years later, at the start of the internet boom, eighty megabytes was about right. Now a desktop computer, selling for about eight hundred dollars, will probably ship to your home with a storage capacity of eighty gigabytes—eighty *billion* characters. At this rate, given the advancing science of storage densities, we cannot be far from terabytes, petabytes, exabytes, zettabytes . . .

What is happening, essentially, is that each new computer has enough disk space to hold everything you've ever stored on all the computers you've ever owned in your life. The equivalent would be a new house that, every time you moved, would be so much larger than all your past houses that all the furniture you've ever purchased would follow you, indefinitely. Board-and-cinder-block bookshelves from freshman year, Goodwill sofa with the dog stain, Danish Modern coffee table from grad school, mountains of mattresses, that maroon velveteen sofa bed you knew you'd made a mistake buying the minute the deliverers put it down on its white plastic wheels—everything—the rug you picked up at a garage sale after a tipsy brunch, that second-hand dining table bought hurriedly after the divorce—all of it, no escaping it, the joy or humiliation of every decorating decision you've ever made, the occasion that brought each object into your life perpetually, unflinchingly present: the brutality of the everlasting.

I looked at my new laptop, its empty gigabytes waiting to swallow up the mere megabytes on my old machine, the siren song of the Microsoft wizard calling me to *copy, copy everything.* And I suddenly wanted to resist. Right then, the ability to take everything with me seemed oppressive, a tyranny of technological progress. I think it had to do with the jolt of remembering my long-ago ex-husband. Right around the time I bought the new laptop, thirty-four years after the end of marriage number one, I got married again, this time to the wonderful Elliot. It's sometimes good, I decided, to free yourself of the past, to wash off certain associations—for instance, the ones previously connected to the word "husband." I wanted to start clean. From my old machine, I told myself, I would take very little, only what I absolutely needed.

Of course, the meaning of "need" is always complicated. I was certain I would indeed need the final version of the book I'd just finished, the book for whose sake the old laptop had just contributed its working life. I decided I'd also copy over a few essays that someday might be useful for something. I knew I could leave behind several folders relating to my work as a software consultant; those contracts were over. But beyond that, everything became fuzzy. What about the contents of the three folders at the top of the screen, named "whatever," "toutes directions," and "I don't know," inside the last of which I found a folder called "Letters for the Drawer," and inside that a collection of anguished, angry, wisely unsent letters relating to a very unhappy relationship? Did I *need* those things? Were they the dead weight of the past, or could they perhaps be called creative "material"?

And what to do about the litter of folders holding the many old versions of the book: folders inside folders inside folders, their names changing as I struggled with the conception of the book, later ones named "start over" and "start again" and "not yet" and "yet again"—a Russian doll of folders, each one a deeper step backward into the murky beginnings of the book that had taken me five years to write? I could not decide what to take and what to leave behind. I would have to leave my fate to the wizard.

Now I had to be careful. This was not like putting your papers in a carton you could store in the basement. Once the wizard program had waved all this over to the new machine, there it would all be, right in front of me. It would do no good to create a folder on the new machine called "basement" or "attic." On a computer, there is no basement or attic. At any moment, while you are whiling away time, maybe avoiding another task, or just daring yourself to think of the past, you might go "click," and then it all pops out at you: fresh, un-yellowed, cruelly unchanged.

The current scientific view of memory is that it is something like an evolving dream. While studying the chemistry of memory forma-tion, two New York University researchers, Karim Nader and Glenn Schafe, were surprised to find that laboratory rats could not recall formerly consolidated memories (those stored in long-term memory) when their brains were denied a protein used to form *new* memories. The rats had learned to associate a tone with an electronic shock. The researchers waited for a day or more, allowing the painful association to become "fixed" in memory. Then they administered a drug that prevents the synthesis of proteins required for new memory creation and again presented the animals with the tone. If previously held theories of memory formation were correct, the drug should have had no effect: the rats should have remembered what they had learned, responding with fear at the sound of the tone. Instead, the creatures barely reacted. It was as if the experience of the tone and the shock—and the fear—had never happened to them.

Why should the creatures need to create new memories in order to recall already consolidated ones? The processes of long- and short-term memory formation were thought to be distinct. The general scientific thinking was that, once something was consolidated in long-term memory, the problem was then to stabilize it, make it durable despite the constant turnover in the cellular matter of the brain—somehow creating permanence in the midst of physical change. The overall goal of research was to understand how we get a memory out of storage, think about it now, then put it back.

What Nader and Schafe discovered, however, was that the brain is not a file cabinet. There is no "back." It is a network of neural connections constantly being strengthened, weakened, broken, and formed, and each time we recall something, the researchers found, the connections become labile again. We make new associations, abandon old ones. We refit the memory into the web of all that has happened to us since we last called the thought to mind. And what we then store "back"—the definitive-seeming "I remember it happened just like this"—is not the original incident, not even the last memory we had of it, but the product of a teeming, plasmatic event, whole portions of the brain rearranged and reconnected: an enlightened but temporary judgment on the meaning of experience.

At first, the researchers thought their findings might apply only to fear. Perhaps other types of memories, those more conscious or declarative, would prove more durable. But in a subsequent experiment, Nader found similar results: conscious memories were also "reconsolidated"—rearranged—each time they were recalled. And now the whole notion of a stable long-term memory had to be reconsidered. The only memories that endure unchanged, it seems, are those we never think of again.

Sometimes experiences you have not remembered rush out at you with a breathtaking immediacy. Your mother hands you a Mallomar cookie: sudden happiness! Terror at first seeing a live horse. The shock as a dog lunges out and rips open your skin. The stab of fear as you open the door to a professor's office. The shine of a fake ring stuck in a hedge: Joy! Someone left it for you. Anything. It is as if the experience is happening for the first time. You want to hold on to that feeling. But it is impossible. The moment you recall it, the memory has become woven into other experiences. The newness, the clarity, is gone forever.

As a mechanism for remembrance, then, human memory is unreliable. And this is indeed what studies of eyewitness testimony and police lineup identifications have shown. People misremember; they make life-threatening errors of recollection; they mix past and present in a constantly boiling stew, recalling people, faces, colors, details that were seen only later. Compared with the hard evidence of DNA, with the clarity of bits on a disk—the undeniability of the digital—what possible use is this shifty, self-deceiving mechanism of human recall?

It occurred to me that, before my old laptop, I'd had an even older one, an Apple PowerBook that had lain for five years in a cheap briefcase at the bottom of the guest closet. Like its successor's tenure, the PowerBook's time with me had been bounded by the writing of a book, my first, and I thought this old-old laptop—what I had and had not carried over from it—might guide me in deciding what I should take to my newest machine.

The PowerBook started up by sounding a chord—E major?—and immediately I was drawn back to the time when this machine was my constant companion, carried everywhere despite its weight, a kind of ballast for my then foundering life. Even before it showed me the files and folders it held, I was taken by the sound and feel of it, the crackling disk drive spinning up to speed, the maddening keyboard I'd cursed for its lack of proper "page up" and "page down" keys, the dim intimacy of its small, blue-tinged screen, the silky touch pad that had seduced me into buying an Apple machine despite its incompatibility with all the software I'd ever owned. It took me back to the first place I'd ever used it: a sublet apartment in New York, the city where I'd grown up but no longer lived, my father dying in a hospital I could see from the living-room window.

On the screen, a different set of Russian-doll folders exposed the nasty struggle to write a book: essays in version after version. Yet another "Letters for the Drawer," with its own collection of anguished, unsent mail. A folder called "Kaddish," where I kept track of my search for a synagogue that did not make me feel like an outsider when I said the prayer for the dead, the file creation and modification times (2:00 a.m., 5:00 a.m.) holding the indisputable record of an intractable insomnia. And then something called "scary untitled folder," inside of which was a file titled "suicide.doc," which began: "Some people are suicides and some are not. Here is a simple test. You wish to die because: a) no one loves you, b) you have just been fired, c) you can't stand being yourself for another moment." The second paragraph goes on to say, almost cheerfully, "The correct answer is C."

I shut down the machine, put it back in the cheap briefcase, and returned it to the dusty floor of the guest closet.

Some days then passed, during which time I didn't think about my computers, new or old. I think this interval let things settle in my mind—let my thoughts rearrange themselves in accordance with the shifting, sifting rules of memory. For when I next took out my old laptop, to consider again the problem of what to copy over to the new one, I noticed, with a shock, that it contained almost nothing from the PowerBook. Not the essays, not the Kaddish journals, not even the final version of the book that had marked that machine's working life.

Who would want to carry all that forward? I thought. When writing the second book, I'd remembered (or thought I'd remembered) that writing the first one had been easier. I recalled (or seemed to recall) the moments of utter engagement, the perfect paragraphs that had scrolled their way onto the screen as the keyboard went *tac, tac* under my hands. But the old PowerBook—all those files and folders, word by word the record of what I'd done, even the hours I hadn't slept—made me remember the pitiless truth of the matter. And in some essential way, I had to forget all that. I needed the unreliable retellings of memory, the balm of revision. If we had to be confronted, daily, with the incontrovertible data proving the despair that attends the writing of books, how would anyone ever begin another? Or (for that matter), forever rereading anguished Letters for the Drawer, how would anyone ever make the breathtaking decision to remarry?

I decided, once again, that I'd take almost nothing. The files were unforgiving, frozen, perfect mechanisms for recall, and I wanted to be what I was meant to be: a bad remembrance machine. I could almost feel the memories run away from me as I approached them, scattering at the touch of thought. Even long-ago ex-husbands might now be wished well. And I realized that the fact that memory changes is what allows us to tolerate something called memory in the first place. If we could not continuously reinterpret the past—could not turn experience over and over, and so interweave it with hope and unknowing—memory would be a tyranny. It would be unbearable, a torture, a bad recurring dream. Like data spinning away on a disk: forever the same, the same, the same.

All that remained now was to decide where to put the old machines. Though I knew I did not want their contents perpetually before me on my ever-renewing machines, threatening to jump out at me at the click of a mouse, I also felt they did not belong on the floor of the guest closet—or cast out on the curb with the dead stereos and forlorn monitors.

For I understood that each was a sort of diary, a record of time bounded by the writing of a book. The arrangements of the folders, the feel of the keyboards, the look of the screens—these were as particular as handwriting, able to stun me back in time. What they held was not "data" but experience. And I knew they should be saved the way you save those other records of experience, journals, which is to say carefully but not ceremoniously, neither thrown away nor read too often, opened only on those mysterious days—and they are always mysterious—when you can bear, and suddenly need, the shock of remembering.

So I cleared a space for them on the bookshelf and stood them up, vertically, like the notebooks they are. And they took their place among the other diaries and journals, treacherously holding the past, their power units crouched behind them like small, sleeping rats.

Dining with Robots

2004

In Memory of Julia Child

On the first day of the only programming course I ever took, the instructor compared computer programming to creating a recipe. I remember he used the example of baking a cake. First you list the ingredients you'll need—flour, eggs, sugar, butter, yeast—and these, he said, are like the machine resources the program will need in order to run. Then you describe, in sequence, in clear declarative language, the steps you have to perform to turn those ingredients into a cake. Step one: Preheat the oven. Two: Sift together dry ingredients. Three: Beat the eggs. Along the way were decisions he likened to the branching if/then/else logic statements in a program: If using a countertop electric mixer, then beat three minutes; else, if using a hand electric mixer, then beat four minutes; else (beating by hand, I suppose), beat five. And there was a reference he described as a sort of subroutine: Go to page 117 for details about varieties of yeast (with "return here" implied). He even drew a flow chart that took the recipe all the way through to the end: Let cool, slice, serve.

I remember nothing, however, about the particulars of the cake itself. Was it angel food? Chocolate? Layered? Frosted? At the time, 1979 or 1980, I had been programming for more than a year, self-taught, and had yet to cook anything more complicated than poached eggs. So I knew a great deal more about coding than about cakes. It didn't occur to me to question the usefulness of comparing something humans absolutely must do to something machines never do: that is, eat.

In fact, I didn't think seriously about the analogy for another twenty-four years, not until a blustery fall day in San Francisco, when I was confronted with a certain filet of beef. By then I had learned to cook. (It was that or a life of programmer food: pizza, takeout, whatever's stocked in the vending machines.) And the person responsible for the beef encounter was a man named Joe, of Potter Family Farms, who was selling "home-raised and butchered" meat out of a stall in the newly renovated Ferry Building food hall.

The hall, with its soaring, arched windows, is a veritable church of food. The sellers are small, local producers; everything is organic, natural, free-range; the "baby lettuces" are so young one should perhaps call them "fetal"—it's that sort of place. Before you go shopping, it helps to have a glass of wine, as I had, to prepare yourself for the gasping shock of the prices. Sitting at a counter overlooking the Bay, watching ships and ferries ply the choppy waters, I'd sipped down a nice Pinot Grigio, which had left me with lowered sales resistance by the time I wandered over to the Potter Farms meat stall. There Joe greeted me and held out for inspection a large filet—"a beauty," he said. He was not at all moved by my remonstrations that I eat meat but rarely cook it. He stood there as a man who had—personally—fed, slaughtered, and butchered this steer, and all for me, it seemed. I took home the beef.

I don't know what to do with red meat. There is something appalling about meat's sheer corporeality—meat meals are called *fleishidik* in Yiddish, a word that doesn't let you forget that what you are eating is *flesh.* So for help I turned to *The Art of French Cooking,* volume one, the cookbook Julia Child wrote with Louisette Bertholle and Simone Beck. I had bought this book when I first decided I would learn to cook. But I hadn't been ready for it then. I was scared off by the drawings of sides of beef lanced for sirloins, porterhouses, and T-bones. And then there was all that talk of blanching, deglazing, and making a roux. But I had stayed with it, spurred on by my childhood memories of coming across Julia on her TV cooking show, when I'd be clicking around the dial early on weekend mornings, then be stopped short at the sight of this big woman taking whacks at red lumps of meat. It was the physicality of her cooking that caught me, something animal and finger-painting-gleeful in her engagement with food.

And now, as rain hatched the windows, I came upon a recipe that Julia and her co-authors introduced as follows:

SAUTÉ DE BŒUF À LA PARISIENNE
[Beef Sauté with Cream and Mushroom Sauce]
This sauté of beef is good to know about if you have to entertain important guests in a hurry. It consists of small pieces of *filet* sautéed quickly to a nice brown outside and a rosy center, and served in a sauce . . . In the variations at the end of the recipe, all the sauce ingredients may be prepared in advance. If the whole dish is cooked ahead of time, be very careful indeed in its reheating that the beef does not

overcook. The cream and mushroom sauce here is a French version of beef Stroganoff, but less tricky as it uses fresh rather than sour cream, so you will not run into the problem of curdled sauce.

Serve the beef in a casserole, or on a platter surrounded with steamed rice, *risotto*, or potato balls sautéed in butter. Buttered green peas or beans could accompany it, and a good red Bordeaux wine.

And it was right then, just after I read the words "a good red Bordeaux wine," that the programming class came back to me: the instructor at the board with his flow chart, his orderly procedural steps, the if/then/else logical decision branches, the subroutines, all leading to the final "let cool, slice, serve." And I knew in that moment that my long-ago instructor, like my young self, had been laughably clueless about the whole subject of cooking food:

If you have to entertain important guests.

A nice brown outside.

Rosy center.

Stroganoff.

Curdled.

Risotto.

Potato balls sautéed in butter.

A good red Bordeaux.

I tried to imagine the program one might write for this recipe. And immediately each of these phrases exploded in my mind. How to tell a computer what "important guests" are? And how would you explain what it means to "have to" serve them dinner (never mind the yawning depths of "entertain")? A "nice brown," a "rosy center": you'd have to have a mouth and eyes to know what these mean, no matter how well you might translate them into temperatures.

To make my machine an intelligent recipe writer, I would have to reproduce in code the equivalent of the complex, labile synaptic connections we hold in our minds. I would have to teach it the associations for each name, action, and object in the recipe: to set off in its operations a resonating, ever-expanding aura of meaning. What, then, was I to do about "Stroganoff," which is not just a sauce but a noble family, a name that opens a chain of association that catapults the human mind across seven centuries of Russian history? I forced myself to abandon that line of thought and stay in the smaller realm of sauces made with cream, but this inadvertently opened up the entire subject of the chemistry of lactic proteins, and why milk curdles. Then I wondered how to explain "risotto": the special short-grained rice, the select regions on earth where it grows, opening up endlessly into questions of agriculture, its arrival among humans, the way it changed the earth. Next came the story of the potato, that Inca food, the brutalities through which it arrives on a particular plate before a particular woman in Europe, before our eponymous Parisienne: how it is converted into a little round ball, and then, of course, buttered. (Then, Lord help me, this brought up the whole subject of the French and butter, and how can they possibly get away with eating so much of it?)

But all of this was nothing compared with the cataclysm created by "a good red Bordeaux."

The program of this recipe expanded infinitely. Subroutine opened from subroutine, association led to exploding association. It seemed absurd even to think of describing all this to a machine. The filet, a beauty, was waiting for me.

Right around the time my programming teacher was comparing coding to cake making, computer scientists were finding themselves stymied in their quest to create intelligent machines. Almost from the moment computers came into existence, researchers believed that the machines could be made to think. And for the next thirty or so years, their work proceeded with great hope and enthusiasm. In 1967, the influential MIT computer scientist Marvin Minsky—he who described us as meat machines—optimistically declared, "Within a generation . . . the problem of creating 'artificial intelligence' will substantially be solved." But by 1982, he was less sanguine about the prospects, saying, "The AI problem is one of the hardest science has ever undertaken."

Computer scientists had been trying to teach the computer what human beings know about themselves and the world. They wanted to create inside the machine a sort of mirror of our existence, but in a form a computer could manipulate: abstract, symbolic, organized according to one theory or another of how human knowledge is structured in the brain. Variously called "micro-worlds," "problem spaces," "knowledge representations," "classes," and "frames," these abstract universes contained systematized arrangements of facts, along with rules for operating upon those—theoretically, all that a machine would need to become intelligent. Although it wasn't characterized as such at the time, this quest for a symbolic representation of reality was oddly Platonic in motive, a computer scientist's idea of the pure, unchanging forms that lie behind the jumble of the physical world.

But researchers eventually found themselves in a position like mine when trying to imagine the computer program for my *bœuf à la Parisienne*: the network of associations between one thing and the next simply exploded. The world, the actual world we inhabit, showed itself to be too marvelously varied, too ragged, too linked and interconnected, to be sorted into any set of frames or classes or problem spaces. What we hold in our minds is not abstract, it turned out, not an ideal reflection of existence, but something inseparable from our embodied experience of moving about in a complicated world. Again, Hubert Dreyfus's example of a chair best illuminates the problem, when he lets flow the myriad associations that radiate from the word "chair":

> Anyone in our culture understands such things as how to sit on kitchen chairs, swivel chairs, folding chairs; and in arm chairs, rocking chairs, deck chairs, barber's chairs, sedan chairs, dentist's chairs, basket chairs, reclining chairs . . . since there seems to be an indefinitely large variety of chairs and of successful (graceful, comfortable, secure, poised, etc.) ways to sit in them. Moreover, understanding chairs also includes social skills such as being able to sit appropriately (sedately, demurely, naturally, casually, sloppily, provocatively, etc.) at dinners, interviews, desk jobs, lectures, auditions, concerts . . .

> At dinners where one has to entertain important guests . . . in a hurry . . . serving them beef in a French version of Stroganoff . . . with buttered potatoes . . . and a good red Bordeaux.

Several weeks after making Julia's *bœuf*, I was assembling twelve chairs (dining chairs, folding chairs, desk chair) around the dining table, and I was thinking not of Dreyfus but of my mother. In her younger days, my mother had given lavish dinner parties, and it was she who had insisted—indeed, commanded—that I have all the necessary equipment for the sort of sit-down dinner I was giving that night. I surveyed the fancy wedding-gift stainless she had persuaded me to register for ("or else you'll get a lot of junk," she said), the Riedel wineglasses, also gifts, and finally the set of china she had given me after my father's death, when she sold their small summer house—"the country dishes" she called them—each one hand-painted in a simple design, blue cornflowers on white.

It wasn't until I started setting the table, beginning with the forks, that I thought of Dreyfus. Salad forks, fish forks, crab forks, entrée forks, dessert forks—at that moment it occurred to me that the paradigm for an intelligent machine had changed, but what remained was the knotty problem of teaching a computer what it needed to know to achieve sentience. In the years since Dreyfus wrote his book, computer scientists had given up on the idea of intelligence as a purely abstract proposition—a knowledge base and a set of rules to operate upon it—and were now building "social robots" like Cynthia Breazeal's Kismet, machines with faces and facial expressions, which are designed to learn about the world the way human beings do: by interacting with other human beings. Instead of being born with a universe already inscribed inside them, these social machines will start life with only basic knowledge and skills. Armed with cute faces and adorable expressions, like babies, they must inspire humans to teach them about the world. And, in the spirit of Dreyfus, I asked myself: If such a robot were coming to dinner, how could I, as a good human hostess and teacher, explain everything I would be placing before it tonight?

Besides the multiple forks, there will be an armory of knives: salad knife, fish knife, bread knife, dessert knife. We'll have soup spoons and little caviar spoons made of bone, teaspoons, tiny demitasse spoons, and finally the shovel-shaped ice-cream spoons you can get only in Germany—why is it that only Germans recognize the need for this special ice-cream implement? My robot guest could learn in an instant the name and shape and purpose of every piece of silverware, I thought; it would instantly understand the need for bone with caviar because metal reacts chemically with roe. But its mouth isn't functional; the mouthpart is there only to make us humans feel more at ease; my robot guest doesn't eat. So how will it understand the complicated interplay of implement, food, and mouth—how each tool is designed to hold, present, complement the intended fish or vegetable, liquid or grain? And the way each forkful or spoonful finds its perfectly dimensioned way into the moist readiness of the mouth, where the experience evanesces (one hopes) into the delight of taste?

And then there will be the wineglasses: the flutes for champagne, the shorter ones for white wine, the pregnant Burgundy glasses, the large ones for Cabernet blends. How could I tell a machine about the reasons for these different glasses, the way they cup the wine, shape the smell, and deliver it to the human nose? And how to explain wine at all? You could spend the rest of your life tasting wine and still not exhaust its variations, each bottle a little ecosystem of grapes and soils and weather, yeast and bacteria, barrels of wood from trees with their own soil and climate, the variables cross-multiplying until each glassful approaches a singularity, a moment in time on earth. Can a creature that does not drink or taste understand this pleasure? A good red Bordeaux!

I went to the hutch to get out the china. I had to move aside some of the pieces I never use: the pedestaled cigarette holders, the little ashtrays, the relish tray for the carrots, celery, and olives it was once de rigueur to put on the table. Then I came to the coffeepot, whose original purpose was not to brew coffee—that would have been done in a percolator—but to serve it. I remembered my mother presiding over the many dinners she had given, the moment when the table was scraped clean of crumbs and set for dessert, the coffee cups and saucers stacked beside her as she poured out each cup and passed it down the line. Women used to serve coffee at table, I thought. But my own guests would walk over and retrieve theirs from the automatic drip pot. My mother is now ninety-one; between her time as a hostess and mine, an enormous change had occurred in the lives of women. And, just then, it seemed to me that all that upheaval was contained in the silly fact of how one served coffee to dinner guests. I knew I would never want to go back to the manners of the 1950s, but all the same I suddenly missed the world of her dinner parties, the guests waving their cigarettes as they chatted, my mother so dressed up, queenly by the coffeepot, her service a kind of benign rule over the table. I put the pot in the corner of the hutch and thought: It's no good trying to explain all this to my robot guest. The chain of associations from just this one piece of china has led me to regret and nostalgia, feelings I can't explain even to myself.

The real problem with having a robot to dinner is pleasure. What would please my digital guest? Human beings need food to survive, but what drives us to choose one food over another is what I think of as the deliciousness factor. Evolution, that good mother, has seen fit to guide us to the apple instead of the poison berry by our attraction to the happy sweetness of the apple, its fresh crispness, and, in just the right balance, enough tartness to make it complicated in the mouth. There are good and rational reasons why natural selection has made us into creatures with fine taste discernment—we can learn what's good for us and what's not. But this very sensible survival imperative, like the need to have sex to reproduce, works itself out through the not very sensible, wilder part of our nature: desire for pleasure.

Can a robot desire? Can it have pleasure? When trying to decide if we should confer sentience upon another creature, we usually cite the question first posed by the philosopher Jeremy Bentham: Can it suffer? We are willing to ascribe a kind of consciousness to a being whose suffering we can intuit. But now I wanted to look at the opposite end of what drives us, not at pain but at rapture: Can it feel pleasure? Will we be able to look into the face of a robot and understand that some deep, inherent need has driven it to seek a particular delight?

According to Cynthia Breazeal, future digital creatures will have drives that are analogous to human desires but will have nothing to do with the biological imperatives of food and sex. Robots will want the sort of things that machines need: to stay in good running order, to maintain physical homeostasis; to get the attention of human beings, upon whom they must rely, at least until they learn to take care of themselves. A robot will be intelligent and happy the way a dolphin is intelligent and happy: each in its own form, each in its own way.

Breazeal is very smart and articulate, and her defense of the eventual beingness of robotic creatures is a deep challenge to the human idea of sentience. She insists that robots will eventually become so lifelike that we will one day have to face the question of their inherent rights and dignity. "We have personhood because it's granted to us by society," she told me. "It's a status granted to one another. It's not innately tied to being a carbon-based life form."

So challenged, I spent a long time thinking about the interior life of a robot. I tried to imagine it: the delicious swallowing of electric current, the connoisseurship of voltages, exquisite sensibilities sensing tiny spikes on the line, the pleasure of a clean, steady flow. Perhaps the current might taste of wires and transistors, capacitors and rheostats, some components better than others, the way soil and water make up the terroir of wine, the difference between a good Bordeaux and a middling one. I think robots will delight in discerning patterns, finding mathematical regularities, seeing a world that is not mysterious but beautifully self-organized. What pleasure they will take in being fast and efficient—to run without cease!—humming along by their picosecond clocks, their algorithms compact, elegant, error-free. They will want the interfaces between one part of themselves and another to be defined, standardized, and modular, so that an old part can be unplugged, upgraded, and plugged back in, their bodies forever renewed. Fast, efficient, untiring, correct, standardized, organized: the virtues we humans strive for but forever fail to achieve, the reasons we invented our helpmate, the machine.

The dinner party, which of course proceeded without a single robot guest, turned out to be a fine, raucous affair, everyone talking and laughing, eating and drinking to just the right degree of excess. And when each guest rose to pour his or her own cup of coffee, I knew it was one of those nights that had to be topped off with a good brandy. By the time the last friend had left, it was 2:30 a.m., the tablecloth was covered with stains, dirty dishes were everywhere, the empty crab shells were beginning to stink, and the kitchen was a mess. Perfect.

Two days later, I was wheeling a cart through the aisles at Safeway—food shopping can't always be about fetal lettuces—and I was thinking how neat and regular the food looked. All the packaged, pre-prepared dinners lined up in boxes on the shelves. The meat in plastic-wrapped trays, in standard cuts, arranged in orderly rows. Even the vegetables looked cloned, identical bunches of spinach and broccoli, perfectly green, without an apparent speck of dirt. Despite the influence of Julia Child and the California-cuisine guru Alice Waters, despite the movement toward organic, local produce, here it all still was: manufactured, efficient, standardized food.

But of course it was still here, I thought. Not everyone can afford the precious offerings of the food hall. And even if you could, who really has the time to stroll through the market and cook a meal based on what looks fresh that day? I have friends who would love to spend rainy afternoons turning a nice filet into *bœuf à la Parisienne.* But even they find their schedules too pressed these days; it's easier just to pick something up, grab a sauce out of a jar. Working long hours, our work life invading home life through email and mobile phones, we all need our food-gathering trips to be brief and organized, our time in the kitchen efficiently spent, our meals downed in a hurry.

As I picked out six limes, not a bruise or blemish on them, it occurred to me that I was not really worried about robots' becoming sentient, human, indistinguishable from us. That long-standing fear—robots who fool us into taking them for humans, from Asimov's Byerley to Breazeal's Kismets—suddenly seemed a comic-book peril, born of another age, as obsolete as an old computer junked on the street.

What scared me now were the perfect limes, the five varieties of apples that seemed to have disappeared from the shelves, the dinner I'd make and eat that night in thirty minutes, the increasing rarity of those feasts that turn the dining room into a wreck of sated desire. The lines at the checkout stands were long; neat packages rode along on the conveyor belts; the air was filled with the beep of scanners, as the food, labeled and bar-coded, identified itself to the machines. Life is pressuring us to live by the robots' pleasures, I thought. Our appetites have given way to theirs. Robots aren't becoming us, I feared; we are becoming them.

Three Stories About What We Owe the Past

While I Was Away

2012

In February 2006, a story began trailing me. This sort of thing can happen to anyone. Something installs itself in your imagination and is pushpinned to your brain.

What pursues you can be anything. Embarrassment that you did a bad job on a computer program; it runs, so you don't tell anyone, but the faults will be discovered one day, you are sure; you think of the scenes that will follow, the shame, the downward road of your life, and you cannot escape what your imagination has brewed for you. Maybe a change of feeling about a close friend because she lied about you to all her other friends; and you dream of strangling her for all the nasty ways she has treated you over the many years, her sly criticisms of your looks ("Oh, your ankles really aren't thin, are they?"); most especially her suggesting that you leave your current, wonderful husband ("Those of us who are your friends hope you find someone better"), invoking an imaginary Greek chorus. And now you try to leave thoughts of her, tear open the plastic-bag packaging of that story—danger of suffocation!—and go on to a happy memory, your father watching you as you go round and round on a merry-go-round on a sunny Saturday in a park called Fairyland, but still you want it to go away, because you recall that he watched you on a merry-go-round only that one time, so even a memory of happiness is terrible.

As I said, anything.

The story pursuing me in February was a grim tale. It included the Holocaust, abandonment, madness—it haunted me. All the darkness in the story was too much a part of my own sensibility—okay, no Holocaust in my personal experience, but yes to abandonment and madness—and therefore it would be better not to let this deep-sea monster swim anywhere near my imagination.

The story came upon me by accident. I read a short article in *The New York Times*. This is why newspapers are dangerous, and perhaps it's a good idea to set up feeds only for things you're already interested in. No risk of being mugged by starvation in Somalia, a murder in the Bronx, twenty-six people killed in a bombing in Iraq, an obituary where you find out someone you knew or admired or loved or hated is dead.

Turn the page. Bottom right. A picture showing prosperous-looking men in business suits and overcoats. The story: a group of men and women who had been born in the displaced-persons camp at Bergen-Belsen after World War II; they kept in touch, met every year when they could arrange it. They had a bond, it seemed. But I could not for the life of me understand the nature of that bond. Why would anyone born in a DP camp want to commemorate such a past? They had been stateless people, in a camp surrounded by barbed wire, no country to go back to, and no country willing to let them in. Stranded in a former concentration camp. Maybe, for them, the story of growing up in the camp was one of those pushpinned things they could not escape.

I hung the article on the wall of my small office. (Mistake! I even used a pushpin!) The paper yellowed, which gave it a sort of glow. I should have taken it down. I was supposed to be thinking about the second rise of the internet, the next episode in the story of code in the world.

In the same year, 2006, I came across another story, one that wrenched me away from my own. It was another emotional hijacking by newspaper: I was traveling; *USA Today* was on the floor outside my room; might as well read it over breakfast, I decided. The article: our government's National Security Agency was performing mass, warrantless surveillance of the citizens of the United States.

The article disclosed the details of the NSA's "secretly collecting the phone records of millions of Americans." AT&T, Verizon, and Bell-South provided information about calls made by their customers—two hundred million citizens. They gave the NSA data including phone numbers, and the date and duration of each call. (Only Qwest refused to cooperate.) The massive amount of information was being stored in what would be "the largest database ever assembled in the world," said a source who remained anonymous. The goal, he said, "is to create a database of every call ever made" within the nation's borders.

The story seemed inevitable, the result of coalescing forces put in place decades ago. I recalled the fiber optic cable being laid in front of my building in a trench heading toward the monolith of AT&T. What bandwidth the company must have by now, enough to track the vast numbers of international phone calls and emails! I remembered the long-term fear among internet creators, such as Tim Berners-Lee, that governments could use the internet for surveillance. And the database systems I had worked on in the mid-1980s, speeding access to information stored on servers. And now the NSA had powerful algorithmic tools to sift through billions of data elements, looking for patterns. The U.S. and UK intelligence services had tapped the transatlantic cable that constitutes a very spine of the internet. Whatever excitement I'd had in 1999 about the internet was extinguished.

There was brief hope when a U.S. district judge ruled that the surveillance program was unconstitutional and illegal. Then the decision was overturned by Attorney General Alberto Gonzales (he of "enhanced interrogation techniques," not to be confused with "torture"). He said that the "Terrorist Surveillance Program" would be overseen by the Foreign Intelligence Surveillance Court, whose proceedings are secret. A black curtain was drawn over the government capture of the internet.

The story faded from the news.

Characters began appearing in the tale of the Bergen-Belsen children. There will be a young woman, born in Belsen, who is adopted by a chain of parents who do not want her; a German psychiatrist who is helping the young woman find her identity, the analyst herself struggling with her family's participation in the Holocaust; the mother who gave birth to the young woman who was then sent away for adoption. The mother comes from a wealthy, assimilated Jewish family in Berlin, and finds herself, in the end, living in Tel Aviv, Israel, a country she "detests."

The time setting also revealed itself. The "now" of the story will be San Francisco in 1974, all the characters looking back to 1945 and the years before it.

Each character was a betrayer, a thief stealing some part of my own life (adoption, abandonment by parents, therapy, therapist who had something to hide from me), pieces of those interior stories that will not go away. I did not know if bringing them to the fore would purge them from my mind or more firmly install them. In any case, the characters seemed inevitable.

A year went by. Two hundred pages written, discarded.

Then came another astounding, irresistible distraction. It was January 2007: Apple introduced the first iPhone. Beautiful! A computer in your hand. Apple would support third-party applications. I knew that programmers by the thousands would flock to writing code for this device; I knew that nothing in computing would ever be the same again.

A few blocks away from where I live is the Moscone Center, two large convention halls that host technology conferences with their legions of attendees. Forty-two thousand at Oracle, streets closed around the center, the diverted traffic honking in vain. The Game Developers Conference, black leather jackets among suits, a more punky crowd, boyish—the exhilaration of fun. The most anticipated of them all, the Apple Worldwide Developers Conference, a chance to see Steve Jobs on the stage, live; what new feats of magic will he perform before the audience?

The sidewalks teemed with young men—overwhelmingly young men, white and Asian—their plastic-covered badges swinging, reflecting light; the men talking, gesturing, energy rising from the streets, the air crackling with intellect; a world more tempting than the pink cotton candy that mysteriously wound itself around a cardboard core in Fairyland.

Sometimes I stood by wistfully. I was not a part of it.

———

One night, about six months after Apple's iPhone announcement, I sat trying to work in my small writing office in an old building on New Montgomery Street near Market—Mark Twain once had an office there. Everyone was gone: there were no sounds but the traffic outside and the anxious electricity of the fluorescent lights in the hallway. A voice came to me—I mean a voice as in a writing voice, not the voice heard by a schizophrenic, although there was something of illness in the way it invaded my consciousness. He was a professor, on leave from a university, for some infraction he has presumably committed; serious or not, he will not tell. He is alone in San Francisco, experiencing, as he describes it, "a particularly obdurate spell of the nervous condition I had been subject to since boyhood."

The voice was dangerous, too much like my own but darker—my being permuted into a strange man who is sitting in an office, like mine, from which he will overhear the therapy of the adopted young woman through a thin door to a neighboring office. Despite all my internal protests, I knew he must own the entire tale; it cannot unfold but for what he says about what he hears. Insanity! The story had pursued me; it had to be told; yet it hid from me, behind a door, in the words of the professor.

In his voice, that very night, in one sitting, I wrote what became the first twenty pages of the story. Here was the trap: fluency. The story that stalked me would not leave me alone unless I spoke through the strange professor, a man, someone subject to spells of a nervous condition.

The world outside the little writing room grew remote. What I saw was the San Francisco of the 1970s. The serial killer known as the Zodiac was still at large. A group of Black Muslims, who called themselves the Death Angels, terrorized the city by waging their revolution as snipers, shooting white people at random, earning "wings" for each kill. The underground group the Weathermen, a leftist, mostly white, revolutionary movement, took its name from the Bob Dylan lyric "You don't need a weatherman / To know which way the wind blows"; the group was inclined to use violent means, and the police tried to capture them by stopping and questioning every woman in overalls walking in the Mission District, including my own then dykey-looking self. Then there was the group called the Symbionese Liberation Army, which famously kidnapped the Hearst newspaper heiress, Patty Hearst, converting her within weeks into someone who renamed herself Tanya, called the police pigs, and helped out, sporting a carbine, at a bank holdup in which a guard was killed.

Meanwhile, the city was in a hot frenzy of physical desire. Men from gay bars overflowed into the streets of the Castro; they practiced whatever sexuality they liked in bathhouses. Lesbian women, reputed to be so tame, jammed into their own bars, sometimes repairing to private places therein to partake of drugs and sex.

I walked through my memories: the wildness of that time, terrifying, exhilarating. I could imagine pre–World War II Berlin as San Francisco's doomed sister, in its own madness and wildness, the frenzy of the Weimar Republic, whose inhabitants could not know what horrors lay ahead.

Modern human beings have existed for two hundred thousand years; human beings who have used the modern web have existed for twenty years. This thought kept me from utter surrender to the excitement of apps, startups, mobile computing, all that was suggested in the iPhone announcement of January 2007. But also unfolding was the continuing story of government surveillance, and surveillance done by technical-industry companies—Google, Facebook—tracking users' movements on the web, selling knowledge of those moves to advertisers; Google became the largest advertising-sales organization the world has ever known. It is not as if I could ignore all that—I wrote a few short pieces—but the events of those years, 2008–12, were like roaring crowds in the street.

I had to close my window, lock it against temptation, pull down the shade. I wanted to think about the countless human beings who had lived before the internet had ever come into existence. A small handful of those humans, my made-up people, was waiting for me in the little writing office—where it is quiet at night, as I've said, no sounds but the traffic outside and the anxious electricity of the fluorescent lights in the hallway.

The past. The several pasts:

San Francisco, 1974, the wildness of that time.

Tel Aviv, 1975, Israel after the Yom Kippur War, the country all but overrun by surprise attacks on two of its borders, the war that nearly ended the existence of the State of Israel. The anxiety of a nation that suddenly understood it could disappear.

Germany, 1945, the Bergen-Belsen camp after Germany's surrender. The concentration camp had been liberated, yet thousands were dying each day of hunger and typhus. The internees could not go "home" to Poland or Russia; Jews who returned were met with pogroms. And so they looked to the hope of going to Palestine. But the British ruled Palestine; they refused entry. Life went on as best it could in the camp.

Europe, 1930s, 1940s. The war. The Holocaust.

Berlin, 1930s. Wealthy, cultured families who were Jewish in name only, who thought of themselves as "Germans of Hebrew heritage."

For each time setting, I tried to imagine a physical existence for the characters. What fabrics were their clothes made of? Did the styles of the shoes make their feet hurt? (No trivial matter. Think about how much the feelings of your feet contribute to your state of being.) What did the ambient world smell and sound like? The birth mother is old enough to remember a time when cars were beginning to replace horses, the smell of horse dung giving way to the acrid, choking smoke of exhaust, horse clip-clops and winter sleigh bells drowned out by the mad screech of engines.

And what did the characters themselves understand of the past: from books and art and music; from their forebears and teachers and dinner-table conversations?

I could not simply take single points in time, 1938 or 1945 or 1974. The characters lived in a pool of their own moment and everything they experienced or remembered of what came before, what their parents told them, and the stories passed down from grandparents. The birth mother's own mother described the opening of Berlin's Great Synagogue in 1886, an event so grand that it was attended by Franz Joseph, the emperor of the Austro-Hungarian Empire.

Pasts receded into pasts into pasts. When I came to the Austro-Hungarian Empire, I knew it was time to come back to the present.

The year two thousand and twelve, and the story is done. It goes out into the world, the words frozen in place; there is no more I can add or subtract. Despite errors and flaws, the story lets me go.

The internet again moves into my foreground. The general public seems to have accepted being tracked and surveilled as a fact of life. I knew years ago that technology would intrude into the intimacies of our lives. But I could not know that so many people would be delighted at that changed state of existence. I could not have imagined that they would simultaneously know they were being surveilled by massive corporations and the government, yet still suppress the thought and go on revealing themselves. This seemed to me a madness of our time.

Readers have asked me why I chose a story that happened before the internet. Fair enough: I have written about technology for several years. But the question comes over and over: Why before the net? Why before the net? Why create a gulf that separates us from the story—that great gulf being the internet?

I answered that the internet is not the culmination of human experience. The web is just another stunning point in the two-hundred-thousand-year history of human beings on earth. The taming of fire; the discovery of penicillin; the publication of *Jane Eyre*—add anything you like. The momentous befores and afters: different worlds on either side of the great divides in life and consciousness.

There was a world before the internet, and there will be a world after it. There will be an end to this internet. Given the omnipresent surveillance entity it has become, the internet as we know it may already be dying.

The characters in the story are searching for the truth in their pasts. I felt I had to reclaim the idea of search, tear it away from Google with its snippets of information. Search is an ancient trope, as old as Homer and the Greeks and the writings humans of the deep past have left for us. We look back again and again. Search is a part of us, one of the desires evolution has woven into us over the eons, to keep us alive.

And narrative. We are narrative creatures and poets. Human history has been passed down to us through story and song and rhyme—the makings of memory, the roots of recall. The act of narration never leaves us. The need for story is in our bodies, in the evolution of our minds. We sleep. The brain is doing its housekeeping, weaving today's experiences into the synaptic connections of all that happened before this day. Shifting moments. Pathways strengthened, or fading.

Meanwhile, we lie sleeping, trying to make sense of it all. We have no choice; we must understand what flickers in our mind. We desperately try to make it coherent—turn the chemical charges into a story, narrate the dream to ourselves. The narration fails. The story will not adhere. The memory of it evaporates upon waking. We fail, we fail. Yet night by night we try. There is no escaping the body that makes us. Sleep is full of stories trying to unfold.

Close to the Mainframe

2014

In 1981, I decided I could not be a real programmer until I had experience on a mainframe computer. This was a completely abstract idea: I had no idea how to program a mainframe computer.

A headhunter got me an interview with a national retailing chain. I was not exactly what they were looking for, he said. I had no experience on a mainframe; they wanted someone who had worked specifically on an IBM/370 running MVS SPF JES2 with CICS. (What?) And I had never written code in the language they were using, COBOL. My being a woman didn't help. The headhunter's success at getting me in the door must have been due to his relentless salesmanship, motivated by the fact that, if I got hired and stayed a year, the company would pay him 20 percent of my first year's salary.

For the interview, I dressed in a wide-shoulder-padded pantsuit and shoes that were not sneakers. I had changed since the early San Francisco days of the mid-1970s, those years of short hair and cats and temp work. I'd had a real job before the one I was applying for: I had worked as a programmer on a midsized computer running an operating system brazenly called "Reality." And now I was determined to get another real job, on an even bigger computer. The gay revolution raged on; lesbian bars were packed; I still went out with women. But here I had to pass for straight.

The company's processing center was on the ninth floor of a large department store in San Francisco. The floor seemed not to exist. The elevator buttons topped off at eight, where I got out and saw a sign over double swinging doors that said "Employees Only." I went through them on the theory I might become an employee and saw another sign showing only "9." An arrow pointed to a narrow staircase where a dim light from above staggered down the stairs.

At the top was a glass-enclosed, harshly lit room. Women—all Filipinas, it seemed—were working, heads down, at keypunch machines. They were exposed to every passing eye, the thick glass forbidding the escape of any sound, the viewer hearing nothing of the chatter of the machines, so it all seemed a pantomime, a mad window display of some imagined past era. I had forgotten that keypunch machines ever existed. Data entry as I knew it was typed directly into the computer system at a terminal. It seemed that the strange staircase had led me not only to a nonexistent floor but also ten years back in time.

Beyond was a short hallway that opened up to a room as large as half a city block. There were partitions so high I couldn't see any people. No one greeted me.

The vast space had a low ceiling. Humming fluorescent tubes

hung about every six feet. At the end of a row of cubicles was a tiny arched, shuttered window that let in only a slit of light. The low ceiling, the single window, the hidden top floor: these combined to create the impression that I had climbed up to an attic; or to the sort of half-story that once topped old apartment buildings, where servants lived.

I wandered at random and, by chance, came upon the triple-wide corner cubicle of Mr. Peter M, head of data processing for the Western region—and my prospective boss. His nameplate hung crookedly on the outside of the partition. Its gold-toned plastic border was chipped. Scraps still clung to three pushpinned papers, one showing a fragment of a calendar from two months ago.

He was on the phone and waved me in. He looked to be about forty-five. But I could have been wrong, since I was thirty, and anyone who looked older than I was, but not yet really old, seemed to be about forty-five. His hair was bristly, salt-and-peppered; he had a mustache, also bristly and salt-and-peppered. His complexion was pinkish, even in the green fluorescent light, and his squashed nose was too big for his face. He had on a sort of nautical blazer, navy blue with brass buttons. A button was missing from the left cuff. The lapels said the jacket had taken one too many trips to the dry cleaner's.

The interview lasted three-quarters of an hour, during which time Mr. M did most of the talking. He described—bragged about—an upcoming upgrade to a POS system. I nodded with an expression I hoped made me look intelligent, since POS was yet another set of letters that made no sense to me. He went on like that for half an hour. With a shock, I realized he was trying to impress me, which seemed bizarre because it seemed it should have been the other way around. I didn't know yet that a bad interviewer uses the occasion to puff himself up, show off his brilliance, his superiority and authority, the manly size of his domain. I was supposed to be dazzled: Mr. M wanted me to want him.

Finally he said "point-of-sale." Ah. POS. Thousands of digital "cash registers." Intelligent terminals connected to a network of servers operating across five states. All the servers communicating with the company's largest mainframe, somewhere in Texas, which soon—a new project I hoped to join—would add a relational database containing millions of data elements. Suddenly I knew why I couldn't think of myself as a real programmer until I got my hands on one of these big systems.

He must have seen it: his success, my desire. I got the job.

By the time I showed up for work three weeks later, Peter M, who, last I saw him, was the commander of two hundred souls, had been demoted to leading a group of five programmers—of which I was to be one. My welcome to the company consisted of Mr. M's glaring at me from across his desk while he explained why he regretted hiring me.

"I thought you might not work out," he said, laughing, "but you were going to be Peterson's problem." Evidently, Peterson was some manager he wished ill, and I was the ill.

With Mr. M's demotion also came his banishment from the company's advanced developments. The point-of-sale terminals that had inflamed my desire: gone to other managers. The vast database containing millions of data elements: given to a group in Los Angeles. The letters CICS, now known to me as the Customer Information and Control System: goodbye to my "kicks." The networks of networks. The nerve center somewhere in the great state of Texas. All the new technology that I had been willing to risk humiliation to learn: I was never going to get my hands on any of it.

Our tattered little band of Peter M survivors was left to tend a set of pokey applications, the Inventory, Stock, Purchasing Analysis System. (At least we had been spared the utter decrepitude of General Ledger and Accounts Receivable.) Our dull charges read files from tapes; did some juggling around with the data; wrote the results of our juggling on new files on new tapes or disks, and finally came to the sole act for which our systems owed their continued existence: the printing of a report. My cohorts, four men about forty years old who wore jackets and ties, seemed already glazed over, the years of early 1970s programs having worn down whatever spikiness might have once pricked their imaginations.

In my case the glaze was produced by the Department/Class Stock Analysis System. Insert tapes; add, subtract, multiply, divide; save new "Master File"; print report. The four programs in the "system" ran automatically overnight, Mondays through Thursdays.

The entire purpose of the little set of programs was to produce one single report for buyers, which was named, not surprisingly, "The Department/Class Stock Analysis Report." A department was something like women's shoes. The "class" was whatever a buyer chose to track in that department. It might be sandals in the women's shoe department, loafers in men's, blue dresses in misses, Estée Lauder in cosmetics. The buyers could change the classes they were interested in—at the change of seasons, for instance, or the arrival of a new line from a designer. But for some unknown reason, some classes had endured, unchangeable, for decades, forcing buyers to ignore the sales figures (or lack thereof) of items like men's evening capes and women's flowered housedresses.

I met weekly with the senior buyers, six gay men and two alluring women, all deliciously perfumed, in a tiny office on the eighth floor, in one of the grubby areas hidden away from the selling floor. The buyers barely looked down at the bug list; had no requests for changes; and, five minutes into the meeting, started making leaving gestures: feet shuffling under the table, hands pressing down on the arms of the chairs, eyes devouring the floor. So I, humiliated, could only mumble on for half a minute. Then their bodies rose, turned, walked out the door.

How could I hide the fact of my incompetence? I learned COBOL without much trouble. Its letters stand for Common Business Oriented Language, indicating it was not used for moon shots. But I had to burrow through the operating environment, deal with all those SPFs and JESs and JCLs; learn how to use the strange terminals that were clumsy compared to the ones I had been using; get code in and out of libraries; move a job into production—all without getting caught as being stupid. There is nothing more humiliating for a programmer than coming to a new system and not knowing how to log on. I told myself that I had taught myself how to code, from scratch, knowing absolutely nothing, so now, having already worked as a programmer, I certainly could learn my way around this new system. And it was my good fortune that my programs ran their useless code without incident. I had time; I could lie low. I made a work buddy who taught me the basics, a fortunate guy who worked on a CICS project.

But most of what I learned was freely given by a veteran programmer universally known as "the old man." He was fifty years old and stooped; he wore short-sleeved white shirts and bow ties; he worked on the General Ledger, a system yet more aged than mine. Two weeks of his tutelage went by. Occasionally, I retreated into a library to read manuals from among the hundreds that filled the shelves. The veteran took me by the elbow and pulled me out of that dark cave of IBM bulletins. "Go fix some bugs," he said.

And so I did.

Three bugs were not hard to spot. Two of them were a result of variables that were not initialized, one not set to zero, the other not filled with blanks, so their values could be anything left lying around in their locations in memory. The other was a misconstructed loop—a block of code that repeats—but the program looped back to the wrong spot. And, with humble thanks to the old man, I fixed the code.

When I reported these facts at the subsequent buyers' meeting, only one person replied, a woman in a cloud of Shalimar. She said, "Well, goodie for you!"

The next day was our group's regular meeting with Mr. M. He had been out of town for a while. As I approached the cracked, crooked nameplate on his cubicle, I was bouncing on my toes with happy anticipation. I went in; sat down. When he got to me, I slid the bug list across the table—no longer a list exactly, because all that remained was one item.

"Where are the others?" he asked.

"Fixed," I said.

Mr. M sat still, stared at me, and said nothing for so long that he almost undid my happiness. Then he raised his bristly mustache and showed me his teeth. I had to get away from this man, I thought, I had to quit. But there was my résumé to think of: at least one year on the job. And what revenge I was extracting by staying and succeeding.

There was yet more revenge to be extracted: the last bug, the column of zeros. The buyers needed to know how a particular class was doing. Sandals, for instance. Were this week's sales up by 2 percent over last week's or down by 3 percent? Unknown, according to the report. The value for each week's change was shown as "%0."

I went to one of the buyers (she of the Shalimar) and asked her about the missing figure. She smiled a purple-lipstick smile and said, "Oh, that's been zero since I came here. Peter says the bug's not in our programs. It's in some little system we bought, or leased—I don't know."

(That liar Mr. M! There was no vendor software in our system. Every line of code was written in house!)

Then she added, "And you should probably know that the yearly department total is junk. It drops any digit to the left of $99,999. No room for it on the report. So you can't know if it's $999,999 or $9,999,999, and so on."

"Are you kidding?" (No one had ever reported it!)

"Hey, sweetheart, the program was probably written when a hundred thou was a ton of money."

I asked her what use the report was. She laughed. "No use at all."

So this was my job: Go to a floor that did not exist as far as the elevator was concerned. Work on programs that were completely useless. Make sure they ran anyway. Keep track of flowered housedresses. Go to a group meeting once a week with Mr. M, a man whose disappointment in life was a warning to me of how not to conduct yourself in the face of failure.

The weeks went by. If the system was useless, I thought, what was the point of working on it? Just put in my time, I told myself; no one cares about the Department/Class Stock Analysis System. It runs on its own in the dead of night, not causing trouble, the operator mounting and demounting tapes, printers spitting out unread reports, code living on past its useful life, a zombie.

I had to do something. I was invisible at the office. My personal life was not going well. A blanket of gloom hung above my cubicle, threatening to drop down and suffocate me. (Long days in a windowless room, doing nothing, the sensory deprivation, can make a person go slightly mad.) Maybe I could work on the lost higher-order digits, I thought; maybe I could find them.

The solution turned out to be laughably simple on a technical level. The potentially missing hundreds of thousands or millions were sitting right there on the tape of the Master File. The problem was the pre-printed form, which had no space for the larger numbers. Changing the report's format was a decision that had to be made at the regional level, an impossibility. I imagined Mr. M sending ignored memos up the chain of command from which he had been banished.

So I worked around the obstacle. I wrote a little program that read the master tape and printed a separate report that listed the full total-sales amounts. At the report's first distribution to the buyers, my darling Ms. Shalimar came to my cubicle, took my hand in both of hers, and gave me a "thank you, thank you, thank you" that sailed on and on, then sweetly sailed off.

Glory. My system was no longer useless.

At seven in the morning, an Edward Hopper white light slashed the façade of the building, and a legless man in a wheelchair sat before the employee entrance, selling yellow number-two Ticonderoga pencils. He was always there, friendly, and I was happy to see him. I bought a pencil every day.

I liked the store in the early morning, the escalators rumbling up and down for no one, the empty selling floor, the mannequins posed to fool you, threatening to come to life. Then up the odd staircase. Past the glass box. Into the gloom of the attic.

Weeks went by. Months. I reached my nine-month anniversary. Two hundred and seventy pencils in a box on the floor.

The boredom became intolerable. I fiddled with the system. I made work friends, but I could not keep interrupting their work. I roamed the store, inspecting the departments and classes of this week's report. Designer sunglasses in notions. String bikinis in women's seasonal wear. Khaki shorts in men's sportswear. I thought of the bug: it deprived the sunglasses and shorts of their potential bestsellerdom, their time to shine, to boast that this week's sales percent had soared over last week's. All the merchandise begged me: I'll do better with a different placement in the store. Help me. Sell me.

It was time now. Get rid of that column of zeros.

The zero-percent bug had a shady past. She was a lady that had been around (the bug seemed to me a woman because of the glamorous buyer). It was first reported ten years ago, which coincided with the very day the system was launched; marked as closed two days after; reported again; again marked closed; most recently reported five years ago by a buyer who had left the store. Had the bug really been fixed or simply banished to the ignore pile? The lady appears. The lady vanishes.

The code logs showed that, before me, six programmers had failed to fix the bug. Which were the dissimulators who had declared it closed? I followed the steps my predecessors must have taken but found nothing that would account for those zeros. I went through the debugging procedures again. And again. Day by day, again. A task that was supposed to fill my idle hours had grabbed me by the lapels—ravaged them until they were as threadbare as Mr. M's.

We came to mid-August: Summer is over inside a department store. Cashmere scarves take over sun hats' prominent perches. Umbrellas banish the flip-flops from the gem location next to the main door. The changing classes mocked me. The new arrivals rebuked me. It was my fault they were still zeros.

Tenth-month anniversary, three hundred pencils in the box on the floor. September in San Francisco: seventy-eight degrees and sunny. In the store: branches and golden leaves and the bunches of red cranberries of an imaginary fall.

Eleven months. November. The California rainy season comes on in earnest. The legless man has disappeared. Where was he? Escaping the cold and rain for someplace dry and warm, I hoped.

It must have been the sudden loss of the man and his pencils—the line of kindness that had connected my days at the job—but a week after his first absence, I stopped running the debugging procedures. I got away from the screens. I did not roam the store, where the classes scorned me.

On that day, I had been sitting at my desk reading Raymond Chandler's *Trouble Is My Business* (thereby reinforcing my vision of the bug as vamp). It was late afternoon, at the hour when I usually tried to convince myself that the light in the windowless room was darkening into night and it was time to go home. I left the book on my desk, put on my coat, and took three steps toward the hallway. Suddenly I found myself stopped under a buzzing fluorescent tube.

Book. Text. Reading.

COBOL: Designed for a human reader. Designed to be easy to read. English-like: subjects, verbs, clauses, sentences.

ADD THIS-MONTH-SALES TO SALES-TO-DATE.

A command. The subject understood to be "you."

A verb: ADD.

A predicate: this month's sales to sales-to-date.

End with: the optional period.

The next morning, I ordered printouts of what I thought were key modules. Then of other parts of the system. The Filipina women who deposited the knee-high piles of fan-folded listings thought I was insane (as did everyone around me). Then I sat down—and read the code.

It was relaxing, a leaning-back experience, like all reading. No terminal screens to hurry me. No literally small windows into the code. Instead, big sheets of paper whose pages I could hum over and turn at leisure.

But code does not follow in orderly pages. Modules call other modules, which in turn call other modules: subroutines within subroutines within subroutines. I had to skip around. Each time, I put a pencil in the listing to keep my place. Soon my little cubicle became a mountain range tunneled through with caves of yellow number-two Ticonderoga pencils.

The zero-bug was no longer an adversary; it had become a mystery wanting me to solve it, the beautiful woman toying with me. I could not stop turning the pages of code. I kept reaching for the next pencil. My one-year anniversary arrived—and went by. The lady had seduced me. I was not going to leave until I found out where she was hiding. I felt I owed that much to the legless man.

Post-Halloween, rain still pelting the streets of San Francisco. In the store: a snowy Christmas. Mannequins with Santa hats. Fake popcorn chains and pretend snowmen. Meanwhile, I sat reading. Mr. M did not bother me; I think he was glad that I had come to what he saw as desperation.

Two days after New Year's Eve. Early morning. Deserted streets, the store not yet open for the hordes. I'm early (New Year's Eve had not gone so well for me, my own teasing lady having vanished). The data-processing department: still closed. The glass box of the punch-card operators: dark. The maintenance crew was just finishing up. I read by the scream of their vacuum cleaners.

Nothing and nothing and nothing unusual. The code, as something to read, had become as boring as the system itself. What is the point? I asked myself. Let these zombie programs rise up in the dark of the machine and go back to their crypt at job's end. (Such was the mood that had overtaken me.)

But on that day, on that morning, on that second day of the new year of 1982, Peter M walked by and gave me a teeth-bared grin. What a useful loathing he invoked in me. Anger! Drive me!

I returned to my code, to my words, numbers, sentences. Hum and hum and hum. Then I saw something I might never have noticed except for the foul, determined mood Mr. M had induced in me. Two sentences:

WS-CLASS-CHANGE-PERCENT EQUALS WS-THIS-WEEK-CLASS-SALES DIVIDED BY WS-LAST-WEEK-CLASS-SALES.

MOVE WS-CLASS_CHANGE-PERCENT TO DS-CLASS-CHANGE-PERCENT.

Sentence one: correctly calculates the weekly change percent for the class as this week's sales / last week's sales.

Sentence two: Moves the class-change percent from the program's internal working memory (working storage, WS) to permanent data storage (DS)—that is, the new master file.

The code seemed completely normal. My eyes went back and

forth over the text, dot-matrix letters on green-and-white-striped paper. But there was something wrong, visually. Some space was ill-formed. Between the letters, a space too high, a space too wide.

Then I saw the villains: the two characters forced to share a single typing key, one riding on the back of the other, shift devils.

Underscore
Dash

WS-CLASS-CHANGE-PERCENT   ← Dash
MOVE WS-CLASS_CHANGE-PERCENT   ← Underscore

The dash version: the true computed value.

The underscore version: Moves something to the master file, but not the true value in the dash version.

What the hell was going on? What in the world was in the underscore element? I searched back up and saw that it was a variable that had been defined by one of my predecessors, used for some debugging gone wrong, then never deleted.

The idiot. He had initialized the underscore version to zero. Then he never again used it in the program. Its value remained as it had been initialized, which was . . . zero. The value the underscore version moved to the Master File on tape was . . . zero!

Ah.

I changed the MOVE statement to use the variable holding the true value, the dashed one. Now the report would show the correct weekly class-change percentage. The umbrellas and scarves and shoes would no longer mock me.

I sat in the gloom of the vast room under the low ceiling. All along, I had imagined the joyous satisfaction I would feel in cornering my illusive, diabolical, beautiful lady—my fantasy of her wearing a stunning gown, smoking a cigarette, and saying to me, So—you finally found me.

What I had found instead was the detritus of some jerk of a programmer who did not know what the hell he was doing, one of the dissemblers who had fiddled with the code and declared the bug fixed. I was too angry to forgive him; years later, after writing my own idiotic code, I would.

I pulled out all the pencils and put them back into the box on the floor. I thanked the legless man and hoped he was well; I hoped that, come spring, he would reappear at the associates' entrance to smile and say hello as the employees arrived in the slanting light of early morning.

Now to tell Peter M. I went by his cubicle and asked if he had a minute. He did. He stood. I handed him the Department/Class Stock Analysis Report. I pointed to the column full of the correct percentages. Mr. M narrowed his eyes and started grinding his teeth.

I thought I would feel triumphant. I had imagined my sweet delight at defeating Peter M. But now I looked at him again, with his bristly hair and mustache adding more salt to the pepper every day, wearing another sports jacket that had taken one too many trips to the cleaner's. I never did learn the reason for his disastrous fall. Had he made a mistake, or was it simply his ordinariness, a dullness of being that could never engender inspiration in anyone?

We stood without speaking. I knew that the anger he was grinding between his teeth was for the next job he would never have, for his age, for the demotion that had doomed him. He was stuck for the rest of his working life in the Inventory, Stock, Purchasing Analysis System. Whereas I had learned what there was to know in his little corner of the mainframe. I could take it with me, and go.

The Party Line

2015

In 1970, while I was a student at Cornell University, in Ithaca, New York, I moved away from campus and into an old farmhouse outside of town. It took about fifteen minutes to get there, a longer drive in bad weather, which Ithaca had plenty of, freezing winters and heavy snows. The area was rural, country roads laid out in perfect mile grids. It was dairy-farming country, some farms to my eyes appearing prosperous, others worn down, others abandoned.

I shared the farmhouse with a lumpy collection of people. I had known only one of them, a guy in my Romantic Poetry class. The others turned out to be my classmate's sister, her excitable artist boyfriend with messianic tendencies, and an orange-haired guy who lived in a room off the back of the kitchen, whom I never got to know. A couple of others came and went, staying on the sofa in the otherwise empty living room. We didn't exactly share the house. We took to putting our initials on the eggs in the fridge.

The house, on Halseyville Road, had occasional hot water and no heat to speak of. My room was upstairs, in an attic under a dormered roof. A small window overlooked the road, where there wasn't much traffic. On clear nights, I could hear car wheels whispering on the macadam from miles away.

I had just returned to Ithaca after a wander year. I had left Cornell, and during that time away I got married and divorced and escaped commitment to a mental institution; drove across the country with a friend, sleeping in a pup tent, avoiding the threat of a creepy guy who kept asking where our camp was, picking up hitchhiking boys, taking up with one of them; later, my friend and I ditched the car and took a milk train into Mexico, where we smoked grass that was—zow!—the real drug, met more boys, and learned the subtleties of tequila; finally, I wound up in freezing Buffalo in the winter, to work as the switchboard receptionist at the Jewish Community Center. One day I picked up the switchboard phone, called the Cornell provost, and asked if I could come back—all of which peripatetic motion, I think, is what drove me out of town to the farmhouse.

It was by no means a rural idyll. During the winter, farm dogs would run off and pack up, and no sane person strayed far from the house. Our landlord had leased the surrounding acres to a nearby farmer, and an evening of sitting in the field to commune with a sunset could quickly turn into the experience of seeing a plow crest over the hill heading for you, its rotating disks chewing up the earth.

The area was sparsely populated. We had rural mail delivery, boxes at the end of the road, and several households had to share a phone number. This was called a party line, which was an antique even then. You knew the call was for your house by the number of rings. But since we were unused to the whole idea, anyone near the phone picked it up automatically, which made us supremely disliked in the neighborhood. A usual response from a fellow party-er was "Hang up, you darned hippies." Making a call involved waiting for the party currently on the line to hang up, which led to all sorts of angry interchanges.

And there was always the suspicion that someone was listening in, and the endless temptation to do the same yourself. I have always been an eavesdropper; I gave in to temptation. I heard gossip about unknown people, but mostly it was just husbands and wives reminding each other to run errands.

One of the people I sometimes heard on the line was a woman with a soft voice and a British accent. Unlike our other shared parties, she was always polite, saying things like "Oh, if it is not too much bother, may I ask you if I may use the phone in ten minutes?" I learned very little about her by listening in, except that they probably didn't have much money: we paid according to our time on the phone, and her calls were always practical, quick, under a minute.

Fall turned to winter. Despite our growing dislike of one another, my classmate, his sister, and her artist boyfriend would often sit together in the low-ceilinged kitchen, trying to stay warm, stove gas burners turned up high, and the oven running with its door open (precisely how you are not supposed to use gas stoves).

One morning, as we were finishing breakfast, there came a knock on the door. This was unusual—a shock, really, since no one ever had to knock. If there was a key to the house, I never knew about it. So someone called out "Who is it?" and in reply came a woman's voice with a British accent saying, "Hallo, hallo. I am your neighbor from across and down the road." I knew her at once as the woman from the party line. I felt a moment of panic over perhaps being discovered, and then, knowing I would never be caught unless I turned myself in, I yielded to the curiosity of seeing her in the flesh.

I was closest to the door and opened it. There stood a woman with peppered gray hair tied into a messy bun. She seemed to be in her fifties. She had on layers of well-worn men's sweaters, stretched out, hanging, one over another, the last one a cardigan.

She put out her hand and introduced herself (I'll call her Mrs. Richard). I waved her in. We told her our names, and as she looked from one of us to another she said, "I know others in this area do not think kindly about your being here, but, well, a neighbor is a neighbor."

We offered her tea, coffee, juice (which must have been the property of the guy in the back room), but she declined everything, saying she just wanted to "pop in." She relayed the simple directions to get to the dirt road that led up to their farm and said, "Please feel free to visit us anytime," she said. She demurred (perfectly Britishly) our further offers for her to join us at the table, then wished us goodbye and left.

I didn't hear a car. She must have come the half-mile on foot.

"How weird!" said the sister.

"Oh wow," said her brother.

Artist Boyfriend stood over the table, pronouncing in transcendent tones what a singular moment that had been.

I thought the visit was strange. Although there was nothing overt in it but kindness, there was also something of desperation. From overhearing her quick phone calls, and seeing the pile of old sweaters over her thin shoulders, I understood I'd just had my first real look at rural poverty.

Sometime later, we at our farmhouse (excluding the orange-haired guy) got involved in the Richards' life. The Richards never asked for it, we never intended it, yet so it happened.

I think it must have begun in the early spring, after the evening when Mrs. Richard brought us a stainless-steel cylinder of milk just barely out of the udder. It had not been pasteurized, had not been homogenized. It was warm, frothy, rich, nutty, suffused with subtle flavors I could not name—clover? I knew I had just tasted milk as our ancestors had known it.

Mrs. Richard liked to tell the story of how she and her husband had come to live on Halseyville Road. Her husband had been a merchant seaman, she said, and when he retired, they affixed an anchor to the front bumper of their pickup and told themselves they would settle down wherever it fell off. This seemed an unlikely story. Did the anchor really fall off a half-mile down the road? Had that particular farm been for sale? Yet we listened and smiled as she told the tale multiple times. I could see it added a sense of glamour to their lives, of happy serendipity, of which they had very little.

It turned out that the family's current situation was fairly dire. Their original farmhouse had burned down, and they were living in a converted outbuilding. It housed Mr. and Mrs. Richard, their ten-year-old son, and Mr. Richard's mother, who occupied the only room that might have qualified as a true bedroom, where she lay slowly dying. Mr. Richard looked to be sixty but was probably ten years younger. He was cranky and pinch-faced, and it was hard to imagine he had ever been a lighthearted man. Their son was what was then called slow. It soon became clear that the boy would not be able to run the farm, and everything would fall to the weary Mr. Richard.

Soon we at the farmhouse were picking up items for them in town to save them the trips. As spring came on, we helped with the yearly thorough-clean of the house and barn. And as the summer ended, we joined the family in gathering the hay bales from the fields, then daisy-chaining them up into the loft of the barn.

Earlier in the summer, I had found myself driving a tractor to pull a hay rake, which turns the cut grass to help it dry. After a row or two, I somehow managed to clog the rake with wet hay. Mr. Richard arrived with a machete to hack away the tangle, all the while muttering, cursing, never turning up his creased face to look at me.

I was twenty years old then, and I still walked blindly from one experience to the next. Having had enough of the cold water and the crazy artist boyfriend, I left the farmhouse and moved into a cheap studio in Collegetown. I lost any connection with the Richards. I would see them again, months later, but not until I had become involved with a media group called the Ithaca Video Project.

The Ithaca Video Project was the conception of Philip Mallory Jones, then a graduate student at Cornell. (The cofounders were Phil, Fred Mangones, Tom Danforth, James Lee Sheldon, Susan Glowski Jones, Roy Fietelberg, Todd Hutchinson, and myself.) What bound us together was our desire to get our hands on the newly released Sony Portapak. You could describe it as a small piece of gear for making videos. But that does not begin to describe a machine that effected a change in the culture. Its introduction was one of those technology-driven moments that ruptured an established order of society, or so we believed—and rightly, I think.

We worked on a grant proposal, and, miraculously, received ten thousand dollars from the New York State Council on the Arts. That was a fortune in 1971, enough to buy us a Portapak (for fifteen hundred dollars—eight thousand in today's dollars), an editing deck (yet more expensive), tapes, cables, accessories, all we needed to get to work.

Making videos before that moment involved equipment that cost tens and hundreds of thousands of dollars. What you could see on a television, that screen that beamed culture into homes across the world, was controlled by broadcasters and large corporate advertisers. Portapaks were expensive for an individual, but groups across the country were buying them through grants and collective funding. That small machine offered the opportunity to break the hold of the corporate controllers, a chance to redefine what one could see on a TV screen. What seems obvious now, video recording machines in the hands of the millions, began with the retail sales of a mass-produced media machine called the Portapak.

Here was the glory of it: One single person could make a video. People could have media-making machines *in their own hands*. No one could tell them what to produce or show to others. They were freed from the tyranny of censors. There were no limits on politics, on the arts, on porn. Indeed, a certain Frenchman smuggled in from Morocco a video of the fugitive Black Panthers Kathleen and Eldridge Cleaver. He also brought some porn. The action would be tame by current standards, but we in the Project, and others around town, enjoyed it with great gusto.

Film requires expertise, but anyone handed a Portapak learned how to use it within minutes. The reel-to-reel recording deck came in a leather case with a strap, and it was light enough to sling over your own shoulder and carry for a while (even over my shoulder, and I weighed 110 pounds). The camera had a zoom lens with a mike on the top. You connected a cable between the camera and the deck. Then all you had to do was press a button on the camera handle to start recording video and sound. You had to focus. You could zoom in and out as you wished. The machine did the exposures automatically. It even operated in low light. You could record political meetings held in dim rooms, people smoking cigarettes and dope and talking of revolution, the low-light exposure producing a peppering haze of black-and-white grain, adding to the sense of subterfuge, as in an underground movie. Protest, activism, art, guerrilla television—all was made possible (or dreamed of) by the coming of the Portapak.

I learned I had no fear of machines. I liked carrying coils of cables on my shoulder; it made me feel tough and cool. I enjoyed unrolling and snaking cables across a room: video out from the deck, video in to the screen; video out from that screen, video in to the next; etc. I liked pushing the buttons on the editing deck, rolling the tape back and forth to find the exact spot, cutting the tape at an angle and joining it to the next spot, cleanly, with dexterity, so the edit didn't make a pop when the finished video played. I used the sync generator that made the video signal compatible with the one on televisions, so scan lines didn't appear on the screen. I went off to a video workshop at Creighton University, in Omaha, which turned out to be a hotbed of art video. For my attempt, I pointed a camera at the screen of an oscilloscope and manipulated the sine waves, colorized the images, recorded my own voice, and added a deep echo. I had glorious fun.

Just up the road from the farmhouse on Halseyville Road, in the tidy town of Trumansburg, was the studio of Robert A. Moog, inventor of the first music synthesizer, the first new musical instrument created since the saxophone. I remember going to Moog's studio with someone from the Video Project. There were keyboards in mahogany-wood cases topped with stacks of electronic metal boxes, all with dials controlling the electronics—wave form, amplitude, frequency; the sustain of the notes—and others I had no idea of. The synthesizers were half fine piano, half basement electronics.

Just when the Project received its Portapak, in 1971, Moog released the Minimoog, a cousin to our machine, one that was portable and could be operated by one musician. Portable visual media, portable new musical instrument; drugs, video, electronic music, media up for wild grabs: this was the charged atmosphere that surrounded us.

Among the works we produced was a video of a desperate addict shooting up, then showing it around town in the hope of dispelling any glamour that anyone might ascribe to heroin. We made one about the Onondaga Indians fighting to prevent the city of Syracuse from building a road through their land; it was shown to the New York State Assembly. On the local cable, then called Community Antenna, I did a piece trying (inevitably failing) to interpret visually a poem by the great A. R. Ammons, who lived in Ithaca and was later the recipient of a National Book Award. Phil did animations. We did photography. We held small classes on how to use the machine; I gave one for women. We were aware of being distantly related to Nam June Paik, the creator of video art, who was redefining the TV screen as an artist's canvas, and to all the others experimenting with the medium, taking back control over that electronic eye that looked into every home, a change rippling through the culture. If this sounds like the coming of the personal computer and the internet— the machines in your hands, the heady dream of technology changing the world—it was.

But the best tape I worked on, I think, was a video about the Richards and the coming of the bulk tank.

In the four months since I had last seen the Richards, their situation had gone from dire to desperate. The local milk cooperative, the organization that sold the farmers' milk into the marketplace, had decided it would no longer pick up the milk in the traditional cans. It would buy the milk only if a farmer installed what was called a bulk tank, which was what it sounded like, a big tank filled with the farmers' milk production. The cooperative would then come around and pump it out.

The tank was expensive, tens of thousands of dollars. The Richards didn't have the money and could not afford the debt. The coming of the tank affected not only their farm, but any small farm depending upon the collective. A farm had to have enough cows to fill the tank to a decent level—sixty, as I remember, double the number of cows on the Richards' farm.

Bulk-tank collection was surely more efficient that picking up individual cans. Consumers might benefit from the lower costs of production. It was technology at what it does best: standardize and homogenize and monetize, create efficiencies in sales and markets and distribution chains.

It was also technology at its worst. The coming of the bulk tank was another of those ruptures in society. Yet this one did not widen the scope of individual freedoms. The tank would effectively drive the small family dairy farm out of existence.

One morning, Tod and I drove out to Halseyville Road to make a video about the Richards and their situation in the face of the bulk tank. Tod, with his billowing blond hair, was at the camera (and very ably), while Mrs. Richard and I walked around the farm, and I engaged her in conversation.

It was a bright early-spring day, and the light and shadows gave the stubble of the fields a bright sheen. In one particularly lovely moment, Mrs. Richard opened the barn door and the cows came galumphing out. "Oh, I love when they prance like that!" she called out. After a pause she added, "Well, of course it's bad for the milk."

She spoke of the bulk tank, the effect it would have on their farm. And the images of shining fields and happy cows fell into the emotional background.

Near the end of our recording, Mrs. Richard stood on a rise, saying nothing for several seconds. Then she rested her chin in the palm of her hand, looked out toward the fields, and said, "Oh, sometimes it is all so . . . hard."

Tod had kept the camera on her as the pause went on for long seconds. I said nothing, to let the silence continue. Then Tod slowly panned the camera in the direction of Mrs. Richard's gaze and gently zoomed out. There was Mrs. Richard, still standing chin in hand, as the farm and its fields and its barn surrounded her in the frame.

We showed the video around as widely as we could, even at a meeting of the farmers who were part of the collective. The meeting hall was a small room with a rough wooden floor. The showing was sparsely attended. The stern-faced farmers were impassive; they asked no questions afterward. We were culturally suspect creatures, hippies from the college, renting on the cheap the houses of failed farms. What did we know of their lives?

In the end, the result was what one might have expected. The milk collective prevailed; their big disruptive machine trumped our little Portapak; we were powerless to prevent the coming of the bulk tank.

Time went on; I graduated from Cornell and moved to San Francisco, where, one day in 1979, I walked past a Radio Shack store on Market Street and saw in the window a microcomputer called the TRS-80. Reader, I bought it.

I never would have considered such a move if it had not been for my experience in the Video Project, where I'd felt the deep pleasure of exploring machines. For me, there wasn't anything scary about the TRS-80. The fact that I knew next to nothing about computers was actually a draw. I could fool around and see what happened, as with the Portapak. To me, the TRS-80 was another new piece of personal technology—*personal*—therefore promising adventures in electronics. What could you do with the TRS-80? Could you make art? All of it—the Portapak, the TRS-80, the exhilaration at getting my first computer code to run—led to my unexpected career as a programmer.

Ahead was the coming of the Mac and the PC, databases, networks, then the network of networks, the internet; soon the machine dreams, the belief that technology would change the world for the better. Then the corporations' moves to control the net; the coming of commercial surveillance; the internet as a vast advertising-sales mechanism, a global retailer. Finally, the Edward Snowden revelations, when the populace finally understood that the United States government was spying on its own citizens and those around the globe—the internet as vast surveillance machine.

Through it all, I embraced the new technologies as they emerged but looked at them with a gimlet eye. I could not succumb to believing in the ultimate goodness of technology; something kept me from the dizzy addiction. I was not surprised to find out the worst of what had happened to the internet.

As I began to recall the story of the Richards, I understood what indeed had held me back, kept me skeptical, wary, even afraid of what technology could do. The bulk tank; the bulk collection of records. The end of the small family farm; the end of privacy. The cautionary tale about technology had come from my knowing the Richards, and their desperation, and the folly of my youthful, dumb belief that our small machine could help them change their lives.

The Hand That Writes
the Code

Programming for the Millions

2016

I.

One day in 1980, my father, an accountant, asked me if I could write a program for a "variable-rate amortization schedule." I was on a visit home to Flushing, Queens, just a few weeks after I'd started my first professional programming job, and I had no idea what amortization was, let alone what the rate was and why it should or should not vary. My father was in many ways an admirable man, but a terrible teacher. I had to clarify everything he said by sneezing my way through molding accounting textbooks I'd found in the basement (no internet then; no convenient Wikis).

A greater difficulty lay ahead. The program was for a client. It had to run on their minicomputer, which was different from the one I used at work. I had never even seen a machine like theirs, let alone worked with it. And the manuals they gave me showed that their system used a version of BASIC that was incompatible with the two I had learned. I was anxious but not undaunted. I would read the manuals; BASIC was BASIC, after all, a beginner's language. I'd figure out what to do, work at the client's office, and get the program running. This plan had an excellent side effect: it gave me a reason to get out of the parental home during my stay for the Jewish High Holy Days.

My plan was not to be realized. The client's office was going to be closed for the full ten days of the Holy Days. I would be back in San Francisco by the time they reopened. If I was going to keep on with the project, I would have to write a program that worked on the machine I had on the job, the aforementioned Reality system, then write a translator that would convert the Reality code to a program that would run on the client's machine.

Right then, I should have said no to my father. This was an absurd set of impediments. But I was still naïve, dizzy with the new happiness of coding, and I bounded forward like a loping puppy just let out to run in the yard.

This was one of those I-know-nothing occasions that let me, self-taught, all unschooled, stumble into a problem I was wholly unsuited to solve. Even if I absorbed quickly all the nuances in the differences between the language versions, I faced the question of how my program would "understand" the effects of the differences, making sure that each version did the same things when it ran, not an insignificant problem, involving test after test with various inputs on both machines, most of which would fail—probably all in my case. And how would I know, from two thousand five hundred air miles away, that the code was working correctly on the client's machine?

But no matter. I wrote the Reality version, which was annoying enough because of that amortization business. But the translator, the translator . . . The subtle differences between operating systems, languages, compilers. A computer-science student could have sniffed at the problem: it would be easy. But, novice that I was, I was pulled into the dark corners of anything I'd ever tried to do with a computer, which was the allure. It was better than something that might be easy. It was irresistible.

Four days after my father's request, he found me with papers flung across the twin beds and wall-to-wall carpeting of my childhood bedroom. He watched me for a while and said, "Maybe you should give it up. You appear to be struggling."

I looked up. I had one of his mechanical pencils behind my ear and a red pen between my teeth. I removed the pen and stared at him. There was nothing on his face to reveal he knew that he had just sucker-punched me in the gut. I knew him. I knew what he was thinking. He pitied me. I had failed. I was expected to excel in everything, and here I was: a disappointment.

I think of that punch to this day; I still see the girlish candy-striped wallpaper loosening along the seams, the scribbled yellow pages on the bruise-blue carpet. From then on, I knew I could be shamed and humiliated by others for my struggles and failures, but that was no reason to give up.

It was my father who had given up, on me. He went on to wave off my questions about amortization. I put the project aside. He and I never spoke of it again.

When I bought the TRS-80 I saw in the window of Radio Shack, in 1979, I thought it would be fun to explore, as I have said. Could it be a tool for political organizing? Could it make art? Better yet: was it capable of doing things I had no idea of? I knew it was nothing like a

Portapak; the computer was not designed to get you up and running with the push of a button. I knew it involved computer programming, something I had never done before and had never even imagined trying.

Yet I had a cocky courage and went ahead, armed with little but some knowledge about video, the understanding that I was not afraid of machines, and an honors thesis on *Macbeth*.

Naturally, I began by thrashing around. The programming was done in the BASIC coding language, which is easy to learn if you stick to easy things, like getting text to appear on the screen, a black-and-white TV that was old technology even then. However, writing an actual program, coding a set of statements that did what you intended them to do, was another matter.

For the first two months, I was maddened, indignant at the machine's opacity, ashamed at my own ignorance. I stayed up nights. I forgot to eat. Afternoons found me in my pajamas. I was still a day laborer in those days, a temp, filing papers, answering switchboards, pumping gas and wiping windshields at a gas-only station—I had to make money somehow. But I turned away all offers for employment. I was not available: I was somewhere deep in a tangle code.

I fell into the traps early BASIC laid all around you. You could jump around in the code. You could GOTO here and GOTO here and GOSUB there, until it was hard to keep track of where you had come from or where to go next. All the variables were "visible" everywhere, not confined to specific blocks of code, so it was easy to step on your values unwittingly. I didn't understand that the GOTOs were traps. Only later did I learn that early BASIC was called spaghetti code for its mess of strands. For me, though, at first, it was more like a pile of entwined hissing snakes.

I began to chip away at the confines of my ignorance. I moved from failure to failure, which, perversely, proved alluring. By "perverse" I mean the sort of experience that drags you into the unknown and abandons you there, and where, against all expectation, you find you like being. In other words, fun.

The snakes turned into lines and arrows drawn on a piece of paper, the variables into a list of line numbers where they were referenced. I told myself if I could follow the flows of time in *Macbeth*— where the past kept being mistaken for the future, as perceived time rolled backward and forward, with a singular startling moment in the present, when Macbeth kills the king—well, all these code tangles were nothing.

When I got my first decent little program running (graphs using x's to show the decreasing amplitudes of a bouncing ball), I sat back with a pleasure that reminded me of the time I'd fixed a carburetor: It works.

In the late 1970s and early '80s, business computing became ubiquitous, and there were not nearly enough programmers to do the coding. Computer science was then generally a subdepartment of electrical engineering, and a trained engineer was not inclined to code up a COBOL program to produce a profit-and-loss statement. It seemed that anyone who had written any code could get a job. I had written code; I needed work; I got a job.

I went on to become an ordinary computer programmer. My code ran at the levels between flashy human interfaces and the deep cores of operating systems. The programs were like altos in a chorus: they give the music structure, but you never leave humming their parts.

In one of my jobs, I flew to a small town in the Southwest to fix the system of one of my company's clients. The owner of the business was a sweaty middle-aged man with pendulous earlobes. He rubbed his clammy hands up and down on my back while I worked to survey his system's problems. I wanted to plant a bomb in his system that would blow up a year after I'd gone. I didn't. Until recently, I told myself that I had had too much pride in getting the code working. But now, on later reflection, I think I was a coward.

I once worked for a man who said at a meeting, "I hate to hire you girls, but you're all so smart." He would also interrupt me often to say, "Gee. You have pretty hair," to which I'd reply, leaning to one side, "I'm just going to let that shit fly over my shoulder." He had indeed hired those so-smart women to work in essential technical positions. And he taught me a great deal about computing. Early digital business-to-business computing. Relational databases. And I was given a great opportunity: porting the company's code, which ran on the Pick operating system, to run on UNIX; from there, becoming fluent in the C coding language. Then I got into the deeper reaches of programming: operating systems, human-computer interfaces. I did have pretty hair; I went on to become a software engineer.

I consulted on projects that succeeded and more often failed. I once worked with engineers and computer scientists whose abilities were so far above mine that I endured humiliation for the chance to learn what I'd had no other avenue to learn. When I was applying for that job, my interviewer explicitly said, "Your work is to translate between the extraordinarily intelligent [he meant himself and his team] and the ordinarily intelligent [the software engineers who would use what the superior intelligences were creating]." The role they assigned to me, translator, is perhaps the most accurate description of everything I have done concerning technology.

Over the twenty-odd years I worked as a technology practitioner, I came to realize that my wrestling with the TRS-80 was not just a beginner's experience; it was a paradigm for all the work ahead. That state of not-knowing proved permanent as I moved from machine to machine, operating system to operating system, language to language, each move a re-encounter with bafflement, as was my introduction to the mainframe. Failing was also a permanent state of affairs. Programs crash. The causes of bugs hide from discovery. Designs lead to dead ends. Goals are ill-conceived. Deadlines are absurd. One must develop a high tolerance for failure, learn to move forward from discouragement, find a ferocious determination, a near-passionate obsession to solve a problem, meanwhile summoning the pleasures of the hunt.

It was not easy for me. I am gloomy at heart and have a propensity for catastrophic thinking, believing that the events of life will inevitably lead to horrible ends. I see my car crashing even as I drive, for instance. It was one thing to wrestle with the TRS-80 in the privacy of my living room. When I worked for others, though, I was always certain my incompetence would be revealed at any moment. I had taught myself chaotically. I learned what I had to know when a job required it and where my interests randomly let me. I was aware at all times that I had only islands of knowledge separated by darkness; that I was surrounded by chasms of not-knowing, into one of which I was certain to fall.

My experience with the mainframe was one of the glorious exceptions. It was like a return to the TRS-80, the outcomes being of no importance except as I, inspired by the desire to play with a little machine, cared about them; except as I was inspired by the legless man and my illusion of the gorgeous teasing lady. Otherwise, the chasms haunted me throughout my career, such as it was, including that night when I darted off like a startled lizard from Larry Page and Sergey Brin and the possibility of working at Google.

I learned I was not alone. I met a postdoctoral student in computer science at Berkeley. I talked with him about my islands, the darkness, the fear. He answered without hesitation: "Oh, I feel that way all the time."

On the other hand, I was once invited to a small computing-and-society class at Stanford to talk about my novel *The Bug*. The story concerns an elusive software bug that plagues the protagonist for a year, a flaw like an actual bug that had once terrorized me. While I was talking about the fear that comes over you when solutions seem to be hiding in deep unknowns—and everyone around you is foot-tapping, waiting, suspecting your incompetence—a young man interrupted me mid-sentence. He said, indignantly, "I would never have a bug I couldn't solve for a year," and walked out.

II.

I dare to imagine the general public learning how to write code. I do not mean that knowledge of programming should be elevated to the ranks of the other subjects that form basic literacy: languages, literature, history, psychology, sociology, economics, the basics of science and mathematics. I mean it the other way around. What I hope is that those with knowledge of the humanities will break into the closed society where code gets written: invade it.

My hope is sorely tested by what I see all around me in SOMA. The last we saw of South of Market, in 2001, the neighborhood had gone dark after the first technology crash. Now, with the second rise of the internet, it has been resurrected as startup boulevard.

Every weekday, legions of technology workers colonize Second Street. They come on foot. They come on bicycles. They come on skateboards. They come on hoverboards. They take over the sidewalks pushing scooters, wearing helmets, like kids whose parents won't let them ride in the street. The crowd, as ever, is overwhelmingly male, white and Asian. Ninety percent of them are between the ages of twenty-two and thirty-four. The older men have shaved their heads, in the hope of remaining cool. The sight of a black face is startling.

They make their way to Salesforce and Yelp and Uber and LinkedIn and GitHub and Dropbox and Square and Instacart and Eventbrite and Spotify, not to mention the startups revealed within just three square blocks of where I live, at Second and Bryant: Yammer, Zendesk, Playdom, Scribd, Flurry, OpenDNS, Stripe, Rackspace, ShopItToMe,

Red Bubble, Optimizely, CoTweet, Chriply, Cumulus, Criteo, Drone-Deploy, PointAbout, Klout, Qwiki, Plum District, PeopleBrowsr, Udemy, SlideShare, Visually, Rdio, AppHarbor, TokBox, Zimride, Whitetruffle, Dropcam, Runscope, Manage, MyTime, CyberCoders, DataSift, Trulia, Disqus, Skillz, Mekanism, Twilio, Okta, and . . . many of which may not exist by the time you read this.

The technical soldiers then repair to their offices with comfortable chairs and sofas and free snacks and, sometimes, an open bar with excellent Scotch, where they are working on the mesh of code that envelops human life.

Meanwhile, on the street, there is the mixed-up variety of the human race: Latinas delivering catered sandwiches for meetings. Black men with push brooms hired by a charity to KEEP SOMA CLEAN. Bus drivers of every skin tone. The Latino and white working-class men getting off their construction jobs at three in the afternoon, hauling yellow buckets filled with their tools. Young white women who work in marketing (one can tell), walking ferociously forward on high heels, trailing carry-ons. Two Latina nannies (nannies: brand-new arrivals in SOMA, as if summoned on demand from the Upper East Side of New York) pushing strollers of white kids, meanwhile talking to each other in Spanish. The black male security guard with a holstered gun in front of the Bank of America. The traffic-control woman riding in her little three-wheeled vehicle, its brand name being INTERCEPTOR, hunting for parking meters flashing red, red, red.

I think of the one-third of humanity with access to the internet. And of the two-thirds living in an electronic darkness—largely in the poorest and politically most chaotic countries of the world—who are nonetheless subject to the workings of that same internet code. For the algorithms of the wealthy surround them as well, controlling trade, allocations of resources, economics, political actions, social interactions . . . life. If in 1994 the computer was poised to penetrate into the capillaries of being, and by 2000 society recognized the depth and perils of our dependence upon technology, then by now the penetration of technology into the interstices of human existence has become nearly complete. And the code that surrounds us is closed to public view: opaque, inescapable.

What, then, are we to do? By "we" I mean the privileged one-third. What are we to do when the great mass of humanity is ensnared within algorithms, *and* a bare percentage of human beings on earth has any idea of what a computer program actually is?

My thought is that we open the door to the coding rooms, spread widely the knowledge of what happens inside. It doesn't matter to what degree an individual learns to code; that knowledge does not need to lead to professional programming. The goal is for the general population to pierce the computing veil; to demystify algorithms; to know that code has biases, that programs are written by human beings and can be changed by human beings; to know the concepts, the patterns of thinking, the paths through which human thoughts get altered as they pass into the language of computers.

I welcome the philosophers and English majors and speakers of Spanish; the immigrants and social workers and teachers of everything from kindergarten to graduate school; and all those who are on the streets of SOMA after the programmers settle into the cocoons of their offices, the caterers and cops and nannies and the women in their INTERCEPTORS. This thought first came to me on Bastille Day, 2015, which certainly affected my image of a citizenry rising up and pounding at the gates of the technical aristocracy.

Perhaps, after your first exposure to programming, you who learn to code may find yourself seduced by it, as I was. You may discover you have a passion for the work and a desire to go forward. Then I see you and your cohort flooding into the closed rooms of the technical world, into the monoculture that exists within. I see you carrying in your civic, literate, diverse lives, the whole mix of gender and color and nationality and language and social class. In a real sense, you will integrate that segregated world of young white and Asian men.

Venture capitalists promote themselves as technology visionaries, yet they know little about programming itself. It is the founders, if they are code-savvy, the project leaders, and the engineers who influence the directions and particulars of what product will ultimately be made. I see you new programmers at a design presentation of a delivery app, and you are saying, "There are opportunities to expand our deliveries to underserved communities, beyond those 'select ZIP codes'" (i.e., beyond the well-to-do). At another presentation, you ask about the target user of the app: "Who exactly is that 'you' we are addressing, and what is the bias in that choice?"

Later, when you are more skilled, I see you confronting the newly anointed oracles called data scientists, "experts" in scanning billions of data points. You say, "The answers you arrived at are mired in the bias of the past. Your information is based upon what has already happened. Those of us who have not succeeded in the past are not in your databases—or, worse, we are, as bad risks."

To my hoped-for new programming army: You are society's best hope for loosening the stranglehold of the code that surrounds us. Enlist compatriots. Upset assumptions. It will take time and perseverance, but you can do it. Stick a needle into the shiny bubble of the technical world's received wisdom. Burst it.

And now to an unhappy reality. How indeed will the general public learn programming?

Ideally, the knowledge of computing should come from the

public schools, from kindergarten through high school through community colleges and state universities. But achieving this ideal would require a complete social and political upheaval: to re-fund public institutions, to provide quality educations in all neighborhoods, for all social classes; in short, a renewed belief in the value of the public sphere and civic life. Such a renewal would require a massive effort to reverse the current political movement away from public education in favor of private and charter schools.

In this drive for privatization, schools become profitable enterprises paid for by public funds: a transfer of wealth from the taxpayers to the rich, all without good evidence that students are better served.

In this universe of privately controlled education, each charter school can choose the curricula of its choice: Evolution is just a theory, the Bible is a literal history, dinosaurs and human beings simultaneously inhabited the earth, men are superior to women, white Christians to everyone else, and so on. Private and charter schools are like websites: they can foster any belief, shatter the idea that there is anything called truth, can blur the distinction between reality and belief.

What is to be done? A tenet shared by internet true believers is the idea that the ills promulgated by technology can be solved by the application of yet more technology. If the web is insecure, add encryption. If self-driving cars crash into other cars, make sure that all cars are self-driven.

Similarly, if public education is failing, online teaching can address the problem. If the general public does not understand technology, use technology to teach technology.

I decided to challenge that circular reasoning; I explored online classes, the massive open online courses, or MOOCs. The classes are generally free; anyone can enroll or just "audit" the videos as a way to browse the offerings that teach programming and technology.

Yet the great problem with MOOCs, of course, is that taking them requires a computer and access to the web. What of the two-thirds in the internet dark? What of the underserved in our own country: rural areas, poorer neighborhoods, households that cannot afford what internet providers are charging?

Nonetheless, for the sake of argument, let us imagine there is a multibillionaire who will take up the hobby of providing computers and reliable internet access to every person in the United States (the problems of the two-thirds in the electronic darkness being too daunting for this individual). This imaginary donor will also pay the fees for optional completion certificates, which show that a student has finished a course with passing grades. Now arises a question. Even if that person follows through and does not become distracted by taking up another hobby, such as going to Mars—even if: Will that person's donations truly educate the public, provide knowledge about technology to society at large?

I wondered what I would find online. I thought about the students who might be taking the classes. I thought about the instructors, how they themselves are rooted in the existing computing culture. I surveyed the programming offerings on the Coursera framework, which organizes the presentation of many MOOCs, and signed up for three of them.

III. Introduction to Interactive Programming with Python, Part 1

The four men who will teach the online programming course face the camera and stand awkwardly in a semicircle. This is the introductory video lecture being streamed to tens of thousands of students around the globe. The instructors are wearing identical blue tee shirts with white circles on them, and they quickly introduce themselves: Joe Warren, Scott Rixner, John Greiner, Stephen Wong, all from Rice University. Warren is the head of the computer-science department. Rixner is an affable-looking guy with glasses wearing a too-wide tie that hangs to the level of his crotch.

"To get things rolling," says Warren in the video, "we've all worn our tee shirts for rock-paper-scissors-lizard-Spock." Each of the instructors points to the circles on his shirt, which may be iconic images of the game's "characters," or may not, since the shirts are not shown in close-up.

Warren then says to the other instructors, "So, guys. Let's just play a game, a sort of battle royale."

And they play.

"Rock-paper-scissors-lizard-Spock: shoot!"

They survey the hand gestures they have shot out into the circle. They start laughing. It's not clear what Warren's gesture is. He motions snip-snip with two fingers. "I'm scissors," he says. For some baffling reason, they're cracking up.

Warren later explains that Rock, Paper, Scissors, Lizard, Spock (RPSLS) is a game played by a character named Sheldon on the television show *The Big Bang Theory*, a program I stopped watching because it perpetuates the figure of the geeky techie young-man-still-a-boy. (Warren does not say that RPSLS is based on the children's game Rock-Paper-Scissors, evidently believing that everyone around the globe should be familiar with it.) To my dismay, I learn that our first required "mini-project" will be to program the *Big Bang* version of the game. Warren tells us the assignment was suggested by his sons, which is a warning about the age and gender mentality involved.

He goes on to tell the students that Python is named not for the snake but for the goofy, crazy comedy show *Monty Python's Flying Circus*. He does not explain the show. As with RPSLS, he assumes that students know about it, about its geek-cult following, like *Star Trek*'s.

The first coding project is simple and optional. The goal is to print out on the screen, "I want a shrubbery . . ."

I have no idea why anyone should want to print out these words. Where is the usual "Hello, World!"? Then I learn: it relates to an in-joke from a Monty Python film.

Warren says, often, that he wants the class to be fun.

"Our goal in this class is to be funny," he says near the end of the first video. "Sometimes we're lame, I admit. But we're trying not to be boring."

I'm not enrolled in the class to learn Python. (I know it well enough to do some debugging and might code up something semi-ambitious in a pinch.) I'm here to see how others learn Python.

It is a beginner's language, a standard for introductory courses, also a foundation for web development. Learning the language can quickly lead to employment, which is why would-be programmers flock to Python courses. Yet the class is more than just an introduction to a coding language. It is an aspiring programmer's first look into the rooms where programs get written, a first exposure to the culture that prevails among the society of programmers. I have enrolled to see what awaits the students as they encounter that culture, also to remind myself of what greeted (or repelled) me when I first met the sentries at the door.

After the introductory video, the class moves on to programming basics: expressions, variables, and assignments of values to variables, mostly taught by Warren. He is a good teacher, heartfelt about the students' learning to program, encouraging them to stay with the course when they feel frustrated. It is the nature of programming, he says, that you have to be persistent in the face of difficulties. He points to the assistance available in code tutorials, documentation, and the online discussion forums, where students can help one another. He hopes they will feel the excitement of writing a program and seeing it run. Warren offers the best encouragement, I think, when he says, "Beginning does not mean easy."

Warren's passion, clearly, is video gaming. In one lecture, we watch him play a game against his colleague John Greiner. We cannot see the screens, only their faces and their hands on the keyboards. Greiner, seemingly, is playing as a good sport, but Warren is in a fierce competition, eyes riveted on the screen, mouth set, fingers flying, breathing "Yeah!" and "Gotcha" each time he scores a point.

Warren is familiar to me. He is someone I might have worked with on any job. Punning, unashamedly silly, with a sense of humor related to children's knock-knock jokes. It is a sense of fun that stems from a steely mind inside a gleeful child, a kid who hangs out with his own geek in-group, where everyone groans at the punchline—and loves it. Being with him is less fun when you're in the out-group.

In one of the videos, we are in Warren's office. In it stands a knight's suit of armor. "The knight," says Warren, "is named Sir Loin."

Week two marches through logic and conditionals, then on to teaching the library of interactive functions written by Scott Rixner, he of the long tie, who is an associate professor. With no offense meant to the other three, Rixner soon becomes my favorite of the four instructors. He projects the sort of geekiness I came to enjoy over the years: a goofy brilliance, ironic statements told with a strange childishness, wide blinking eyes that affect an innocence barely hiding a fierce intelligence; meanwhile, he is a generous teacher. In every video, he wears that same wide tie (which, we learn, has the RPSLS symbols on it), which is a running joke, a visual reminder that all this technical information is simultaneously rigorous and delightfully weird. Yet again, it took me years to warm up to colleagues like Rixner. All that childishness; and I was a grown-up woman. I understand that he may not be for everyone.

Week by week, the project assignments come due.

The project submissions are peer-graded. I want to go through the evaluation process, and so I submit my own simple little RPSLS program. That done, I have to assess the work of five other students, then assess myself. I worried about the idea of peer grading—my old experiences of living through brutal code reviews. But the instructors are doing a good job of creating a clear and specific grading rubric. When Warren showed the example "I want a shrubbery," he deliberately made a typo, writing "shrubery." It was his way of telling the peer graders not to concentrate on trivia; the important thing was to learn. Automated grading programs see the text literally; they can't tell a typo from a mistake in logic. "If the code were machine-graded," Warren says, "you'd be dead."

The ultimate project, which will determine whether one has successfully completed the course, is the coding of a video game called *Space Rocks*. In the game, a rocketship you control with arrow keys has to zap rolling asteroids; if you don't zap them, you may crash into one and die. It's a simple game, but not trivial for a first effort. The instructors have made available what they call sophisticated sound effects. The rocketship fires: Kuh-TSHOO! Kuh-TSHOO! Kuh-TSHOO!

There is nothing wrong with rocketships and space rocks, per se, if you like such things. But the world of computer gaming is hugely overpopulated by, again, white and Asian men, and famously hostile to women. When the organizers of the 2015 technology conference SXSW put on the agenda two panels about sexism and sexual harassment in the gaming community, they received threats of violence if they did not remove the panels. They removed the panels.

As we arrive at the final project, I wonder how many of the tens of thousands across the globe are still with the class. Women, men, U.S. citizens or not, students just out of college, laid-off fifty-year-olds hoping to retrain themselves for twenty-first-century jobs. Curious laborers. Students aspiring to escape the bounds of their social class. How appealing do they find this introduction to the world of programming? How many want to be part of the culture portrayed in this class? How many who came for new professions are offended by the youthful goofiness that makes no sense in their current lives? The entryway was clogged with barriers from the very start: *The Big Bang Theory*, RPSLS, "I want a shrubbery," in-jokes, Sheldon and Spock and U.S. television programs. And then, all through the course: the underlying assumption of male, white, geeky American culture. The crucial question, the answer to which determines how easily one crosses into the programming room—indeed, into any room—is this: Do you feel invited in?

The course's atmosphere is not an anomaly in the coding world, I fear; it portrays that world all too accurately. A friend suggested that the nature of this online course is a good thing. The techie culture is what it is, my friend said, and maybe it's a good thing to warn off people who won't feel suited to it. (Let the reader imagine the fury I felt at hearing those words.)

Yet there is a truth to what my friend said. I do not mean the warning off; I mean the inoculation, if you will, a chance for the online observers to know what they will be getting into, and prepare for it, internally.

For the world of programmers is not going to change on its own. Many who enter are going to find themselves in the company of sweetly boyish men who bristle at the very idea of anyone unlike them invading their territory, climbing into their treehouse, men who want to humiliate the newcomers, find every error in their work, trap them in a shooting gallery without apologies, as was my life in the group alias twenty years ago. And they will find themselves in the company of morose men who will not or cannot communicate, like my co-worker on the user-interface project. More often, though, it will be men like Warren, apparently unaware of their internal biases, off-putting, but trying to be jovial and helpful. And then there are the programmers I've met who were like Rixner, with sparkling, playful minds, for whom I developed an abiding affection.

This may not be a popular sentiment, but I urge new students to appreciate some of the weirdness, at least see it as distinct from overt or covert hostility. The puns and knock-knock humor can be tiresome. Yet they are the instructors' attempts, if bad ones, to preserve the spirit of programming—through all its bafflements and frustrations—as fun.

I could not have said anything like this twenty-two years ago. Over time, though, my memories have become more rounded. I can remember the good parts, jobs where there were women in highly placed technical positions. I can recall my own little core of geekiness. And through it all, no matter what prejudices I had to confront, there were the moments of pleasure, perhaps too rare, when I leaned back and breathed to myself: It works. If I could not remember this pleasure, if I recalled only hostility and humiliation, there would be no reason for me to encourage anyone to learn to write code.

The Python course includes access to online discussion forums. There are perhaps a hundred of them, each with tens of threads, with topics ranging from the current assignment to general questions about coding. An often repeated question is: Is anyone else having trouble with this course?

I spend hours roaming there. They are the heart of the class, I see. The videos are dead, but the forums are live. This is where the aspirations of the programming-outsiders express their determination to come in; where they also express their fears and failures. The conversations are courteous. There is no trace of the nastiness of internet trolls. Students work hard to solve problems together. I worried that peer forums would be the blind leading the blind (there is some of this), but overall the volume of replies usually shakes out the problem. If not, in the case of blind alleys in key subjects, online teaching assistants, "Community TAs," step in to help.

Now and then I get busy with the adult errands of life, and I quit following the lectures and attending the forums. Then a day goes by, two. And I find myself drawn back in. There was a furious conversation going on inside my laptop, it seemed, and I felt compelled to open the cover and rejoin it. In there were the thousands of students talking to one another from across the world, and I missed them.

The last forum I visit is for general questions, about anything—the course, classes, life. The leading post is from a male student who feels he is failing. He is afraid to get back the grade for the project he submitted. He is not fit for coding, he writes. He cannot keep up with the class. He is going to quit. This confession expresses the sting of failure, the shame of inadequacy. I marvel at how the student has made himself so vulnerable. As I read the post, I worry for him.

Yet what follows is kind and sweet and supportive. There are women in the discussion, but it is mainly other men responding. One by one, they cheer him on: I'm having trouble, too. Don't worry, the purpose of the course is to learn. I had to take the course twice before. Stay with it. The grades aren't important. It's too soon to say you can't do programming; this is just your first try.

The urging on is gentle. It is a chorus of camaraderie. I don't know the ages of the students, but the conversation has the feel of the sweetness young men can have at fifteen, sixteen, before they cross into manhood and must try harder to maintain that sweetness. For all the boy-geek atmosphere of the course material, I'm surprised and glad that the culture has not completely pervaded the forums. As I read on, I can only hope that the atmosphere of openness and goodwill stays with the students as they move more deeply into the coding culture; that they remain vulnerable, unafraid to express their fears; that they keep their tenderness as they cross into the rooms where they will write the algorithms that surround us.

IV. The Design and Analysis of Algorithms, Part 1

Tim Roughgarden, an associate professor of computer science at Stanford, looks directly into the camera as he introduces the course, speaking freely from memory though occasionally glancing down at his notes. He seems well rehearsed. He is a pleasantly handsome man, easygoing in manner. The sleeves of his blue shirt are rolled up to the elbow.*

This course corresponds to the first half of a ten-week computer-science class he teaches at Stanford, says Roughgarden, a course required for anyone working toward a computer-science degree there,

---

* The video I am describing here is based on the course as I watched it in 2013. At that time, we saw Roughgarden's actions, such as his writing on a whiteboard. The earlier videos had a nice, improvised feel—for instance, a camera looking up at Roughgarden's face as he inserts slides into an overhead projector. The "now" as he described it at that time was 2012. In the 2015 class, the audio is the same, but we see very little of Roughgarden. His head and shoulders appear, sometimes, in a small box at the lower right-hand corner of the screen. Overall, there are many PowerPoint slides, and we hear his voice behind them. The intent, I think, was to professionalize the video. We do see the whiteboard writings much more clearly. However, the effect of the 2015 version is to make the MOOC an even more disembodied experience.

whether undergraduate, master's, or Ph.D. In both the online and on-campus classes, he will introduce the key algorithms created over the last fifty years of computer science, what Roughgarden calls "the greatest hits." And, indeed, I can see we will go through the creations of revered computer scientists, such as algorithms for sorting and merging, computing shortest routes, the closest pairs, the connections between nodes in a graph. They are among the procedures that constitute the basis of the code that surrounds us, including the structure of the web.

A fortunate side effect of understanding these key algorithms, Roughgarden will say later, is that you will impress a prospective employer. You will "ace your technical interviews." You can become "a card-carrying computer scientist." You will have the lingo to fit into the higher levels of the technical community. "No longer will you feel excluded at that computer-science cocktail party when someone cracks a joke about Dijkstra's algorithm."

If Introduction to Python was a first step into the programming world, Algorithm Design represents the sentried gateway into the inner and deeper reaches of that world. Beyond this course are the mightily guarded secrets of companies like Facebook, Google, Uber, Amazon, and Goldman Sachs, where the algorithms are modified and tinkered with and tweaked and sent out to fill the capillaries of human life.

Thirteen minutes into the first video, Roughgarden begins the process of winnowing out the unprepared among the online tens of thousands. He plunges into a familiar algorithm, the procedure for multiplication we learned in the third grade. He shows how many steps it takes, how the number of required steps increases with the growing sizes of the multiplicands and multipliers.

Then he moves on to analyzing a procedure different from our grade-school version: Karatsuba's algorithm for integer multiplication (which was devised by Anotoly Alexeyevich Karatsuba in 1960, published in 1962, a history not discussed in the class). The algorithm uses recursion (where procedures invoke themselves as a subroutine with smaller inputs, a concept he assumes the students know), and a strategy called "divide and conquer" (which Roughgarden says the students will not understand yet; he will teach it later). He dashes off mathematical expressions on the whiteboard behind him, math that should be as easy as breathing for anyone who remembers high-school math, but those with rusty memories are perhaps breathing somewhat harder. (I am somewhere between the two categories at this point in my life.)

He says we will not yet be able to have intuition about the algorithms. He wants to show us something exciting about algorithms, that there are "a dazzling array of options for solving a problem." He expects we will feel "some mixture of bafflement and intrigue," which is the perfect expression of learning computing as I experienced it: feeling baffled and intrigued, maddened and seduced.

Roughgarden turns to the whiteboard. He speaks quickly. Numbers and letters fly onto the screen. He finishes up by saying that the process involves "elementary algebra that suggests a recursive approach to multiplying two numbers, which you can code up quite easily in your preferred programming language."

He pauses, then says, "If you made it here, you're good to go."

The rush of talk and text is a warning to those who are too mathematically rusty, or who do not have a background in programming, the math and logic constructs. Roughgarden's students at Stanford come prepared with the prerequisites: knowledge of programming, recursion, discrete math, logic proofs by induction and contradiction. They are what he calls his canonical students. When he looks into the camera, it is those canonical Stanford students he sees. But the unknown tens of thousands on the other side of the screen may not qualify for card-carrying membership in the canon; they could be anyone who does or does not conform to the image of students Roughgarden holds in his mind.

Nonetheless, incongruously, recognizing that he has no way to drive off anyone in the streamed-in thousands, Roughgarden says that even if some students do not have the prerequisite knowledge, they should not necessarily leave the class. "I am happy to teach you algorithms," he says.

Here is where I hope the programming newcomers will stay the course, literally. You do need a background in programming, some fluency in proofs, in mathematical analysis. But you do not have to be completely prepared. You can watch the lectures, sit back, and let the images and words roll over you. You may find that, once you're released from having to understand it all, a certain fascination gets through. It can be like those times you hear someone playing the piano beautifully or a sax wailing through jazz improvisations, and the sounds ignite a longing in you, a desire to take up the difficulties, and learn how to play that music.

However, there are more challenges involved, even for those who are well prepared. At one moment in the introductory lectures, Roughgarden looks directly into the camera, talking to us on the other side of the screen, and he says, "What do I expect of you?" Then: "Well, honestly, nothing."

Fair enough. It is an online course, and the students are under no obligation to give it more time or effort than they choose. Yet it is discouraging, dispiriting, when nothing is expected of you. "Nothing": it stings.

And then there is the grading. Says Roughgarden: "The course has tens of thousands of students, so it's absolutely essential that assignments can be graded automatically. We are still in the 1.0

generation of free online courses such as this one. So the tools for auto-graded assessment available are still rather primitive."

What he goes on to say is yet more deflating. "We are trying our best, but I have to be honest with you. It's difficult and maybe impossible to test deep understanding of the design and analysis of algorithms using the currently available set of tools."

In other words, no matter how well we do on assignments, the verdict of how well we have learned algorithm design, or if we have learned anything at all, will be determined by inadequate methods. We are in a tangle of code from which there is no escape: trying to learn algorithms graded by faulty algorithms.

Now I think fondly of Joe Warren and the successful process he and his co-instructors devised for peer assessment. I think of him saying that if a typo were machine-graded "you'd be dead." Here, with Roughgarden's 1.0 auto-grader, you will be dead.

The most damning realization for me goes beyond Roughgarden's description of the inadequacies of the 1.0 grading program. The problem is that, in both 2013 and 2015, he introduces the early version as being "current" in 2012. Evidently, it had not been worked on since. It made me wonder why Roughgarden and his colleagues, or whoever wrote the auto-grader, did not see the need to progress to something better, did not see it as a pressing obligation to tell the online students if they had indeed learned anything.

At the very opening of the introduction section, Roughgarden had said that the course corresponded to the one at Stanford. Later, we can see the hedging used in the choice of the word "corresponded." Roughgarden says, "While the lecture content in this online course is in no way watered down from the original Stanford version, the required assignments and exams we will give you are not as demanding as those that are given in the on-campus version of the course."

We are not at Stanford. We are in a lesser land, where we may or may not be coming to his course prepared; where we will not know if we have succeeded or not. I can almost hear the clicks of the windows being closed, the silence of the missing page-views. Why should anyone keep going? The answer is, to get a glimpse of the beauty that resides in the best algorithms of computer science.

As the video lectures go on, I feel my brain shaking off the crusts of time. My thoughts go back twenty-five years, to when I first studied algorithms in Donald Knuth's magisterial work *The Art of Computer Programming*. I feel again the wonder of a great algorithm's logical beauty, its elegance of thought, the sheer intelligence and creativity it reflects—as Roughgarden describes them, "a rare blend of creativity and precision." The algorithm for random selection is going to be "quite elegant," he says. Dijkstra's algorithm, which computes the shortest paths between points, as in driving directions, has "beauty," is "elegant" and "pretty." I can almost feel the heat of my synapses firing, as in the experience of reading great literature and poetry. It is in these moments when I most want the technical outsiders and beginners to make it this far, to come in, fill the ranks, understand that the beauty in logic is as powerful as the beauty in any creative human endeavor.

As Roughgarden correctly points out, the procedures he is analyzing are not new. He cites the dates of their invention. The algorithm that underlies the web's hyperlinking, social networks' "friend" finding, used so successfully for the Google search engines, dates back to work done as early as 1948. The algorithms are the contributions of computer scientists, mathematicians, philosophers (yes, philosophers), social scientists, and a few Ph.D. dropouts, including the former Stanford students Larry Page and Sergey Brin. A cumulative effort, a collaboration over time.

The analysis of algorithms, as Roughgarden teaches it, centers on how long algorithms take to run, on their "time efficiency." For instance, if a web application works well with five thousand users, how will it perform when there are five million users? The goal there would be for the time increase per user to level off, or at least not soar into the stratosphere. The overall question is: How well does an algorithm scale, how well does it perform as the number of basic steps it must perform grows arbitrarily large?

The goal of the analytic method is to evaluate algorithms abstractly, unencumbered by the particulars of any specific computing environment. Code that runs quickly in one place (on a machine with a faster processor) may run slower in another (same processor but much slower network). Therefore, when the environment is part of the benchmarking, there is no way of evaluating an algorithm in general. Here, though, we forget about the operating system, the chips, the network, even the abilities of the programmers. As someone who worked for years enmeshed in the givens of systems—the mandated hardware, the scarce resources of memory and storage, the networks that were down, the software interfaces that failed, the servers that crashed, the programmers on the project not always up to the task or overworked, the unrealistic schedules, the breathing-down days of deadlines— I recall the days when I first explored the design of algorithms, the pleasure of washing away those contingencies, freeing the code, as much as is possible, from the muck of physical reality.

Nonetheless, despite the pleasure of evaluating algorithms in their abstract sense, when I first enrolled in the algorithm course in 2013, the public was becoming aware, finally, of the NSA's mass spying upon U.S. citizens. The texts of the documents taken by the NSA contractor Edward Snowden were flooding the news. (I say "finally" because a great deal of the information was known as early as 2006.) The political reality is a mental invader; I cannot clear my mind of the uses to which our algorithms are being put. In one of the class forums, I start a thread, asking if anyone is thinking about how the algorithms are being used. I receive two replies. The first is "Uhm." The second is a rebuke, saying that the political considerations are "not appropriate" to this course.

Yet Roughgarden himself takes a moment to step out of the abstractions. He is writing on the whiteboard, discussing the steps in an algorithm. He is proceeding as usual, with a mathematical and logical analysis, when he suddenly stops and turns to the camera. About the algorithm he says, "If the future of your startup [depends on this code], make it as fast as you can."

Mathematical purity has just now opened its doors to the muck of reality. This must be done in nearly all computing systems, which have to work with all the givens in the technical environment, as I've discussed. Yet that is not what Roughgarden said: the tweaks are for your startup.

Now the "you" out there in the audience has changed. You are no longer someone with the course prerequisites who intends to go forward in computer science. You are not taking the course for the pleasure and challenge of learning algorithms. You are an entrepreneur; you will go it alone; do a startup; make the code run faster; make money.

In no way do I wish to impugn Roughgarden's teaching. He is a fine professor, obviously devoted to his subject, passionate about the principles of algorithms. But it seems to me he carries within him an unconscious bias. He lives in a world where the favored few have assumptions about how the world should function. The ether of the internet does not purify the values imbued in the teaching of technology. It does not filter out social biases. Far from muting the social context, the internet is an amplifier. It broadcasts its value-laden messages around the world.

At this point, you may wonder about the computer-science parties where they joke about Dijkstra's shortest-path-between-points algorithm. How can you possibly be invited? And even after learning more about the algorithm, you may ask what the joke could possibly be. Roughgarden certainly wasn't referring to a rude version that circulates widely on the internet: "Your mother is so fat, even I couldn't find my way around her."

A video of Roughgarden's corresponding on-campus Stanford course is available online, running at the same time as the 2013 offering of the MOOC. The video was made with just a camera at the back of the room and a mike on Roughgarden. In the class, he apologizes for the early hour, and you can see the weariness of the students as they drag in late. Meanwhile, he keeps running out of chalk as he pounds the lecture notes on the blackboard. His speaking pace, rapid on the videos, is manic in class. I can barely tolerate it, and I am not one of his sleep-deprived students. As I watch, I remember the unrelenting sleep-deficit of being in college, the 8:00 a.m. class hour that never seems to end. Roughgarden goes over the course requirements: the tests, the assignments, the deadlines. In this class, the final is scheduled, nightmarishly, for the last slot of the last day of the exams period. And I recall the anxiety of looming grades. I pity the sophomores who are taking the course with juniors, seniors, and graduate students. I almost feel sorry for them.

Then I don't. Roughgarden tells the students about his availability to help them. Email him, he says; come to his office hours, to those of his assistants: We are all here for you.

Then there comes a spontaneous moment in the lecture—unscripted, as it were—something that does not appear in the prepared videos of the MOOC class.

Roughgarden is attacking the blackboard. He is discussing a certain mathematical conjecture. He says, If you write a book about this, and prove the conjecture, you'll win a prize of a million dollars. In the online class, there is a passing mention of the prize, a few words on a PowerPoint slide that quickly yields to another.

But here, at Stanford, Roughgarden stops at the mention of the conjecture. He turns to look over his shoulder. He stares at his students for a moment and says of the million dollars, "For most of you, that would be nothing."

I considered the two nothings: the nothing expected of the online students, the million dollars that would be nothing to the Stanford students, of whom everything is expected. I thought of how difficult it would be to narrow the chasm between them. The internet might work as a teacher at the entry levels, but not in this course. The students cannot even know if they have learned much about algorithms. The online class can arouse desires, may instill an attraction to the beauty inherent in the work, ignite a passion. But it cannot assure students that the course will fulfill those desires.

At Stanford, the professors are there for the students, making sure they are well prepared and supported by all the resources the exclusive university can muster. Their students stand before the gateway to the summits of knowledge and riches, which is open wide for them. The gateway is otherwise well guarded. A note shown on the web page introducing the online class states clearly, understandably—but coldly—that taking the web version in no way permits the students to use the facilities of the university.

There are hundreds of technology-related classes among the Coursera offerings. I looked for humanities courses and found exactly two that involved reading actual literature, one for novels, one for poetry, which is offered by the University of Pennsylvania. The introductory video for the poetry class shows the instructor, Professor Al Filreis, sitting in a humble room. He speaks proudly of the school's substantial collection of recordings of well-known poets reading from their own works. One can sense his loneliness. He invites the students to come by and visit if they are in the area. They will not find the library doors closed to them. He says the students are welcome to listen to the treasured recordings "anytime."

V. Programming for Everyone

I had one last hope for opening the door to the great millions. Among Coursera's offerings, I found a class named Programming for Everyone. Each course has a start page with a short video in which the instructor describes the class. And as I watched that class description, I thought I had found what I was looking for.

The instructor is Charles Severance, an associate professor at the University of Michigan School of Information. In the video, he expresses his desire that everyone will indeed learn to code. He doesn't just want to teach programming to his students, he says. He also wants to help other instructors teach programming, offering them free access to his curricula, to start a wave that would roll outward. "I see Programming for Everybody as much more than a single class," he says with some passion. "I want this to become a movement, an expanding, open ecosystem that brings us all closer together where programming is truly for everybody." I feel I have found my champion. A programming evangelist! A proselytizer of coding for the millions!

The course was not running yet. (The short introductory videos on the class's page can be seen anytime.) I enrolled and would have to wait several months. Then, two months before the course was set to begin, Severance sent out an email saying we could "check out a recording of our most recent office hours with special guest Colleen van Lent." I was a little confused; he did not say who van Lent was.

Nonetheless, excited about the course, I immediately clicked the provided link that led to a YouTube video, which Severance describes as his digital office hours. He and van Lent talk about their classes, meanwhile receiving questions from potential students via Twitter and Google Hangout, like those radio call-in shows where listeners send in questions by email.

As the video goes on, I remain somewhat confused. I'm still not entirely certain who van Lent is. It will take my Google search to learn that she has a Ph.D. in computer science and is a Lecturer III in the School of Information. She and Severance talk about the role of persistence in attaining proficiency in technology. He says becoming a professional programmer takes patience, years and years of hard work studying computer science. "How long did you go to school?" he asks van Lent. "Ten years," she answers. "Twenty," says he.

They sit side by side at a table. He is bearded and looks a little husky, from what you can see of his upper body. She is blonde and slim. Clearly, he is older, over forty, given his twenty years of post-undergraduate education. Using the same metric, she must be in her thirties.

Their interchanges are informal. Van Lent's class, Web Design for Everybody, is not intended as a path toward becoming a professional designer, she says. It is more a guide for people who want to build their own web pages by learning the standard tool set: HTML5, Cascading Style Sheets, JavaScript. (These tools will be challenging for complete novices but are eminently learnable.) She is animated, infused with the spirit of bringing people into technology, to make them feel they belong there. I am more certain than ever that I have come to the right place. Another coding proselytizer! A woman after my own heart!

When it's Severance's turn, I find out that my anticipated perfect course, Programming for Everybody—which was to be the seed of a movement—has become a series of four courses designed to lead students to professional programming. What has happened to the expanding ecosystem of "everybody"?

By taking this series, says Severance, students can see if they have the passion for programming, passion being the essential driver toward more advanced classes. This seems perfect at first: classes designed to let students see if they want to reach more deeply into computing science. If so, he offers a clear path forward.

Then Severance talks more about the series of classes. The four courses will be self-paced. There will be no discussion forums, no participation of community TAs, none of the live-humans-there-*now* who so animated the Python class. Only after students have completed and passed the four courses will they be able to take a scheduled course, with all the associated help and camaraderie. They enter that more advanced course with "known skills," he says. I see this is Severance's winnowing process. But I wonder about all the beginners trying to learn without having living companions. Where will they find the encouragement to keep going through the real difficulties of programming? Where will they find that sweet community encouraging them to struggle on? How much passion can they discover while sitting alone with the code?

Up until now, Severance has let van Lent do most of the talking. But as the video moves on, the balance changes. He begins talking over her. As her potential tens of thousands of students listen in, he interrupts her, makes clarifications of what she has said. There is an interchange that is painful to watch:

Van Lent is discussing "tags," icons that, when you click on them, do some action, such as bringing up a map. The tags are part of the class she is teaching. She is describing what they look like on the screen:

SHE: I just learned that when you go to a website, and the navigation goes away, and you see three little lines, that's called a hamburger.

HE (incredulous): You never knew it's called a hamburger?

SHE: I didn't know it was called a hamburger.

HE (abruptly leaning toward her): Do you know what it's called when there's three little lines when there's a shape of a human cut out in the three little lines?

SHE: No.

HE: It's called a manburger.

SHE (with a little laugh, moving her head aside): A manburger.

HE: It's because there's a little man plus a hamburger with a man on the side.

SHE: Manburger.

HE: Manburger.

HE (lecturing): See, if you're in responsive design, you have to know what the hamburger icon is, and you gotta know what the manburger icon is.

SHE (softly, behind his talking): I need to learn all these things. And—

HE: You gotta know the hamburger icon, like, it's had its hypercycle. So the hamburger is past its point. Don't tell your class that the hamburger is, like, the latest thing, because you'll lose your credibility.

I can't believe what I'm looking at. Has Severance forgotten that this meeting is being streamed live on the internet? He is not talking to van Lent in the privacy of his office. He is questioning her competence before the tens of thousands.

Severance is turned toward her, almost blocking the view of her body. Now van Lent moves away, as if surprised by his casual display of disrespect. Then, perhaps to defend herself, she reaches for the reassurance of her credential. "The thing is," she says, "I'm a computer scientist, so my job description is to be uncool."

There will always be men like Severance in the coding rooms—or anywhere, for that matter. Yet it is precisely here, with him, that you must not be deterred. This video is helpful, the ugliness of the scene a gift, a perfect opportunity for another inoculation against the worst of the programming culture.

Go on and try out the professor's online courses; maybe they will be good. Take them with a couple of friends, create your own living discussion group. You can download the videos, and offer them to schools and community centers for local showings. Then anyone taking the course—whoever you are, from whatever background—can go on with confidence; no one can scare you off; you already know this stuff. Power lies in the refusal to be intimidated: in technical fearlessness.

Take your time looking at the classes; roll the videos backward and forward until this teacher looks like a cartoon character. Get what you need from this man; just get it. All prejudice is meant to slap you back and put you in your place. Use your anger to fuel your determination. It is very hard to face such prejudice. But here the perpetrator is only pixels on a screen, mere packets streaming off the internet. How helpful is the web! Pause the video; stab your finger in his eye; stick your tongue out at him; he cannot see you. Use his empty presence to practice your reactions. Here is your chance to learn the difficult feat of looking at prejudice and refusing to be diminished. Here you may learn how to sustain your dignity, your angry dignity.

In Severance you have met one of the sentries at the door, the ones who shame and humiliate you for your struggles and failures, and yet, as with my father, that is no reason to give up.

Boom Two: A Farewell

January 2017

I.

I knew it was getting time to leave SOMA, and maybe even San Francisco itself, when I saw what was happening to South Park.

Until a few months ago, the park was still surrounded by tall, rangy trees. The grass was still the rough-bladed crabgrass. The picnic tables were weathering. The dirt paths turned to mud when the winter rains came on. The park retained a certain wildness, untrimmed, left alone for the trees to grow and dandelions to bloom on the grass. It went its own way after the technology crash of 2000–2001, the cell-yellers gone, the restaurants dark, the oval seeming to sigh with relief at the abandonment. And even as this new boom was inflating all around it—a building frenzy, high-rises piercing the skyline—South Park remained nicely desolate, fortunately neglected, a reassurance that there could be a little patch of dirt where SOMA might hide from this second rising of the internet.

It was a place I had often escaped to. On those early fall days when the marine layer recedes and the wind blows from the inland valley, and the temperature rises to desert-hot with an unrelenting sun, I sought the coolness of the park. When I moved into SOMA in 1996, it wasn't a neighborhood yet, as I've said. It was an abandoned industrial zone with a few weathering Victorian houses that had once housed the working class and still offered rough, affordable flats. The park provided all there was of shade for a mile around, except for a few streets here and there that had trees at the curbs. When I was confronted with problems, personal or technical, I would go there to sit on a park bench and watch dogs catch Frisbees and hear children squeal in the small playground in the middle of the oval, see the birds living their own lives, careless of us, finches and sparrows, and mourning doves in their pairs for life. I let the problems sink to the back of my mind, into the mysterious background processes from which solutions tend to arrive if you don't talk, sit still, and do nothing in particular.

This year, I was away from San Francisco for several months and returned on one of those fogless hot days. My husband, Elliot, and I decided to go to the South Park Cafe, which had arisen anew, with a new owner, after the technology bust. We took the three-minute walk, turned right from Second Street into the east side of the oval.

Something was wrong. The space to my left was bare. Sun blared where there should have been shade. My understanding of what had happened came on slowly, the way time slows down to microseconds when you know you will be in a car crash and you see the disaster unfolding ahead.

The entirety of the South Park oval was imprisoned behind a

six-foot-high, chain-link fence. Everything had been dug up. No grass, no benches, no playground, just mounds of dirt and rubble. A backhoe commanded the tallest mound, its jaw still hanging open, ready for another bite. Three-quarters of the trees were gone; the entire north rim was naked. The dust-covered trees that remained looked as lost and dazed as I was.

We learned what had happened from the café's bartender, Marty, whom we'd come to know over the years. "Some community group got together to dig it all up," he said. He shrugged. "It started months ago."

Houses, apartments, and offices ring the park. I asked him if that "community group" had gone around and talked to anybody about their plans.

Marty laughed. "First we knew of it is when they put up the fence."

He handed me a postcard-sized notice. He said the group had slipped them under doors after the project had gotten started. It was from "The South Park Association," which said it was a "Parks Bond Recipient."

I'm studying that card now, as I have done every day since Marty handed it to me. The longer I look, the more hopeless I feel about the city I have lived in for forty-odd years, about the neighborhood that has been my home for over twenty.

The front of the card shows an architectural rendering of the park, the sort of image where the designers put in people and trees and bicycles and make up a reality. Renderings like this have been standard practice for architects since digital tools allowed for the creation of plausible, soothing illusions. The result is an urban planner's idea of a park, a benign setting for cheerful people.

Both the card and the group's website show all the trees that had existed in the park, a false image, since most have been cut down. There is a path made of concrete rails with spaces between them, about three strollers wide. Someone is indeed wheeling a stroller, and it is a man, which is so unlikely as to be funny in this neighborhood of young male engineers working seventy and eighty hours a week. One thing about the rendering is accurate: there is not a black face in sight.

The website of the "community organization" says that the park needed work—better drainage, for example (which it did). It describes the new design as having ample seating, which the rendering belies. Women are perched on the ledges of two-foot-high retaining walls. The picture shows those small metal tables around which you can pull two metal chairs, maybe three. I don't see any new picnic tables where groups could gather. Of course, the nonmillennial gentlemen—who had enjoyed their beverages in paper bags—would never again own their picnic table at the lower slope of the park.

In the architectural plan view, from above, you can see that the park's concrete path slashes what is left of the grass into five discrete sections; can see the path's even, trigonometric sine waves—nothing meandering here. Goodbye to uneven beauty, I thought. Goodbye to rawness, aging, wildness. Farewell to the messy place where random thoughts can ramble and collide and maybe cohere in the tumultuous background regions of the mind.

On the second day after I got the postcard, I suddenly noticed that it showed, to the southwest, a view of a massive high-rise. The building did not exist. Why, then, had the designers put it in? I looked out my window to see new cranes. They were not high enough for the forty-story building in the rendering, but a new, taller one must be about to stick its finger up into the sky. If the park organization wanted to depict a happy scene, surely it would not have a rendering showing a forty-story building looming over the west end of the oval.

It seemed that the "independent group" must have known what was coming—if not coming right now, then soon (and for the rest of our lives, I cannot resist saying). The San Francisco Planning Commission, always on its knees to technology interests, also must have known. They had all worked this out long ago, I thought. I felt their collusion. The beautified, sterilized park; the high-rise taking over an arc of the sky: the value of one identical to that of the other, as if the park was not a place of nonhuman nature but an opportunity for the social cleansing of a neighborhood, was like the building, a development adjudged as good.

There was a time, in 2012, when the master plan for South of Market was supposedly still in formation. One evening, I went to a meeting of the planning commission. I had been involved with a group of people who lived and owned businesses in the area around South Park, and I had kept up my visits to the commission and the San Francisco Board of Supervisors.

The planning-commission meeting was in a small room with three tables at the front set up in a horseshoe, around which sat five men in their late thirties or early forties. Facing the table were about twenty chairs where the public might sit and participate. That evening, as far as the public went, I was it.

The plans the commission had approved for the South of Market area included the footprints of stores that would be on the ground levels in the soon-to-exist residential and office buildings. I raised my hand and was recognized begrudgingly. I stood up to say that the footprints for the ground-floor stores were too large.

"Too large?" one of the men said, as if my idea was preposterous. They turned to one another and chuckled.

There I was, in the role I had wound up in again and again, the girl at the meetings of technical guys, and, worse this time, a brotherhood of construction men: I was someone to be swept away as a no-body knowing nothing. They had no idea of who I was, of course. There was no opportunity to introduce myself and explain my background. If so, I would have told them that my father, with many partners, had purchased a small, C-grade building in the Wall Street area of New York City in 1962. When he died, overseeing the management of the building fell to me.

And I mean "fell." I lived across the country, in San Francisco, and my father had kept his business affairs to himself. It was a learning curve steeper than any I had attempted in programming. The other partners were aging and relied upon a modest income from the building. I could not rely on the manager my father had hired, who had made deals that, to put it mildly, had worked against our interests. And so, while the sharks of would-be building purchasers circled me—"What is that girl doing in the middle of these negotiations?"—I came to know that the main income from the building had come from the little businesses at the street level: A bag shop. A fast-food joint. A jeweler. A woman selling handmade candies. The stores were tiny by the standards of the laughing city planners of San Francisco. Yet I came to know the keepers of those shops. They were the first generation of immigrants and the children who had succeeded them. The moms and pops and cousins and aunts and uncles. They believed in America. Their shops were the way to join the culture and send the next generations to college.

I asked dismissing planners to think about opportunities for families to rise from being immigrants and increase their fortunes. Where were the spaces for the dry cleaners, shoemakers, convenience stores, all that goes into making something that is not just a building but a part of a neighborhood? We were all ready to talk about affordable housing, I said. Where was the drive to address affordable capitalism?

They barely listened. A few talked among themselves as I went on. I knew it was hopeless. The forces were in motion, and I, little girl that I was to them, was spitting into the wind. The mom-and-pop stores are disappearing from Manhattan. San Francisco had a chance to keep what was best about New York's life at the street level. There was that moment in 2012 when we might have preserved the neighborhood—no, created it. We might have avoided the construction of housing for the well-to-do, with services on the ground floor where employees in chain stores and franchises would be lucky to make more than the minimum wage.

There is a convenience store downstairs from my office. It's tiny as stores go, narrow—only three people can squeeze in side by side—with a small room at the back for storage. I go there every day on my way upstairs. A Palestinian Christian family leases it. The head of the family wears a four-inch-high brass cross on a chain around his neck. He calls me darling, pronounced "DAH-link," which in former days would have sent me into a fury: I hated men who called me "dear" and "doll" and "honey." But over the years, I had come to see it as a word of affection from him, to see him as the sort of friend one makes through the long-standing relationship between buyer and seller. When I don't have the right change, he waves my hand away from my wallet. Take that green banana, he says, knowing I like bananas that way.

I don't spend much money there. A Diet Coke. A yogurt. A bottle of wine sometimes. They sell the usual sodas and chips, making more from the sales of wine and beer, lottery tickets, cigarettes, and cigars. Their profits grew when they finally got their liquor license (the owner had kept me apprised of all the headaches he endured during the process), with ready buyers from the Palace Hotel across the street, who are happy to escape the predations of their minibars. The little store is not much in the grand scheme of an economy. Yet it supports his family: himself, his wife, twin sons, and a daughter. He makes what was once the modest objective of one's labor, formerly known as "a living."

II.

The crane index I used in 2000 to measure a boom is useless now. There is not a direction you can turn to, not a street you can walk down in SOMA and neighboring South Beach, where cranes do not pierce the sky. Parking lots have been turned into foundations. Unused buildings have been demolished. Lanes everywhere are closed for construction vehicles. Cars clank over trench plates. Drivers hang like dead men on their horns. Trucks haul the extracted sandy soil of the Bay in trailers shaped like bathtubs for giants, long enough to block an intersection. The monster semis roar under my window on their way to landfills. The drivers are supposed to cover their loads with canvas but rarely do; the particles of dried bay-bottom swirl into the air like dirty steam.

The excavations have changed the bird neighborhood. The mourning doves were the first to go, then the little finches. The digs uncovered mice and rats and other tasty treats for crows, who took over the area. Crows are big, sleek, shiny black, and smart. They often alight on the utility pole next to our window. They turn one eye, then the other, to look at us, calm, unafraid. They are the perfect representatives for what is happening here: predators.

Yet all vital cities must change. A city that does not extend its boundaries into underused areas is a dead city. The question is, into which boundaries and what sort of change?

SOMA was a classic underused area. It was once the working-class part of San Francisco—printing plants, steel rollers, stone cutters, collision repair shops, electrical suppliers, warehouses. Tracks are still in place where trains once rode directly to the front of the William Henry Steel company, at Second and South Park, its name fading on the brick façade, now seen in ghostly silver paint.

By the 1980s, during the decline of manufacturing across the United States, the plants were abandoned, the warehouses emptied, and they remained that way into the early 1990s. Gay male S&M leather bars had taken over the southern end of Folsom Street; a few have survived. The collision repair shops are still here, as are the gas stations, social-service agencies, and soup kitchens where SOMA extends down toward the Mission District.

Technology companies have moved into the best of the abandoned historical structures. Twitter is the main tenant of the fine Art Deco building of the former wholesale Furniture Mart. Yelp's headquarters is in the tower where the Bell System reigned, then the tallest building in San Francisco, its insignia carved into the façade, signifying the monopoly company's belief in its perpetual dominance. The lobby is dark; the atmosphere mixes *Flash Gordon* with Dracula movies of the 1930s. The ceiling is stenciled in black and red and gold, depicting phoenixes, clouds, unicorns (as if foreseeing the coming of the billion-dollar-valued startups), and fanciful creatures (likewise).

The supply of empty historical structures is limited, of course, and there came (and still comes) a frenzy of construction for new office buildings. For a time, builders could not get enough architectural glass—the manufacturers had the glass on back order. Salesforce will occupy the new Transbay Tower being built at First and Mission Streets, the tower now to be the tallest building in San Francisco. It is not even large enough for all of Salesforce's employees; a second building is under construction across the street. A black-glass-clad Darth Vader monolith, to house LinkedIn, has risen at the corner of Second and Howard, on the spot where that 1998 billboard had advertised a new world that revolves around you. The building is a suitable bookend to the AT&T aluminum-clad video-game warrior up the street. Between them—still here, as I'd hoped—is the marble-faced Marine Firemen's Union hiring hall, with its medallion over the door of the muscled worker pulling a man-high lever. There is something wonderful about the hiring hall's survival.

I love walking by the signs taped to its windows that say "Proud Union Home."

Someone had to build apartments and condos for the swarm of technology workers, and would-be workers, arriving in San Francisco by the thousands. The prices of condos are in the multiple millions. I have been besieged by Realtors wanting me to sell my loft, promising I'd get what seem absurd sales prices. By 2015, in SOMA/South Beach, over five thousand rental units had been approved, were in the review process, or were already under construction. The median rent in San Francisco is nearly $2,900 a month, barely under Manhattan's, according to Zillow. And the rents in SOMA and the adjoining area named Dogpatch are the highest in the city, rising even above the traditionally richest enclaves of Pacific and Laurel Heights.

Only those with salaries in the hundreds of thousands can afford to live here. Alan Morcos, a real-estate agent (and friend), describes how some of his clients wanting to buy in SOMA are entrepreneurs even with regard to their living situations. They look at a condo and calculate how many roommates they need, charging them substantial rent over the cost of their own mortgages, simultaneously being well-paid employees and landlords. Overall, he deals with a mostly male population in which both women and men remain unpartnered, unmarried, and childless even into their mid- and late-thirties, a generation that is delaying entering adulthood, as Morcos sees it.

The premium condos are near the bus stops where luxury transports pick up the employees of Google and Microsoft and Oracle, and their like, and carry them to their offices down the peninsula. The buses idle in city bus stops waiting for their riders, and the Municipal drivers' union was not even consulted about the arrangement, leaving public employees to compete for space at their own bus stops with private drivers in their McMansion-sized coaches.

One of Morcos's clients refused to look at anything farther than two blocks away from a Google stop. There the buyer will join the technology cadre who sit high above the angry battles of the drivers below, sealed into a quiet, private world with comfortable seats and Wi-Fi, from which they see not SOMA but the screens of their laptops; working, working, always working, pampered to keep them working from the moment they step out of their doors, the transports like the village in the 1960s television program *The Prisoner*, both a haven and a trap. Then they will arrive at their corporate campuses, like the one for the company I worked with in 1996, but lusher now, with gyms and organic catered meals and nooks for playing and napping like weary kindergartners, the Googleplex being the most famous—more pampering to keep them from going home.

The result is a population of programmers and engineers and technology planners, who, after the buses drop them off in the evenings, use San Francisco as a bedroom community, reversing the former order, in which one worked in the city and lived in the suburbs. They sleep here; they use what the urban environment can offer—bars and restaurants, conventions and events—but their more intense lives are elsewhere.

It occurs to me that most of the new inhabitants of the new SOMA don't need a neighborhood as we once knew it. Maybe the city planners were right in their careless and unfeeling way. The new residents have a different idea of what a city is; their primary concern is finding comfortable, affordable quarters, not necessarily a community. They won't miss the local dry cleaner or drugstore or convenience market. They do need places where the actual physical body must be present—the hair salons, yoga studios, and gyms. Otherwise, their needs will be satisfied by delivery people.

In 1998, I spoke of a society becoming divided between those who receive the goods of the world at their doorsteps and those who bring the goods to them. Then the goal for the receivers was to stay at home and connect to the world digitally, while other people, those in a different and lower social class, had to work in the realm of the physical, not lifting weights in a gym but hoisting boxes.

At that time, the deliverers were mostly unionized workers, UPS, FedEx, the United States Postal Service. Not to romanticize the work they did, but they had benefits, health care, workers' comp, bargaining rights. In 1997, UPS drivers went on strike, the first nationwide strike in UPS's history. The drivers' union wanted part-time workers promoted to full-time, wanted to keep control of its pension fund. The strike lasted for fifteen days and stopped the delivery of 80 percent of shipments. What UPS did not count on was the anger its corporate customers felt toward the company during the strike. Over the years, customers had come to know their drivers, to say hello and how's your day and thank you. The recipients had *relationships* with their drivers. UPS caved: new full-time jobs would be created; the union kept control of its pension fund.

And we come to now, nineteen years later. I see the packages piled up in front of the doors in my building. Most of the recipients are not home; they are working seventy- and eighty-hour weeks as they run the technology startup marathon. When they get back, the boxes from Blue Apron await them with all the ingredients for dinners to be cooked in minutes—none of Julia Child's finger-painting glee in preparing food. They can get hot meals delivered by Amazon in thermal bags. (I tried the prepared dinner from Munchery: not so great.) Clothing, furniture, household goods. Stacks of boxes with that Amazon arrow trying to be friendly by mimicking a smile.

My neighbors don't know who the deliverers are now. UPS and FedEx still exist, but so many of the goods are delivered by people in the gig economy, one person with a car easily exchanged for another, as fungible as pieceworkers, paid by the run, or by the hour, as if the Chinese women in the old sweatshop on the next block had somehow returned to SOMA. The deliverers deposit the goods by the door and are gone, faceless servants. The recipients have no idea who has come by to fulfill their desires. They come home to see their wishes fulfilled as if by magic, materializing out of an ethereal, disembodied world.

I see delivery people wandering the halls of the Clocktower, lost in the midst of our improbable layout and horrible signage. What relief they show at seeing an actual human being who can give them directions! One day I admired the compact and lightweight dolly an Amazon guy was using. He was probably no older than twenty. He said the dollies broke all the time; the plastic bottoms would just crack or fall off. "The company is supposed to be giving us new ones," he said. Months later, I saw Amazon deliverers still using the dollies with the crappy plastic bottoms.

I enjoy shopping for food. I like to go around testing the broccoli for freshness, gently squeezing the avocados to see which one is good for today and which for tomorrow. But when my back aches or I can't get out for some reason, I use Instacart. I always ask the delivery people how they like their job. The students are happy; they can work around their class schedules and exams. Not so the black man, about fifty years old, who came to my door one evening. It was clear he was not a student pleased with part-time income. His face was sweaty with the effort of carrying heavy bags. He was rushed. I asked him how the job was working out for him. "I work seventy-hour weeks," he said, "and I barely get by." When he left I thought: The seventy-hour weeks of the engineers and programmers earning hundreds of thousands a year, the seventy-hour weeks of a man wanting to earn that modest thing: a living.

Yet this moment of the chasm between the receivers and the deliverers is just a blip on the way to the complete peonization of the working class. Amazon wants to get rid of those guys with their flimsy dollies; the company is moving to replace them with drones.

Uber drivers, the ultimate symbol of the sweep and penetration of the gig economy, are on their way to be supplanted by self-driving cars. The starkest and most terrifying description of this fulcrum moment comes from the media-and-technology critic Douglas Rushkoff, who wrote: "Uber's drivers are the R&D for Uber's driverless future. They are spending their labor and capital investments (cars) on their own future unemployment."

III.

The startup culture has overtaken San Francisco. It was once a place for kids running away from home, where people in their teens and early twenties came to get away from the lives they were supposed to lead but didn't want to, to be gay or bisexual or other combinations of sexuality, all looking for some version of the old, wild, open San Francisco: the Beats, hippies, free love, the gay revolution. Yet nothing abides forever, and now we live in a city whose former identities, however mythical, have been swept away. A new wave of youthful seekers has come a-searching for yet another mythical San Francisco: a place where dreams of founding a successful internet startup are born, and fulfilled.

Dreams of internet success impose a heavy burden on the recent immigrants. The newcomers soon find themselves buzzing like flies in the sticky paper of the startup life. The ethos that surrounds them says that founding a successful company—getting round after round of venture-capital funding, their startup then valued in the billions—is the measure of the highest personal achievement. It is best to be the CEO; it is satisfactory to be an early employee, maybe the fifth or sixth or perhaps the tenth. Alternately, one may become an engineer devising precious algorithms in the cloisters of Google and its like. Otherwise one becomes a mere employee. A coder of websites at Facebook is no one in particular. A manager at Microsoft is no one. A person (think woman) working in customer relations is a particular type of no one, banished to the bottom, as always, for having spoken directly to a non-technical human being. All these and others are ways for strivers to fall by the wayside—as the startup culture sees it—while their betters race ahead of them. Those left behind may see themselves as ordinary, even failures.

The hopefuls pride themselves on the role they believe they will play as members of a vanguard that will disrupt the existing social, economic, and political structures. But the would-be CEOs can more accurately be called conformists. They want what they are supposed to want; they are the men in the gray flannel suits of our time: tee shirts and jeans, casual business khakis. They are not wild. They march down the startup alley of Second Street not as assemblies of punks but like a disciplined army on maneuvers—yet ever anxious. Their ventures are likely to fade away, as a fickle public disposes of both the soldiers and the code, app by app.

It amazes me what would-be founders will go through to fulfill their dreams. There is no shortage of organizations standing ready to fan the flames of their desires, groups that arrange events that entice the hopeful to come and make their pitches, to hone their PowerPoint slides, their "decks," to practice catching the investor's interest in the first two sentences, most of all to fulfill the dream of getting funding. As I left an event one night, I imagined a hundred rooms across San Francisco and Silicon Valley in which the heat of the strivers' desires was swirling like cyclones, churning counter to the usual air currents. To go against the prevailing winds!

One event involved a big spinning wheel like ones used on old game shows such as *Dialing for Dollars* (which is exactly what this event turned out to be). Would-be founders had attached their names in the places where money amounts normally appear. Then the wheel went spinning. A hundred or so attendees cheered and whistled while the hopefuls prayed, and the wheel slowed down and down, one name after another moving past the winning spot. Until the wheel stopped. Whoops and hollers: one lucky dreamer was the winner. His prize: the privilege of giving a pitch lasting no more than one minute, to an audience that may or may not have included potential investors. The compensation: he had practiced his moment. He assured himself he would do better next time.

The most elaborate event I attended was one from Live Sharks Tank®. Everyone, including the presenters, had to buy a ticket, which cost about twenty-two dollars. Three hundred and seven paying customers were in attendance.

That night there would be sixteen strivers making presentations and seven "certified investors," according to the email invitation from the organizers. As per many other events, pitches could last no more than two minutes. The judges were seven "sharks," who sat at a table on the stage, ready to question the presenters.

The hopefuls were trying so hard. Most were in their mid- to late-twenties, yet they were like high schoolers auditioning for the holiday play. The most common question from the sharks was direct: "If I invest in you, how do I make money?"

The presentations were a blur of the usual delivery services, life planners, craft products. One can see why venture capitalists have become jaded, cynical about the onslaught of pitches. It's not clear that the presenters understand the depth of the skepticism they face. There was one standout, however, a man who proposed building virtual-reality devices that would allow the blind to see that alternate world. Given the two minutes, it was hard to tell how he might do this. Nevertheless, it was a reprieve, something meant to benefit not the well-to-do but the needy.

The sharks chose five finalists, who came onstage and sat on metal folding chairs. The sharks, however, would not choose the winner. That determination would be done by the audience, decided by how loudly they whooped for each finalist. And there came another television moment. The master of ceremonies placed his hand over the head of each finalist in turn. Yays, yells, claps, whistles, whoops, and shouts. More softly for the next. Quieter yet for the next one. Until we came to the finalist in seat four. The audience exploded. The winner: the man with the virtual-reality devices for the blind.

Then it was all over; the stage was bare. Rather than the grouchy slouched exits of the disappointed that I expected, what followed was a round of furious networking, as had occurred in the hour before the presentations. Many stayed to demonstrate their work on their laptops, and others went from demo to demo with genuine interest, expressing approvals, asking questions, or not impressed and moving on. The three hundred in the room wanted to make connections, maybe friends. They seemed happy, joyful even. I realized that, for them, the pitch events were not all trials and humiliations. The meetings were also a chance to be among their own kind, to support one another, sustain their hopes that founding a startup could be realized. The whooping and hollering, the hooting as the wheel of fortune turned: These were their raves. Their fervor was the stuff of ecstasy. These events were their fun.

After the Sharks event, I spoke with one of the judges, Roger King. He is the founder of the Bay Angels, a group that organizes events where hopefuls give pitches to wealthy individuals, rather than to venture capitalist companies. I asked him what he thought of the evening. "A circus," he declared it; "not professional," by which he meant presenters should get at least eight minutes while they show their deck of slides.

I wondered what tonight's winner would get. "Nothing," he said. "Maybe an interview somewhere." He waved his hand as if that somewhere were in a faraway fantasy land.

Despite King's saying that the Sharks winners received nothing, the event organizer, Jose De Dios, sent me an email in which he averred that the proportion of winners who got funding was nearly 100 percent.

Roger King's Bay Angels event took place in a well-appointed law office on a high floor of the tower Embarcadero One. It had sweeping views across the Bay, from the San Mateo–Hayward Bridge in the southeast to the Golden Gate in the north. This aerie—the tower in the sky, the reassuring hush of the ventilators—physically enacted an inherent tenet of the startup culture, I thought. Venture capitalists stand on the heights. What happens in the startup world does not rise from the ground up but descends from the VCs on down.

I stood and looked across the Bay to Oakland, to the wide arc of the evening, where clouds were drifting off after a day of rain. I thought of Google X's Project Loon, which is a plan to fill the skies with glittering polyethylene balloons. Each balloon, flying with the stratospheric winds, will provide internet access to those on earth within the balloon's wireless range. The goal is to build a network that will eventually serve the two-thirds of humanity living in the electronic darkness. But I could find no mention on the project's website of what Google X will give to the people below: reliable electricity, clean water, security from the ravages of ethnic wars, not to mention computers and cell phones and software. Even Bill Gates was skeptical. "When you're dying of malaria, I suppose you'll look up and see that balloon, and I'm not sure how it'll help you," he told *Bloomberg Business Week*. "When a kid gets diarrhea, no, there's no website that relieves that."

The Bay Angels' event was indeed more professional than the Sharks' gathering. The price of admission, about eleven dollars, was waived for presenters, five of them that night, each of whom would get his eight minutes. The forty or so seats for the audience were mostly filled, not a black face among the attendees, nor would there be among the presenters. Then the pitches began: Yet another travel app, this one involving personal valets. 3D printing. Outlook viewers installed at national parks, like the ones that have telescopes, except these will show virtual reality, the history of the place, etc., as if being there in person was not a sufficient experience. An app to simplify real-estate searches. (Yet more disparagement of women: The typical user, the presenter said, is not fond of tech—in their view, a fifty-five-year-old woman. The common slur: "Even Grandma can use it." Never mind Grandpa.)

Finally there was something interesting, again a medical application. The presenters described algorithms they had developed for reading MRIs. A woman taking part in the presentation was the chief designer of the algorithms. MRI machines produce images in slice after slice, and it is tedious for doctors to look through them; it's easy to miss anomalies. The presenters' software would do the searching. This seemed plausible to me. Computers don't get tired; they are good at pattern recognition. If I'd had money to invest, I would have gone over to talk to them.

While listening to the MRI presentation I had a moment of believing that, in this grueling winnowing process, something good for society might emerge. I don't mean a grand scheme to rearrange the lives of human beings around the globe, but a targeted application that would improve the lives of those in need of the technology.

Then the inevitable networking followed. A tall man of about thirty approached me. Enthusiastically, he described the app he was creating. Its algorithms would let employers scan résumés to see which applicants were a good cultural fit for their organization.

My reaction was swift. I told him that "fitness" was another word for selecting a person the group would be comfortable with, a type of person they already knew: guys like themselves. His app, I said, was a way to maintain the existing segregated technical culture.

He listened patiently. "Well, all that may be true," he replied. "But I'm not working for society. I'm working for the company."

IV.

Beyond the landlords offering rentals at premium prices, beyond Alan Morcos's clients making money from every square inch of their condos, beyond the pitch-promoters charging admission, there is yet another ring of businesses standing ready to profit off the startup strivers: the purveyors of shared workspaces.

The new arrivals need co-working spaces for practical reasons. Starbucks can't offer reliable places to sit, printers, conference rooms, secure Wi-Fi. But more than the physical requirements, the lure of a co-working space is its aura: Here is where you are supposed to be, it says. Here you join everyone who is like you. Here is the next step on your quest.

One day, as I took a casual walk along the blocks surrounding the Clocktower, I counted thirty co-working companies tucked into formerly disused buildings, inside each a warren of spaces for rent. The companies are landlords, in essence, although their role as such is disguised by the hipness of the places. The offices have a scatter of furniture from IKEA; more upscale ones include mid-century knock-offs. Free coffee, beer, and wine are the usual amenities. The facilities have brick walls and exposed beams. Spaces in newer buildings have left their infrastructure open: ducts as the new exposed beams. The very interiors speak of the desired life to come: This is what your own startup office will look like.

The available rentals range from a seat in a communal area, to your own desk, to a tiny space for you alone, to offices for two, three, more, as your startup's fortunes rise. The prices go from hundreds of dollars up to tens of thousands. All but the most expensive spaces are open to general view, some separated only by sheets of glass or plexi-glass, physically enacting a great contradiction for would-be CEOs. To be alone: emulate the secretive culture of Steve Jobs's Apple. To be together: embrace the networking ideal and openly share your plans.

To spend time in a co-working facility is to inhale the atmosphere of the startup world, a drug something like cocaine mixed with the free beer and wine. The new arrivals pass through in great numbers. For many it is the first stop on the road to their fortunes. The facilities have an outsized effect: they imprint upon the newcomers the norms of technical society they are about to enter.

The co-working facilities are the first indoctrinators. The gatherings of fellow believers, the conversations among aspiring entrepreneurs, all reinforce the belief they will succeed in their drive for success and riches. Signs on the walls, banners splashed on websites, slogans painted on windows:

"Do what you love," as if that choice were possible for the vast vast majority of people on earth.

"If you don't like your job, create one," another impossibility for most of humanity.

"Make a life, not just a living," as if life and work were to be inseparable; as if earning "a living" was not an admirable goal in itself, meant to support all the rest of life, family, culture, the basic need to pay the rent on an apartment and keep the lights on.

And then there is the overarching motto, indeed the mantra, chanted and repeated and proclaimed as the goal of a startup: "Change the world!"

The assumption is change for the better. But rarely have I met would-be founders who consider how the "better" world they envision may be entwined with one that is worse. Without that introspection, the motto of change devolves into an egoistic motive, a willful blindness to the contributions of the past, not realizing that with every advance there also comes some aspect of life that is diminished, or will vanish, for good or ill; and we are at least obliged to look back and recognize what was before and what may never be again.

Change the world! Uber is changing the world. Amazon is changing the world. Facebook is changing the world. In their wake follow struggling drivers and deliverers, disappearing opportunities for immigrants to join the middle class, fake news, echo chambers in which anyone can choose to believe anything . . . this list too long to continue here. But inside the hatcheries of the startups, the founders and engineers must pitch their ideas as bringing light onto the universe, meanwhile assuring investors they will make money.

What assures venture capitalists is the promise of disruption. What makes money is smashing existing structures to replace them with new ones that can be owned by private investors. Wages earned across a wide spectrum of the existing order—small retailers, booksellers, taxi drivers, reporters, editors, schoolteachers, and more—are swept up like chips on a roulette table, everything going into the hands of the winner: the wealth of the many concentrated into the riches of the few.

The drive is to make a fortune, and it hardly matters what follows in its wake. "Change the world!" is but an advertisement, a branding that obscures the little devil, disruption, that hides within the mantra, a slogan to rally the youth, tell them it's fine, you are not here just to make money: You are noble.

The foremost co-working landlord is the international behemoth of WeWork, which, as of this writing, has one hundred and thirty-seven locations in the United States and abroad, including five in San Francisco.

One day I decided to visit WeWork's facility in what the company describes as the mid-market area of San Francisco. In fact, it is in the Tenderloin, the roughest, highest-crime part of town. It is the world of SROs and desperately poor people. The inhabitants are mostly black, with a small enclave of Vietnamese immigrants who came after the war. Alcoholics and junkies loll on the sidewalks. On early mornings, people line up at food banks. On my way to the WeWork facility, I crossed the street to avoid two cops with guns drawn on four men.

I took a brief tour of the co-working spaces, and, on my way out, I met the CEO of a startup that had an office there. The CEO and I talked for a while, and I learned that the company's goal was to set up mobile Wi-Fi access in both outdoor and indoor locations. The company, with seven men, envisions Wi-Fi networks that are put up and taken down as needed, in neighborhoods, for festivals and events, and inside malls, so shoppers can find the stores they're looking for.

At some point, I asked him, "How do you deal with what is outside the door?" The new CEO had a ready answer. He was going to use the Tenderloin for his first Wi-Fi test bed. He spoke of partnering with the Mid-Market Business Development group, a sort of Chamber of Commerce association, which is working to bring retail stores into a blasted blocks-long expanse of Market Street. He has a plan to connect to the community, he said. He wanted to lure tech workers out of their offices to shop and eat locally. They will get points for doing so, eventually winning a month of free Uber or Spotify.

As we talked, I was impressed. I thought it was great that he hoped to form relationships with those in the neighborhood. I was happy to find a startup founder with a social conscience.

Then I left. Outside was a gauntlet of the desperate, the homeless, the drug-addicted, the alcoholics, the psychotics who might or might not be dangerous. I had to pick my way past bodies lying on the sidewalk. One man was screaming, another throwing up. The homeless don't panhandle here. In a sense, for them, here is home.

By the time I got to my office, I wondered: What in the world was I thinking when I liked the CEO's plans to "connect to the neighborhood"? Luring Twitter engineers out onto the street—did he really think they would give up their free, catered, gourmet, organic meals to risk finding a cockroach in a bowl of noodles (this has happened to me) at the Thai place next to a drug-sale site? To shop at bodegas where there is nothing in the way of fresh food? Spend more time than needed on the dangerous streets?

What struck me most was how the CEO was using technology to make changes from above, based on dreams he and his colleagues had devised in the hotbox atmosphere of the co-working spaces. They were seeing the Tenderloin from on high, like Larry Page's Loon balloons in the sky, not aware of the existing structures on the ground for helping the poor of the Tenderloin. The Mid-Market group is about business development, which is important for the future of the area. But what about the helpers already there: the shelters, community centers, and food banks; the iconic Glide Memorial Church, which has been supporting the neediest in the area for decades? For him, I supposed, these organizations address only small local needs, and therefore cannot scale outward—cannot change the world! I was struck again by the avoidance of any "partnership" with government, as if such a relationship would tarnish the brilliance of the Wi-Fi umbrella by joining forces with the underfunded, overworked, understaffed agencies. He, like so many true believers, envisions a clean technical solution to human problems, conceived of in co-working spaces, clear glass boxes, and conference rooms, whereas the government is anathema, a pit, the muck in which dreams of changing the world will forever sink.

I don't mean any disrespect for the CEO personally; he is an affable, intelligent man; he wants to do good, and he thinks he will. What finally depressed and enraged me was the unconscious bias, the terrible cheerfulness amid a neighborhood where reality is two cops drawing guns on four guys.

I remembered my own belief that technology could change the

world for the better; my youth, ignorance, self-importance; the video-tapes and monitors and cables we hauled into a nearly empty room. How far away was and is the true work of creating a more egalitarian world, the slow, hard job of organizing, the hours of contentious community meetings: the clash of need against need. Only those who work close to that ground, and take the code into their own hands, can tell us what technology is good for. For them.

V.

The night after Donald Trump was elected president, about thirty people met at Treehouse Space, a co-working facility above a tourist-trap-store in Chinatown, to hear pitches from "5 Terrific companies," as the organizer had described them in his email invitation. The election had left me in a state of dread. I went to the event in a sort of sleepwalk, slogging through my plans for the day because I couldn't think of anything else to do. I'd registered; I stumbled over.

It was bizarre to sit there while the pitch-making machine churned on as if nothing unusual had happened. More improbable dreams: Certified "green" water to be sold in the usual disposable plastic bottles. Another travel app, to arrange local guides, the audi-ence pointing out the problem of vetting the hosts for safety. Two more pitches I found incomprehensible.

One presentation so contributed to my sense of the startup world's unreality that I wondered if I was having a nightmare. Their pitch to employers: Hire people who are passionate about traveling, and send them down to our own resort in Latin America, where they will work connected remotely to their home office; meanwhile, they scuba dive, bungee jump, go fly-fishing, have fun, bond, become loyal to their employer. I had an image of women in bikinis: a Trumpian fantasy, a Mar-a-Lago of the mind.

I left the event dispirited. I walked home through the deserted streets of Chinatown and thought of what was about to descend on the United States.

The Trump presidency has arrived like an underground nuclear test that has somehow broken through the surface of the earth to explode in the sky. The majority of the nation that did not vote for him stands stunned, as ugly, angry forces spread wide through the atmosphere.

There are many reasons for Trump's unexpected election. Among those reasons, I believe, is the role that technology has played in bringing us to this moment. I don't mean just looking at how Trump is using Twitter right now. I mean the unspooling of a thread that started at least twenty-eight years ago.

When I read a tweet from Trump, I think back to 1998, to the coming of disintermediation, the process of removing the intermediaries who for centuries had been part of our economic and social relationships. We were witnessing a moment when the public was being coerced into believing that the brokers, jobbers, agents who traditionally had been involved in their transactions—even librarians and journalists—were incompetents, out for themselves, dishonest, the next thing to snake-oil salesmen and mustache twirlers. The intermediaries were useless; you could trust only websites; go directly to the internet.

In two decades, that tendency to dismiss the intermediaries has come to ground, at the feet of Donald J. Trump. It is a direct evolutionary line. Websites could proclaim whatever truths they wished. The "mainstream media" was not to be trusted. Anyone who stood between you and your desires was an interloper. Trump inherits all of that history. He humiliates and bullies. Scoffs at the veracity of any source that challenges him. Disdains the professional press.

Refuses to believe the findings of our country's intelligence services. This last one could be deadly. Every government needs to know what other countries in the world are doing. Twitter is the perfect agent of disintermediation. It was designed so that every utterance could be sent to everyone, going over the heads of anyone in between. No matter what one feels about technology, or about Trump himself, one must be afraid of the power that a tool like Twitter has given to one man, who is already among the most powerful people on earth. Trump can say anything. He tweets outright lies. He attacks individuals he dislikes, assails anyone expressing negative views about him. He circumvents the experts who have served presidents, to the extent that he can no longer evaluate the entire collective wisdom of the state. He even avoids the intermediary of his own introspection, if he is capable of any; he rejects any pause to reflect. In short, he is doing exactly what Twitter was designed to do: shout out the emotion of a moment, broadcast a thought fart. Each of which resounds across the globe.

VI.

Last week, while I was in New York, I marched up Fifth Avenue along with four hundred thousand other people, headed for the Trump Tower. We were part of the millions around the globe protesting the presidency of Donald J. Trump, which was already unfolding.

It was exhilarating to step into the middle of that crowd: A sea of pink caps with ears—pussy hats, which I know will become symbols of female defiance. Young women carrying painted posters showing fearless vaginas and cunts so dangerous that they would flay the hand of any Trumpian grabber. Witty creations such as "Super Callous Fascist Racist Extra Braggadocious." The event was organized as a women's march, yet nearly a third were men, as best as I could see from those around me; a largely white crowd but also with blacks,

Latinos, and Asians. Fathers and mothers pushing strollers, one mother with four sons together holding up a sign that said, "Women will rule the world."

It thrilled me to see how many women in their early twenties were there. It seemed they had awakened to the actions of the past, had come to realize what women before them had achieved only after years of political struggle (if I may dust off that 1970s word "struggle" and make it safe to say again without irony). They understood what they would lose under the Trump regime—their reproductive rights, the legal supports for their social, economic, and political equality—unless they put up a fight. I hoped they would learn another lesson from the past, how the women's movement of the 1970s lost its momentum and power with divides, however real, over class, race, and identity.

It was joyous, though. So many of us! It was fun! Fun to chant "Hands too small, can't build a wall!" and "We need a leader, not a creepy tweeter!" Better yet were the yells, screams, and hoots that moved in a wave from one part of the crowd to another, sometimes from behind you, sometimes from ahead, each section keeping it going for the next, shouts echoing between the buildings all along Fifth Avenue, so you knew you were part of a long, loud, protesting snake of people: in one march.

We were happy while we were there. We went home feeling we had done our part, standing up to be counted. Now comes the hard part. Those audacious women have to get themselves organized, I thought, form coalitions with others, groups that can survive losses and failures yet keep fighting on.

Back in San Francisco, the work on South Park has been moving along. The dirt inside the chain-link fence is now level, ready for the sod to be rolled out. The concrete spine of the walkway has been laid down, and the three-foot-high walls separating the zones of the park have been built, also made of concrete. It turns out that there are indeed park benches and picnic tables, despite their absence in the digital rendering, but they all have the off-white color of unfinished maple. The sun was bearing down from the west, and the whiteness of everything blared in the light. Too clean, I thought, too spare in feeling, a true extinction of the fortunate messiness of what had been there before. How careful people would have to be as they moved through this architectural, gallery-white space, as if walking into the house of someone who has white carpeting and upholstery. Then again, I thought, all this spareness was just a folly of the planners and architects, something that looked good on a digital mock-up. The oval is outdoors, after all; there will be rain; people won't wipe their feet before entering. Concrete ages terribly. The pale benches will show wear and weathering years before darker ones would. And soon will come graffiti, all that cleanliness just too tempting a target for a spray can.

Here and there, strange little round tables and stools, silver-toned, sprout up from the ground like giant mushrooms. Silver, white, shiny metal. They will get too hot to sit on in the sun, I thought. Metal stalks of light poles have been installed, cylinders about a foot in diameter. On the park side of the cylinders are half-rounds of glass that look like the visors of knights in armor—sentries guarding the park from unwelcome visitors. Young trees, maybe eight feet tall, have been planted between the old survivors. The new trees will not offer shade for decades.

It was a fine afternoon. The sky was clear blue, and a breeze rose up from the Bay. As I walked home, I passed coffee shops and cafés filled to capacity with young men and a few women talking intently, laughing, holding up phones displaying pictures to one another. Exclamations of pleasure sounded. I saw how happy this fortunate class of seekers was. To found a startup, to be an early employee of a startup: everything around them says these achievements are the very hallmarks of a successful life. And there they were, in the epicenter of what is happening in the technical world, exactly where a whole generation is supposed to be, inside the defining culture of their era. They were having the time of their lives.

This privileged part of the millennial generation has bet its future on the internet. I wonder if they know the peril and folly of that bet.

All around them, the boom has begun deflating. Fewer startups are succeeding. As of this writing, major internet companies are under pressure. Salesforce's stock runs hot and cold while its tower is still surrounded by cranes. LinkedIn was struggling even before the doors to the Darth Vader building were opened; the company has been swallowed up by Microsoft. Investors are abandoning Twitter, which is shedding employees at a rapid rate and is trying to sell itself to another company. No one is buying.

Meanwhile, other technology companies threaten to reap great riches when they sell stocks on the public markets. Uber and Snap plan to go IPO this year. The two companies have been in private hands, owned by a select in-group. As in the first boom, the valuations of these startups are based not on profitability but on the dream measures of revenues and growth: Uber lost some $800 million in its third quarter of 2016 alone.

The general public has been left standing on the sidelines, watching the valuations soar into the multibillions of dollars, their appetites whetted: they, too, want to get into the game. I fear that, on the IPOs, the public will rush in to buy, as was true in 2000. Share prices will soar on the clamor. Then insiders and employees will start selling. Prices dip; the former outsiders see this as a buying opportunity, once more rushing in; and so on. In the end, the last ones to enter the market will have spent their savings and retirement funds, while the insiders can walk away with billions: another transfer of wealth from society-at-large to the rich.

I hope I'm wrong about all this.

I wonder if the groups enjoying themselves in the cafés know much about the first technology crash. I want to tell them what happened, not just to the internet companies but to society as a whole.

And what of the internet itself, its infrastructure and protocols and servers? Even the builders and creators are despondent about what it has become. Everything that Tim Berners-Lee had feared would happen in 2000, at the Computers, Freedom, and Privacy Conference—complete surveillance by the government and corporations—has come true in ways more extreme than he and others at the conference could have envisioned at the time. Phil Zimmermann, creator of PGP encryption for email, also at the conference, was offering a secure email service called Lavabit until 2013. In that year, the government asked him to divulge the identities of the users of the service; Zimmermann shut it down rather than comply. Whit Diffie, co-author of the important security algorithm, said in 2000 that the internet could not be secured by cryptography alone; the government is now demanding backdoors into encrypted systems and is working on tools to break into encryption protocols. Berners-Lee, researchers, key internet inventors, and old hackers are trying to imagine a more secure internet infrastructure: some distributed system, some new internet, something, somehow, that can let us all escape the digital panopticon. The most heartbreaking speech I have heard about the internet was the keynote at the 2014 Black Hat conference given by Dan Geer, a respected computer security analyst who warned of network vulnerabilities before the risks were understood. He gave a mournful talk, sorrowfully accepting the reality that the system we have now cannot be protected from surveillance. He ended by saying that some might consider him an old curmudgeon, but, as much as possible, he was staying off the internet. Geer's story is another cautionary tale the kids in the coffee shops ought to know: compared to the early hopes for the web, the internet is a god that failed.

After I left South Park, I started walking home through the heat and exhaust of the cars fighting to get on the Bay Bridge. I had to get away from there. I turned back, and the breeze picked up where Second Street slopes down toward the water's edge.

I went by the cafés again. Suddenly I wanted to race in and shake those privileged young people out of their internet dreams. I wanted them to see the damage the net is doing to our culture: banishing privacy, widening the divide between rich and poor, hollowing out the middle class, the creation of a segregated, cloistered society of technologists who barely see the real lives of the majority of human beings on earth.

Yet I must force myself to see the good the young dreamers might do. I must hope that those who barely remember life before the internet, or never knew it at all, will find their way through the dazzle and disappointments of technology, the seductions and the traps. I have to trust that, as they await future wonders, they will also look back to see the world as it was before this moment of the internet, and find guidance there on how to live now.

It is up to a new generation to turn a sharp eye on what is happening all around them. It's their turn. I wish their future well.

PERMISSIONS ACKNOWLEDGMENTS

Grateful acknowledgment is made to the publications in which the following portions of this book originally appeared:

"Outside of Time: Reflections on the Programming Life" first appeared in *Resisting the Virtual Life: The Culture and Politics of Information*, edited by James Brook and Iain A. Boal (City Lights Books, 1995).

"Come in, CQ" first appeared, in very different form, in *Wired Women: Gender and New Realities in Cyberspace*, edited by Lynn Cherny and Elizabeth Reba Weise (Seal Press, 1996).

"The Dumbing Down of Programming" first appeared on *Salon*, May 12 and 13, 1998.

Some portions of "What We Were Afraid of As We Feared Y2K" first appeared in "The Myth of Order," *Wired*, April 1, 1999.

"Off the High" first appeared, in somewhat different form, as "Twilight of the Crypto-Geeks" on *Salon*, April 13, 2000.

"Programming the Post-Human" first appeared in *Harper's Magazine*, October 2002.

"Memory and Megabytes" first appeared in *The American Scholar*, Autumn 2003.

"Dining with Robots" first appeared in *The American Scholar*, Autumn 2004.

A small part of "Close to the Mainframe" first appeared as "Pencils" in *Wired*, April 16, 2013.

Grateful acknowledgment is made for permission to reprint "On the Death of a Cat," from *God's Silence* by Franz Wright, copyright © 2006 by Franz Wright. Used by permission of Alfred A. Knopf, an imprint of the Knopf Doubleday Publishing Group, a division of Penguin Random House LLC. All rights reserved.

A Note About the Author

Ellen Ullman wrote her first computer program in 1978. She went on to have a twenty-year career as a programmer and software engineer. Her essays and books have become landmark works describing the social, emotional, and personal effects of technology. She is the author of two novels: *By Blood*, a *New York Times* Notable Book; and *The Bug*, a runner-up for the PEN/Hemingway Award. Her memoir, *Close to the Machine*, about her life as a software engineer during the internet's first rise, became a cult classic. She is based in San Francisco.